Information Structure in Discourse Representation

Maarika Traat

Information Structure in Discourse Representation

Computational analysis of theme, rheme and focus with Unification-based Combinatory Categorial Grammar

VDM Verlag Dr. Müller

Impressum/Imprint (nur für Deutschland/ only for Germany)

Bibliografische Information der Deutschen Nationalbibliothek: Die Deutsche Nationalbibliothek verzeichnet diese Publikation in der Deutschen Nationalbibliografie; detaillierte bibliografische Daten sind im Internet über http://dnb.d-nb.de abrufbar.

Alle in diesem Buch genannten Marken und Produktnamen unterliegen warenzeichen-, marken- oder patentrechtlichem Schutz bzw. sind Warenzeichen oder eingetragene Warenzeichen der jeweiligen Inhaber. Die Wiedergabe von Marken, Produktnamen, Gebrauchsnamen, Handelsnamen, Warenbezeichnungen u.s.w. in diesem Werk berechtigt auch ohne besondere Kennzeichnung nicht zu der Annahme, dass solche Namen im Sinne der Warenzeichen- und Markenschutzgesetzgebung als frei zu betrachten wären und daher von jedermann benutzt werden dürften.

Coverbild: www.ingimage.com

Verlag: VDM Verlag Dr. Müller Aktiengesellschaft & Co. KG
Dudweiler Landstr. 99, 66123 Saarbrücken, Deutschland
Telefon +49 681 9100-698, Telefax +49 681 9100-988
Email: info@vdm-verlag.de
Zugl.: Edinburgh, The University of Edinburgh, 2006

Herstellung in Deutschland:
Schaltungsdienst Lange o.H.G., Berlin
Books on Demand GmbH, Norderstedt
Reha GmbH, Saarbrücken
Amazon Distribution GmbH, Leipzig
ISBN: 978-3-639-21833-6

Imprint (only for USA, GB)

Bibliographic information published by the Deutsche Nationalbibliothek: The Deutsche Nationalbibliothek lists this publication in the Deutsche Nationalbibliografie; detailed bibliographic data are available in the Internet at http://dnb.d-nb.de.

Any brand names and product names mentioned in this book are subject to trademark, brand or patent protection and are trademarks or registered trademarks of their respective holders. The use of brand names, product names, common names, trade names, product descriptions etc. even without a particular marking in this works is in no way to be construed to mean that such names may be regarded as unrestricted in respect of trademark and brand protection legislation and could thus be used by anyone.

Cover image: www.ingimage.com

Publisher: VDM Verlag Dr. Müller Aktiengesellschaft & Co. KG
Dudweiler Landstr. 99, 66123 Saarbrücken, Germany
Phone +49 681 9100-698, Fax +49 681 9100-988
Email: info@vdm-publishing.com

Printed in the U.S.A.
Printed in the U.K. by (see last page)
ISBN: 978-3-639-21833-6

Many people participated in the completion of the doctoral dissertation that the present book is based on. First and foremost, I would like to thank my supervisors Mark Steedman and Johan Bos for their guidance: Mark for supporting me till the end and nourishing my brain with interesting ideas; Johan for giving me a helping hand when I most needed it and helping me focus my efforts in a specific direction. Furthermore, I am very grateful to Jason Ahad, John Beavers, Lexi Birch, Julian Bradfield, Chris Callison-Burch, Trevor Cohn, Samson Tikitu de Jager, Timothy Jones and Merily Plado, who helped me with the last minute proof-reading. I would like to thank my examiners, Ewan Klein and Claire Gardent who suggested some improvements to my thesis. Last but not least, I would like to thank all the wonderful people I met during my studies in Edinburgh, and whose company I had the pleasure to enjoy.

Contents

Chapter 1

Introduction

1.1 Theses proposed

There is a level of linguistic meaning that is usually ignored by the currently available spoken language systems: the level of information structure. Information structure refers to the way people organise the content of their utterances (see Chapter 2). It is usually manifested in the intonation of the utterances. For some languages (e.g. English), intonation is the primary means for expressing information structure, for others (e.g. Czech) it is present in addition to other means, like permutation of word order.

It is a widely held belief that incorporating information structure has the potential to greatly improve the performance of spoken language systems. Knowledge of information structure would be useful for fine-grained interpretation of user utterances, and, even more importantly, for generating natural sounding speech output.

However, it still remains to be decided precisely how information structure should be included in a natural language system. Incorporating it in the semantics that the system is using seems to be the most natural solution: after all, information structure contributes to the meaning of an utterance, and the contextual appropriateness of an utterance heavily depends on the choice of information structure.

This idea is not new: there have been a few proposals about how to go about including information structure (see Chapter 2). However, I consider these approaches unnecessarily cumbersome and complicated to implement in actual systems (see Chapter 3). The present book promotes a practical ap-

proach. If the natural language system also uses automatic inference, it is
highly preferable that the semantic representation used be compatible with
first order logic: first order theorem provers and model builders are the best
and the most efficient tools for automatic reasoning that are currently available (Blackburn and Bos, 2003a). This book offers an approach to including
information structure in semantics, which both has a simple representation,
and is compatible with first order logic. I believe that as such, the framework
presented here is a very attractive choice for use in practical applications like
natural language systems. However, it has to be noted that in this book I will
use the information-structural marking in Discourse Representation Theory
(DRT) (Kamp and Reyle, 1993) to determine the appropriate intonation, and
will not be concerned with specifying semantic computations with information
structure (some pointers for this topic will be provided in Chapter 3).

The choice of Discourse Representation Theory to provide for the semantic
representation is due to a number of attractive properties that it has: first, it
has the potential of covering a very wide range of linguistic phenomena, second, it is extensively used in the computational text analysis and generation
community, and third, it uses an uncomplicated and visually explicit box representation (see Chapter 3). Besides, DRT is especially suited for processing
discourse, providing tools for phenomena like anaphora, presupposition, etc.

Thesis 1. First order Discourse Representation Structure is well suited for
representing information structure in semantics.

Providing a semantic representation that incorporates an account of information structure is half of the solution. We also need to provide a mechanism
for linking this semantics to the surface linguistic form. Steedman (1991a,b,
2000a,b, etc.) has demonstrated the particular appropriateness of Combinatory
Categorial Grammar (CCG) for natural language analysis that takes information structure into account. Due to CCG's flexible constituency, it is possible to
view information-structural and syntactic constituents as being congruent. In
theories which only recognise the "traditional" syntactic constituents, a parallel
analysis of syntax and information structure is often impossible. Therefore the
latter have to postulate separate dimensions for syntax and information structure, while in CCG both of them can be integrated in a single level. However,

in CCG, information structure has been used in the context of a higher-order semantic representation. I am going to use CCG as the starting point when developing my own formalism to provide a path between the first order DRT semantic representation annotated with information structure (IS-DRS) and intonationally marked text.

> *Thesis 2. Combinatory Categorial Grammar provides a sound starting point for developing a formalism to supply a path between an IS-DRS and intonationally annotated text.*

I implement my ideas as a unification-based formalism, because the operation of unification is computationally highly efficient. Besides, it allows for a clean, straightforward and visually attractive representation. I use insights from Unification Categorial Grammar (Calder et al., 1988) to make the various levels of linguistic representation: syntax, semantics, and information structure, work in cooperation.

> *Thesis 3. Unification provides a suitable means for facilitating the collaboration between the different levels of linguistic representation: syntax, semantics, and information structure.*

I call the new formalism *Unification-based Combinatory Categorial Grammar* (UCCG). I believe that UCCG has the potential to boost a considerable improvement in the intonation of the output of spoken language systems. I also maintain that both the IS-DRS semantic representation and the UCCG formalism are very flexible and can easily be extended or modified according to the particular requirements of a task, or in order to accommodate advances in the theory of information structure.

> *Thesis 4. Both the first order DRS with information structure and the UCCG formalism are easily extendable.*

I will evaluate the claims made as follows:

- For Thesis 1 the semantic formalism needs to be tested as to whether it has enough expressive power. Therefore, I will take a small corpus of linguistic data annotated with information structure, and establish which per cent of the sentences can be represented using the IS-DRSs proposed in the present book.

- For Thesis 2 I show how to compute the information structure from intonationally annotated text in a compositional way. I will analyse a variety of linguistic structures with various permutations of information structure.

- To prove Thesis 3 I implement a parser for a medium size fragment of English.

- For Thesis 4 I will discuss some ways to develop the IS-DRS and UCCG further, including the attractive avenue of semi-automatic extension of UCCG for treebank grammars.

1.2   Structure of the Book

This section outlines the general structure of the book. The main body of the book can roughly be divided into four parts: Chapter 2 gives the general background to the topic of information structure, Chapter 3 describes my approach to incorporating information structure in DRT, in Chapters 4, 5 and 6 the UCCG formalism is being developed, and Chapter 7 provides an assessment to the formalism and reviews the principal theses of the book.

Chapter 2 introduces the concept of *information structure*, and the terminology related to the topic. It briefly discusses the different ways information structure can manifest itself in different languages. Since the book is especially concerned with the relationship between information structure and intonation, this issue receives particular attention. Finally, I focus on a specific theory of information structure in the English language. This theory, which was proposed by Steedman (1991a,b, 2000a,b, 2003), relies heavily on prosody.

Chapter 3 is dedicated to issues pertaining to the semantics of information structure. First, I summarise three model theoretic approaches to information structure. Two of them, Alternative Semantics and the Structured Meanings approach examine the meaning and function of focus. The third approach models the semantics of topic in a similar vein as Alternative Semantics. I proceed by discussing previous accounts of representing information structure in semantics, and zoom in on the ones which incorporate information structure into the DRT framework. Finally, I present my own approach to including information structure in DRT, which involves attaching information-structural flags to DRS-conditions. These flags represent different aspects of information structure from the prosodic account to information structure that was introduced in Chapter 2. Besides theme/rheme and focus the flags include two further dimensions: "commitment" and "agreement". I call the new information-structurally marked discourse representation structures *IS-DRSs*.

In Chapter 4 I develop the core of the *Unification-based Combinatory Categorial Grammar* (UCCG) formalism. Prior to introducing UCCG itself, I discuss the main characteristics of the two generalisations of classical Categorial Grammar that are the closest relatives of UCCG: Combinatory Categorial Grammar (CCG) and Unification Categorial Grammar (UCG). Then I embark on devising the UCCG categories and feature structures called *signs* for different sentential constituents, and specify the mechanisms which govern their combination. In the preliminary version of UCCG we use predicate calculus for semantic description. This provisional representation will ultimately be replaced by IS-DRSs.

Chapter 5 elaborates further refinements to the UCCG formalism. Most importantly, here the predicate calculus semantics is replaced by the traditional DRT representation. The consequence of the changes is that all the UCCG signs from Chapter 4 need to be revised and modified. In addition, the chapter discusses two more advanced topics, coordination and type-raising, that were previously omitted, and shows how UCCG handles them.

In Chapter 6 information structure finally makes its second appearance. Before demonstrating how information structure is incorporated into UCCG, I explain the role of information structure in CCG. In this chapter the DRSs in the semantics feature of UCCG signs are replaced by IS-DRSs. Introducing semantics with information structure calls for further adjustments inside the feature structures: we need to add new features corresponding to the DRS-flags of themeness/rhemeness, focus, "agreement" and "commitment". Finally, we examine different configurations of information structure, including, but not limited to, unmarked themes, split themes, multiple foci and focus on function words.

Chapter 7 presents an assessment of the UCCG formalism. This assessment mainly concerns UCCG's treatment of information structure. The formalism is approached from both the parsing and the generation directions. Finally, I review the evidence that has been provided for the four principal theses throughout the book.

Chapter 8 summarises the work presented in the book and discusses some directions for further development.

The conclusion is followed by three appendices containing a description of the main predicates of my implementation of UCCG in SICStus Prolog, the test suite which I used for the purpose of assessing the parser and the formalism, and a sketch of UCCG's treatment of cleft constructions.

Chapter 2

Information Structure Basics

This chapter explains the concept of information structure and the role it plays in discourse. Section 2.1 presents some definitions of information structure, as well as discussing the terminology used for information-structural partitionings. It briefly touches upon the different ways information structure can manifest itself, and illustrates the phenomena with examples. Section 2.2 discusses the connection between intonation and information structure. Finally, Section 2.2.1 gives a brief overview of a particular theory which closely couples prosody and information structure (Steedman, 2000a,b) which will play a crucial role in the rest of the book.

2.1 What is Information Structure

There are usually multiple options for communicating the same propositional content. However, only one of these options can be realised at a particular occurrence of an utterance. By *information structure* (IS) I mean the way people organise the content in a particular utterance. Chafe (1976) informally describes information structure[1] as follows:

> [The phenomena at issue here] have to do primarily with how the message is sent and only secondarily with the message itself, just as the packaging of toothpaste can affect sales in partial independence of the quality of the toothpaste inside.

Choosing the information structure for one's proposition is by no means random. Depending on the choice of information structure, the same proposition

---

[1]Chafe himself uses the term *information packaging*.

13

can be either appropriate or not appropriate in a given context. Thus, information structure plays an important role in ensuring the coherence of a text or a discourse.

According to the most common view, information structure divides an utterance into two parts: one that relates the sentence to the previous discourse, and another that advances the discourse either by adding entirely new information or by modifying the information that was established in the previous discourse. In this book I will mainly use the terms[2] *theme* and *rheme*[3] for these two parts. Utterances do not always need to encompass both theme and rheme. There are also the so-called "out-of-the-blue" or all-rheme utterances. Such utterances predominantly occur at the beginning of a discourse or as an answer to the question of the type *'What happened?'* Somewhat more controversially, also all-theme utterances exist (see Steedman, 2000b, 2003).

The following definitions for the two parts of information structure are adapted from (Kruijff, 2001, page 153)[4]:

> Theme states how the meaning of the sentence *purports* to relate to the established discourse. It helps to set, as it were, the conditions under which the meaning of the sentence can be true, provided these conditions are met.
>
> Rheme says something *about* theme, by qualifying or modifying the meaning it is related to in the context.

Different names have been used for the subdivisions of IS: topic and focus, theme and rheme, ground and focus, topic and comment, relatum and attributum, to name just a few of them. The proliferation of terminology is illustrated in Figure 2.1. What all these divisions have in common, with minor differences, is that they divide an utterance into two major parts, one of which links the utterance to the previous discourse, while the other is a novel contribution. Some approaches distinguish further subdivisions in these two parts. For a more extensive overview of different approaches to IS and the relationships be-

---

[2]When I describe other people's approaches to information structure, I adhere to their terminology.

[3]The terms *theme* and *rheme* were introduced by the Prague circle of linguists. Halliday used the same terminology, but his definition of the notions was slightly different (see Halliday, 1967) from how they are used here. I use theme and rheme in the sense of Steedman (2000a,b).

[4]In the original definition Kruiff used the terms *Relatum* and *Attributum* instead of theme and rheme.

tween different IS partitionings see Vallduví 1993, Vallduví and Engdahl 1996, and Kruijff 2001.

Information structure can manifest itself in several ways, depending on the typology of the language. For example, in the so-called "free word order" languages (e.g. Czech, Russian, Catalan, Hungarian, Turkish, etc.), the ordering of words, more often than being an arbitrary choice, is dictated by IS. Languages with relatively fixed word order (e.g. English), on the other hand, use prosody as the main means of indicating the information structure of an utterance. Yet another means for realising IS is provided by morphology, of which the special topic marker *-wa* in Japanese and focus markers in Navajo are often-cited examples. In realising their IS, languages tend to use a combination of these different approaches, rather than using any one of them in isolation. For a longer discussion of IS in a variety of languages the reader is kindly referred to Vallduví 1993, and Vallduví and Engdahl 1996.

Information structure does not usually affect the propositional content of utterances. However, whether an utterance is felicitous in a context crucially depends on information structure. For example, while 2.1a is a suitable answer to the question in Example 2.1, 2.1b is not acceptable in the given context:

(2.1) Who did Aristotle teach?
    a) [Aristotle taught]$_\theta$ [young ALEXANDER the GREAT.]$_\rho$
    b) *[ARISTOTLE]$_\rho$ [taught young Alexander the Great.]$_\theta$

The words in upper case in Example (2.1) carry the main intonational accent of the utterance. As illustrated by the example above, the placement of this accent determines whether the answer given to the question is appropriate or not. As mentioned above, in English, prosody is the main means for realising information structure, hence the two answers in 2.1 differ in their IS.

Each information-structural unit in Example 2.1 is enclosed in a pair of square brackets. Themes are marked with a subscript θ after the closing bracket, while rhemes are marked by the subscript ρ. The theme of 2.1a contains information present in the question, while the rheme contributes the information that was requested by the question. The information structure of 2.1b, on the other hand, is incompatible with the question.

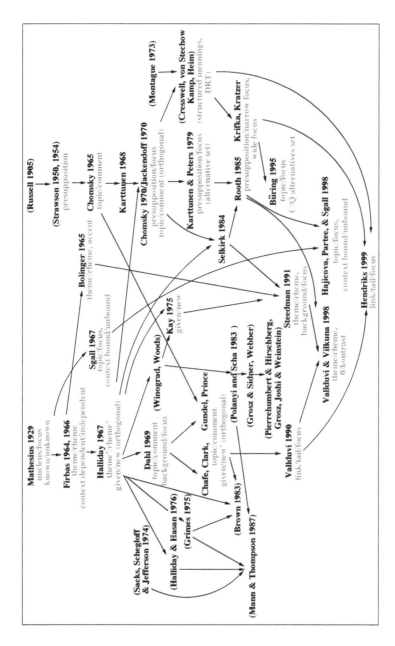

Figure 2.1: Information structure terminologies and their dependencies (Kruijff-Korbayová and Steedman, 2003).

I use an example from the Estonian language[5] to demonstrate the close relationship between information structure and word order. The effects of information structure on word order have been reported to be even stronger in some other languages (Catalan, Hungarian, Czech, Turkish, etc.; see Vallduví 1993, Vallduví and Engdahl 1996, Sgall et al. 1986, etc.). In Estonian both the subject-verb-object (SVO) and object-verb-subject (OVS) word orders are possible. The SVO order is more common and therefore more neutral, but the OVS order is widely used, too. Example 2.2 illustrates the aforementioned property of Estonian.

(2.2) *Q: Ma tean, kes   Kallypost   õpetas,*
        I   know who$_{nom}$ Callippus$_{acc}$ taught,

        aga kes   õpetas Aleksander Suurt?
        but who$_{nom}$ taught Alexander the Great$_{acc}$

    'I know who taught Callippus, but who taught Alexander the Great?'

a) *A1: [Aleksander Suurt   õpetas]$_\theta$ [Aristoteles.]$_\rho$*
        Alexander   the Great$_{acc}$ taught   Aristotle$_{nom}$ (OVS)
        '[Aristotle]$_\rho$ [taught Alexander the Great.]$_\theta$'

b) *A2: [Aristoteles]$_\rho$ [õpetas Aleksander Suurt.]$_\theta$*
        Aristotle$_{nom}$ taught   Alexander   the Great$_{acc}$ (SVO)
        '[Aristotle]$_\rho$ [taught Alexander the Great.]$_\theta$'

Even though both the SVO and OVS word orders are possible in Estonian, there are constraints that block the usage of one of them on certain occasions. These constraints seem to be associated with information structure: it appears to be the case that an object cannot be at the beginning of a sentence if it is a rheme (see Example 2.3).

(2.3) *Q: Ma tean, keda   Platon   õpetas,*
        I   know who$_{nom}$ Plato$_{acc}$ taught,

        aga keda   õpetas Aristoteles?
        but who$_{acc}$ taught Aristotle$_{nom}$?

    'I know who Plato taught, but who did Aristotle teach?'

---

[5] Estonian belongs to the Finno-Ugric group of languages.

a) A1: [Aristoteles   õpetas]_θ   [Aleksander   Suurt.]_ρ
        Aristotle_nom   taught   Alexander   the Great_acc   (SVO)
        '[Aristotle taught]_θ [Alexander the Great.]_ρ'

b) A2:[Aleksander   Suurt]_ρ   [õpetas   Aristoteles.]_θ*
        Alexander   the Great_acc   taught   Aristotle_nom   (OVS)

One explanation for this phenomenon would be to assume that there is a certain preference for the SVO word order over the OVS word order in Estonian, and a preference for the theme to precede the rheme. If this were the case, then 2.3a satisfies both of the preferences, 2.2a only satisfies the "theme-first" condition and 2.2b complies with the preference for the SVO word order, whilst 2.3b does not fulfil either of the two preferences.

Although information structure often manifests itself in syntax in Estonian, it does not mean that intonation is not important. On the contrary, intonation definitely still plays a crucial role in the cognitive process of interpreting the utterances.

As we observed above, information structure performs an important function in ensuring the coherence of a discourse or a text. Even though information structure does not usually have a direct effect on the truth conditions of a proposition, there are some cases when it does. For example, when focus sensitive particles are used, then the choice of information structure does influence the truth conditions. One such case will be discussed in Section 3.1.2 of this book. For more information on truth conditional effects of information structure see König 1991.

Now, how does one determine the information structure of a particular sentence? The most fool-proof test to my mind is the question-answer test, which can be formulated as follows:

> Given a sentence S, determine the question Q that S is an answer to. The content present in both S and Q is the theme of the utterance; the content present in S and absent from Q forms the rheme.

Re-examining Example 2.1, the question-answer test appears to work very well. If we ignore the finicky details of the English grammar, the content that the question in 2.1 and its answer 2.1a share is *'Aristotle taught'*. Hence, this is the theme of the utterance. Subtracting the theme from the rest of 2.1a we obtain the rheme: *'young Alexander the Great'*.

Another version of the test is that of elliptical answers. If, instead of answering the question with a full sentence, a fragmentary answer is given which only contains the most relevant information, then the whole answer corresponds to the rheme (see Example 2.4). The theme being already established, it is not of vital importance to repeat this information.

(2.4) Who did Aristotle teach?

[Young ALEXANDER the GREAT.]$_\rho$

A third test, that has been mainly advocated in approaches which use the information-structural notion of *aboutness topic*,[6] is to reformulate the utterance using the phrase *'as for'*. The word or phrase following the expression 'as for' would then be identified as the topic of the utterance (see Example 2.5).

(2.5) [Aristotle]$_{Topic}$ [taught young ALEXANDER the GREAT.]$_{Comment}$
As for Aristotle, he taught young ALEXANDER the GREAT.

So far things look nice and clear. Unfortunately, in reality things are much more complicated. There are still many open questions in the area of information structure. The tests really only work for simple declarative sentences. Very little has been said about the information structure of questions and imperatives. It is far from obvious how complex sentences should be analysed from the point of view of information structure: whether information structure is a recursive notion, or each part of complex sentences has their own independent information structure. Section 2.2 describes an approach which provides a mechanism that allows for a unified treatment of the information structure of both simple and complex sentences. The central idea of the approach resides in a transparent relationship between intonation and information structure.

Another mystery is whether information structure respects the boundaries of traditional syntactic constituents, or there are no such constraints. Steedman presupposes the existence of NP-island constraints which prohibit an information-structural boundary in the middle of an NP (Steedman, 2000b, page 116): the entire NP has to belong to the same information-structural

---

[6]In these approaches the utterance is divided into *topic* and *comment*. The topic picks a referent, and the rest of the sentence says something about the topic.

unit. At the same time, he has vehemently argued for flexible constituency regarding verb phrases (see e.g. Steedman 2000b (pp. 4 and 85) and Sections 2.2, 3.3.1 and 6.1 of this book) that would allow VPs to be split between different information-structural units. Kruijff (2001) and Sgall et al. (1986) do not assume NP-island constraints. In their approach NP modification can belong to a different information-structural unit than its head (see Example 2.6 adapted from Kruijff 2001, page 186[7]). This is also allowed by the *Sense Unit Condition* defined by Selkirk (1984, page 286).

(2.6) (Which teacher did you give what book?)
    [I gave the book]$_{Topic}$[on SYNTAX]$_{Focus}$[to the teacher]$_{Topic}$[of ENGLISH.]$_{Focus}$

2.2   Information Structure and Intonation

A connection between intonation and information structure has long been suspected. More precisely, the idea that intonation contributes to the meaning of the utterance has been around for a long time. Bolinger (1965) was probably the first to attempt a principled classification of pitch accents. He described three types of accents: A, B and C accents. The shape of these three accents is illustrated in Figure 2.2. Besides noting the differences in their form, Bolinger also attributed the three accent types a distinct meaning, or rather, the meaning differences provided the basis for his formal classification of accents (Bolinger, 1965, page 51):

> The procedure that I have followed in grouping the accents about certain norms has been first to look for similarities and differences in meaning, and then to try to match them with similarities and differences in form. This reverses the approved order of business, but had to be adopted because pitch contours are if anything more fluid than meanings.

Thus, for Bolinger the accents were meaningful units: morphemes rather than phonemes. He described accent A as assertive, contributing to the word or phrase that it occurred on, a quality of "newness" or "separateness". Accent B

---

[7]In the original, Kruijff performs the topic-focus division on the semantic representation rather than on the surface string.

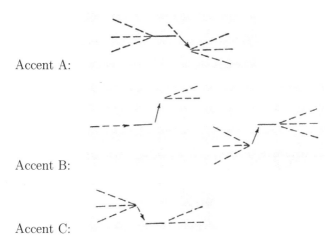

Accent A:

Accent B:

Accent C:

Figure 2.2: The pitch movement of Bolinger's accents A, B and C (from Bolinger, 1965, page 50): arrows represent a skip, solid lines denote an essential movement and dashed lines indicate an optional movement

had the meaning of "connectedness" and "incompleteness". Accent C was kind of an anti-accent A in both form and meaning: it was anti-assertive. Figure 2.3 presents some examples of the accents A, B and C is use. Even though Bolinger did not explicitly use the terminology of information-structural partitioning, he did express the idea that the choice of the pitch accent reflected "how much information was centered in the lexical items on which the accent was to fall" (Bolinger, 1965, page 67).

His theory of the meanings of the different accent types fitted in very nicely with the general idea behind information-structural units like theme and rheme, or topic and comment. Indeed, Jackendoff later started to use Bolinger's accents A and B exactly in this connection: A accent being the typical comment accent and B accent the typical topic accent (Jackendoff, 1972, page 262):

> ... the difference in intonation is due to the order in which values for the variables [in the presupposition] are chosen. The B accent occurs on the variable whose value is chosen first, the one which [the sentence is about]. The A accent occurs on the variable whose value is chosen second, so as to make the sentence true for the value of the other variable.

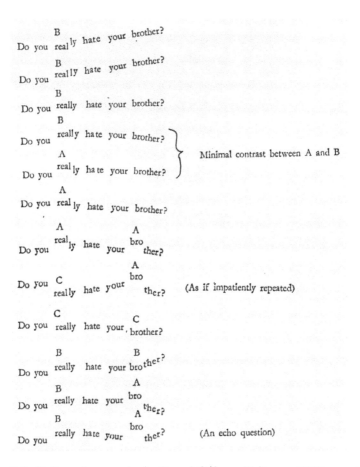

Figure 2.3: Bolinger's accents A, B and C(from Bolinger, 1965, pp. 50-51)

Halliday (1967) was the first to suggest the close relationship in English between intonation structure and information structure. According to him an *information unit* corresponds to a phonological unit, which he calls a *tone group*. Halliday's and Jackendoff's proposals have been developed further by Schmerling (1981), Gussenhoven (1983), Selkirk (1984), Ladd (1980), Zubizarreta (1998) and Steedman (1991a; 1991b; 2000a; 2000b) among others.

Pierrehumbert and Hirschberg (1990) made a new contribution by analysing the meaning of intonational tunes as being compositionally made up of the independent meanings of pitch accents, phrasal tones and boundary tones.[8] Their approach was motivated by the observation that the tunes which share certain tonal features also seem to share some aspects of meaning. They assume the intonational phrase as their primary unit of meaning analysis. Pierrehumbert and Hirschberg do not explicitly bind specific tune elements with specific information-structural partitionings. However, they do say that different prosodic elements assign a different informational status to the linguistic item they occur on (for example, the high pitch accent H* marks the item as "new"). By choosing a particular sequence of pitch accents, phrasal tones and a boundary tone to make up an intonational phrase the speaker specifies how s/he would like the hearer to update the common ground, or in the words of Pierrehumbert and Hirschberg "to modify what ([speaker] S believes) a hearer H believes to be mutually believed".

As a matter of fact, there is a lot of controversy surrounding the theories which tightly couple information structure and intonation. A frequent criticism is that such theories are primarily based on artificial examples and personal intuition. Hedberg and Sosa (2001) tried to empirically evaluate the relationship between intonational contours and information structure in free-flowing discourse. Their conclusion was that they were unable to establish any such regular pattern. However, they do not deny the possibility that systematic correlations between information structure and intonation exist.[9] As also noted

---

[8] Their approach is based on the the system of prosodic elements proposed in Pierrehumbert 1980. Pierrehumbert's taxonomy of English prosodic elements consists of pitch accents, phrasal tones and boundary tones. All of these are made up of high (H) and low (L) tones. The set of pitch accents includes H*, L*, L+H*, L*+H, H+L*, H*+L and H*+H. The phrasal tones are either high (H) or low (L). They are followed by a high or low boundary tone — H% or L%.

[9] The results of Hedberg and Sosa (2001) were based on ToBI (tones and break indices) annotated data. The way the accents L+H* and H* have been defined in ToBI annotation scheme (Beckman and Hirschberg, 1999) makes them especially difficult to tell apart. In fact, very low inter-annotator

by Steedman (2003), identifying the precise information structure in free discourse is a very complicated task, because people make extensive use of the mechanisms of accommodation and inference. Another reason why it is hard to analyse the relationship between intonation and information structure is due to the fact that the present definitions of information-structural categories are rather vague. Moreover, the numerous terms used for information-structural partitionings are often used in an inconsistent manner; neither is the precise nature of the relationships between the various systems of information-structural partitionings fully clear. The third issue complicating the matters is that it is not easy to differentiate between certain prosodic categories. The L+H* and H* pitch accents, which have generally been viewed as the theme and the rheme pitch accents in English (see e.g. Steedman, 2000a,b), anecdotally belong among the ones that are very difficult to tell apart (see the discussion in Steedman, 2003, pp. 13,14). It has been questioned whether the two accents really are categorically distinct (see summary in Ladd and Schepman 2003). The fact that the same pitch accents and boundary tones can take a slightly different form at their different occurrences, due to co-articulation effects and the like, does not make the problem any easier.

A relatively recent attempt to shed light to the connection between information structure and intonation was made by Calhoun (2004). In a series of production and perception experiments, she looked at whether there was a consistent phonetic difference between thematic focal accents and rhematic focal accents per se. The only consistent phonetic difference she found was that theme accents have relatively lower f0 peaks than their corresponding rheme accents. In the production study, she found that while rhemes are almost always followed by falling boundaries (L% and LL%), themes are equally likely to be followed by rising boundaries (LH%) as falling ones. On the basis of these findings and later corpus-based work, Calhoun (2006) proposed that information structure is not primarily marked by pitch accent type, but by the metrical prosodic structure of the utterance. Within both the theme and the rheme phrase, the focus is associated with the most structurally prominent word in that phrase (see also Ladd 1980, Truckenbrodt 1995). Then, at the level of

---

agreement has been reported for annotations based on this scheme. For further discussion of this issue see Steedman 2003, pp. 13,14.

prosodic phrasing that includes both the theme and its corresponding rheme, the theme is prosodically subordinate to the rheme. That is, the rhematic focus is nucleus of the higher phrase. Calhoun's proposal is compatible with Steedman's theory (see Section 2.2.1), which in essence requires that themes and rhemes be phonologically distinct; the marking of this distinction by tonal pitch accent type is of secondary importance. Calhoun did not directly address the marking of speaker orientation and mutual belief (see Section 2.2.1), i.e. the meaning of boundary tones and low versus high accents, however, it seems feasible that these are marked as Steedman claims on top of the metrical prosodic structure.

I conclude this discussion by admitting that more research into the interdependency between intonation and information structure is needed. Likewise, more research is needed into the fields of information structure and intonation separately, that would enable us to formulate more precise definitions of theme and rheme (or other information-structural partitionings for that matter), and also to provide more exact descriptions of pitch accents, and better guidelines for recognising them. In the meantime, I choose to rely on the strong intuition that people do not randomly assign prosody to their utterances, but rather, make conscious choices with the aim of communicating a particular meaning.

2.2.1 Steedman's Prosodic Approach to Information Structure

Steedman (1991a,b, 2000a,b) divides information structure into theme and rheme. In his approach, prosodic phrasing in English reflects IS division. Both theme and rheme can be further divided into background and focus. The words which carry pitch accents represent the focused part of theme or rheme, while the unaccented words form the background. The most common kind of theme is the so-called "unmarked" theme, where no words are focused. Marked themes are only used when some item stands in explicit contrast with another item in the previous discourse. Steedman's information-structural division is illustrated in Example 2.7. Here the word *'admire'* in the answer stands in contrast with the word *'likes'* in the question. Hence, we encounter a marked theme. As a matter of fact, there is a contrast in the rheme too: the word *'directed'*

stands in contrast with the word *'wrote'*. The issues concerning how the focus
(foci) of an intonational phrase is chosen will receive some illumination later
in Sections 3.1.2 and 3.1.3 of Chapter 3 where Alternative Semantics (Rooth,
1985; Büring, 1995) will be discussed.

(2.7) I know that Marcel likes the man who wrote the musical.

But who does he ADMIRE?

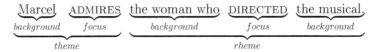

Steedman (2000a,b) argues that there is a specific set of pitch accents in
English that can accompany theme, and another set that accompany rheme.
The most common theme pitch accent is L+H* and the most common rheme
pitch accent is H*.[10] The full taxonomy of English pitch accent can be seen in
Table 2.1. The first row of the table contains the theme (θ) pitch accents, and
the second row the rheme (ρ) pitch accents. A pitch accent marks the whole
intonational phrase that it occurs in as a theme or a rheme.

Table 2.1: The Meanings of the pitch accents (Steedman, 2003)

	+	−
θ	L+H*	L*+H
ρ	H*,(H*+L)	L*,(H+L*)

In his 2003 paper, Steedman introduces a second dimension into the meaning
of pitch accents: $\pm AGREED$. This feature reflects whether the speaker expects
the hearer to share his/her opinion about what s/he says regarding the focused
item, or not. The first column of pitch accents in Table 2.1 demonstrates the
pitch accents that signal that the issue under discussion is uncontentious as
perceived by the speaker, while the second column contains pitch accents that
the speaker uses when s/he anticipates a divergence of beliefs. Example 2.8
illustrates the use of two different rheme pitch accents, marked by +AGREED
and −AGREED respectively. 2.8a° and 2.8b° attempt to clarify the contribution of meaning made by the H* and L* pitch accents by paraphrasing the

---

[10]The intonational notation used is due to Pierrehumbert (1980, see also the footnote on page 23).
According to her, each intonational phrase is made up of a pitch accent (pitch accents), a phrasal
tone and a boundary tone. In Steedman's (2000a; 2000b) representation the last two have been joined
together under the name *boundary tone*. L stands for low pitch, and H for high pitch.

original versions 2.8a and 2.8b and providing some more context. However, the particular interpretation of these pitch accents crucially depends on the specific context they occur in. The accents themselves do not even determine whether the opposition or doubt is coming from the side of the hearer or the speaker (see Steedman, 2003, pages 7,8).

(2.8) a) A: You appear to be rich.
  B: *I'm a MILLIONAIRE.*
           H*   LL%
        +AGREED

   b) A: You appear to be poor.
    B: *I'm a MILLIONAIRE.*
               L*   LL%
           −AGREED

  a°) A: Wow, you have such a cool car! You must be real rich.
    B: Yes, indeed I am:
       I'm a MILLIONAIRE.

   b°) A: What tacky clothes you're wearing! You must be real tight on money.
     B: You are gravely mistaken:
        I'm a MILLIONAIRE.

Boundary tones delimit prosodic phrases. In Steedman's version, Pierrehumbert's (1980) phrasal and boundary tones have been combined into a single unit. This gives us the six boundary tones that can be seen in Table 2.2. The low boundary LL% and the rising boundary LH% are the most frequently occurring boundary tones. There is a tendency for LH% to occur at the end of an intonational phrase containing the theme pitch accent L+H*, and for LL% to occur after the rheme pitch accent H*. (Steedman, 2003) suggested that by choosing a particular boundary tone the speaker shows whether s/he or the hearer is responsible for, or committed to, the corresponding information unit. Assigning this semantics to boundary tones would explain the phenomenon of the so-called "continuation rises", and particularly their occurrence at the end of declarative questions (for example, notice the different effect of saying 'okay' with a low boundary or a rising boundary). The boundaries that mark speaker commitment are shown in the first row of Table 2.2, while the second row contains the boundaries that mark hearer commitment. Examples 2.8a and 2.8b both demonstrated speaker commitment. Example 2.9 shows a case where the speaker delegates the responsibility for the veracity of the proposition to the hearer (for more relevant examples see Steedman 2003).

(2.9) A: Congratulations. You're a millionaire.

B: *I'm   a   MILLIONAIRE?*
          L*   LH%

Table 2.2: The Meanings of the Boundaries (Steedman, 2003)

$[S]$	L, LL%, HL%
$[H]$	H, HH%, LH%

In this Section I discussed an elegant approach to information structure which provides explicit semantics for pitch accents and boundary tones, while the precise interpretation and, possibly "paralinguistic", side-effects of each occurrence of a particular pitch accent or a boundary tone still crucially depends on the specific context they occur in. In spite of its merits, the approach still succumbs to the same criticisms that other approaches which tightly couple intonation and information structure have to endure (see the discussion above).

2.3   Conclusion

This chapter attempted to shed light on the concept of information structure and explicate its role in discourse. I presented some definitions of information structure, and discussed the proliferation of terminology used for information-structural partitionings. We noted that information structure plays a crucial part in ensuring the coherence of a discourse or a text. We also saw that IS has different means at its disposal: it can manifest itself through word order, intonation or morphology. Different languages use different means for expressing information structure. I illustrated information-structural partitionings with examples from English and Estonian. Then I discussed some tests that have been proposed for revealing the IS of a particular utterance. I also highlighted some questions about IS that still need to be answered. Among those were the nature of IS partitioning in complex sentences, and the relation between IS and syntactic constituents.

I proceeded by discussing the connection between intonation and information structure. I briefly reviewed the contributions made to the issue by Bolinger, Halliday, Jackendoff, Pierrehumbert and Hirshberg. They proposed various ways how intonation contributes to the meaning of an utterance. The main idea put forward here was that there is some kind of a systematic relationship between the prosody used and the IS of the sentence. Then I reviewed some criticisms that have been made to approaches which closely couple intonation and information structure, namely, that they tend to be based on artificial examples and personal intuition, rather than on empirical data from natural discourse. I indicated some reasons why studying IS in free-flowing discourse is extremely difficult, and acknowledged that further research was necessary.

Finally, I gave a brief overview of Steedman's prosodic approach to information structure (Steedman, 1991a,b, 2000a,b). This approach equates information-structural phrases to intonational phrases. It gives a compositional account of how the meaning that intonation contributes to the meaning of an utterance is built up of the meanings of separate building blocks: pitch accents and boundary tones. The meanings offered to each prosodic element, while being general and consistent, still have enough pragmatic flexibility to allow for a slightly different interpretation in different contexts.

Chapter 3

Information Structure in Semantics

This chapter explores issues related to the semantics of information structure. It starts by discussing the model theoretic interpretation of information structure (IS), which serves as the general background or frame of reference for the rest of the book. The problem of representing information structure in semantics is then discussed. Since one of the primary concerns of this book is incorporating IS into the dynamic framework of *Discourse Representation Theory* (DRT) (Kamp and Reyle, 1993), I am most interested in previous approaches that include information structure in DRT. Finally, I present my own ideas about how to represent information structure in DRT.

More precisely, the structure of this section is as follows. Section 3.1 looks at some model theoretic explanations of the meaning of information structure. Section 3.2 explores how aspects of information structure have previously been integrated into semantic representations, focusing on approaches set in the framework of DRT. The suitability of these approaches for the task of generating text annotated with information structure from an IS-marked Discourse Representation Structure is briefly discussed. Finally, in Section 3.3 I propose my own approach to representing various aspects of information structure in DRT.

3.1 Model Theoretic Semantics of Information Structure

In this section I will provide a brief overview of the two major approaches to model theoretic semantics of focus and an approach to model theoretic semantics of contrastive topic. The approaches to focus that I am going to outline are the Structured Meanings approach (von Stechow, 1981) and Alternative Semantics (Rooth, 1992). After having discussed these, we turn our attention to Büring's account of the meaning of topic (Büring, 1995), which, in essence, is a further development of Alternative Semantics.

Model theoretic semantics is concerned with the relationship between the language and the world. More formally, it is concerned with mapping a system of symbols and formulae onto a model. The present book is by no means profoundly engaged with model theoretic semantics: my objectives are of practical nature. I aim at providing an uncumbersome semantic representation with explicit representation of information-structural units, which would be convenient to use in areas such as content-based speech generation. However, it would be advantageous to allow for automatic inference about information structure in addition to that concerning the standard semantic content. Therefore, it needs to be possible to combine the semantic representation with a model theoretic interpretation for information structure. When I propose my representation of information structure in DRT in Section 3.3, a model-theoretic interpretation is assumed along the lines of the theories outlined in the next section.

Certain linguistic phenomena have received special attention in the model theoretic literature about focus and information structure in general: focus-sensitive operators, second occurrence expressions, and the influence of information structure on accommodation process are but three of them. I will not include a long discussion of such phenomena in this book, since my main interest lies elsewhere: namely, in providing a semantic representation which reflects information structure, coupled with a grammar formalism to allow for the generation of utterances with context-appropriate intonation. Therefore, the interested reader is kindly referred to other sources. There are many relevant publications; to name some of them: Krifka 2005, 2006; Gardent 2000; Gardent and Kohlhase 1996a,b; von Stechow 1991; Rooth 1992; Geurts and van der Sandt 2004.

3.1.1   Structured Meanings

In Chapter 2 I showed that a string of words in English has the potential to communicate several slightly different messages. In other words, depending on the choice of intonation (or in the case of some languages on the exact ordering of words), the same string of words can make a slightly different assertion. I explained the phenomenon by the difference in the way information is structured in the particular occurrence of the string of words. In the *structured meanings approach* (von Stechow, 1981, 1982; Klein and von Stechow, 1982; von Stechow, 1991; Cresswell and von Stechow, 1982) the difference in information structure is reflected in the visual organisation of the semantics of the utterance. The principal thesis about focus structure, as expressed in Klein and von Stechow 1982 (page 38) is as follows: "Fokusstrukturen drücken gegliederte Gedanken aus."[1] Stechow elaborates on the meaning of the above saying that structured thoughts are more complex than ordinary propositions.

A structured meaning is a pair $<P,<a_1,...,a_n>>$, where the first element, P, is an n-place property and the second element is an n-tuple of individuals, the arguments of the property P. The property P is "ascribed" to its arguments. For example, in Example 3.1a the property of *'Miss Marple seeing somebody'* is ascribed to *'the murderer'*. A structured meaning representation reflects the topic/focus division of the utterance: the first element of the pair corresponds to the topic of the utterance and the second to the focus or foci. In Example 3.1a *'the murderer'* carries the intonational centre of the utterance. In 3.1b, however, *'Miss Marple'* is the focus and the entity who the property of *'having seen the murderer'* is ascribed to. In the corresponding structured meaning representations, the focus of the utterance is first abstracted from the topic, and then moved into the focus position: the right-hand element of the structured meaning pair.

(3.1) a) Miss Marple saw [the MURDERER]$_F$.

   $< \lambda x$ [Miss Marple saw x], the murderer$>$

b) [Miss MARPLE]$_F$ saw the murderer.

   $< \lambda x$ [x saw the murderer], Miss Marple$>$

The property P can also be conceived of as the question that the focus or

---

[1] Translation of the original: "Focus-structures express patterned thoughts."

foci of the utterance, $<a_1,...,a_n>$, give an answer to (see Example 3.2).

(3.2) Q: Who saw the murderer? λx [x saw the murderer]
       A: Miss Marple.   Miss Marple

Von Stechow (1981) defines the notions of topic and focus in terms of old and new information. However, being new or old information cannot be viewed as a property of referents. To illustrate the point, von Stechow provides the sentence seen in Example 3.3 below. *'Hans-Robert'* constitutes the topic of the utterance and has to be old information, whilst *'himself'* being part of the focus, is new information. Since *'Hans-Robert'* and *'himself'* refer to the same individual, the referent is simultaneously both old and new information.

(3.3) [Hans-Robert]$_T$ [likes HIMSELF]$_F$.

Von Stechow (1981) finds a way around the problem by defining new and old information in terms of *material implication* between the topic and focus (see Example 3.4).

(3.4) If Hans-Robert exists then he likes himself.

Using his structured meanings representation, von Stechow defines the notions of *local relevance* and *informativity* (von Stechow, 1981). Whether an utterance is appropriate in a given context crucially depends on these two notions. Based on them, von Stechow shows how common ground[2] gets updated after each utterance.

Some of the controversial linguistic problems that have been accounted for within the structured meanings approach are: question-answer compatibility, essential indexicals and interrogative-embedding operators (von Stechow, 1982), focusing operators (e.g. only, even) (von Stechow, 1991; Krifka, 2006), and *de re* beliefs (Cresswell and von Stechow, 1982).

3.1.2   Alternative Semantics

According to the *Alternative Semantics*[3] of Rooth, originally stated in Rooth 1985 and revised in Rooth 1992, each linguistic expression α has an ordinary semantic value $[\![\alpha]\!]^o$. In addition to the ordinary semantic value, focused phrases

---

[2]In Klein and von Stechow 1982 the author uses the term *Diskussionsstand* in place of common ground.

[3]The name "Alternative Semantics" was first used for the theory by von Stechow (1989).

also have a special semantic value, *focus semantic value* $[\![\alpha]\!]^f$. Rooth (1992) gives the following informal definition for the focus semantic value:

> ... the focus semantic value for a phrase of category S is the set of propositions obtainable from the ordinary semantic value by making a substitution in the position corresponding to the focused phrase.

The elements of the set of the focus semantic value of an expression have to match the type of the ordinary semantic value.

Example 3.5 shows how the above definition works. If we have a sentence *'Mary likes Sue'* where *'Sue'* constitutes the focus of the sentence, we can obtain its focus semantic value by substituting *'Sue'* in its ordinary semantic value with each entity in turn that Mary might possibly like. The logical forms acquired by these substitutions, together with the ordinary semantic value of the original sentence, form the alternative set which is the focus semantic value of the original sentence. In 3.5a the focus semantic value of *'Mary likes [Sue]$_F$'* is spelled out. However, the alternative set may be rather large. Example 3.5b gives a shorthand for representing the focus semantic value. The entities that qualify as valid alternatives are somewhat debatable, further clarification of this issue is provided below.

(3.5) a) $[\![_S \text{ Mary likes } [\text{SUE}]_F]\!]^f =$
　　　　$\{like(mary, peter), like(mary, bill), like(mary, ann),$
　　　　$like(mary, tom), like(mary, sue), \ldots\}$

　　b) $[\![_S \text{ Mary likes } [\text{SUE}]_F]\!]^f = \{like(mary, y)|y \in E\}$, where E is the
　　　　domain of individuals.

The usual effect of the placement of focus is that of separating the contexts in which the utterance is appropriate from those where it is not. However, the effect is not limited to that: in some cases focus placement has also truth-conditional effects. This is true of focus in combination with the focusing adverb *'only'*. Rooth's theory offers a credible explanation for such cases.

The following provides a case study for two sentences where focus placement has truth-conditional effects. The sentences are taken from Rooth 1992, and can be seen in Example 3.6. We study the sentences in the context where Mary introduced Bill and Tom to Sue and did not introduce Bill to anybody else. In that case 3.6a is true, while 3.6b is false.

(3.6) a) Mary only introduced Bill to $[SUE]_F$.

    b) Mary only introduced $[BILL]_F$ to Sue.

In 3.6 focus determines the domain of quantification of the adverb. The domain of quantification is the set equal to the focus semantic value of the verb phrase. Example 3.7 shows how the focus semantic values of the verb phrases in Example 3.6 differ, thereby allowing the correct predictions about the truth values of the propositions to be made.

(3.7) a) $[\![_{VP}$ introduced Bill to $[SUE]_F]\!]^f = \{\lambda x[introduce(x, bill, y)] | y \in E\}$

    b) $[\![_{VP}$ introduced $[BILL]_F$ to Sue$]\!]^f = \{\lambda x[introduce(x, y, sue)] | y \in E\}$

In order to complete the analysis of the sentences in 3.6 we need to define the lexical semantics for the adverb *'only'*. Rooth proposes for it the semantics seen in 3.8a (adapted from Rooth 1992). The adverb *'only'* quantifies over properties. C stands for a set of properties, namely, those equal to the focus semantic value of the *VP*. Basically, the semantics says that whenever an x has a property P belonging to the set C, then P is the property expressed by the ordinary semantic value of the verb phrase. 3.8c attributes this property P to Mary (see also 3.8b). Finally, 3.8d provides a generalisation of the semantics for either of the sentences in Example 3.6. It is a generalisation, since we still need to determine the value of C, which is different in either case, as was shown in 3.7. In the case of 3.6b the focus semantic value of the *VP* includes properties of the form *'introduce y to Sue'*. The semantics of the whole sentence in 3.6b, complete with the semantics of *'only'*, makes a statement meaning that whenever Mary has the property of *'introducing y to Sue'* then this property is *'introducing Bill to Sue'*. Since *'introducing Tom to Sue'* is distinct from the property of *'introducing Bill to Sue'*, sentence 3.6b is false if besides Bill, Mary also introduced Tom to Sue. Similar reasoning applies to 3.6a, making it true in the given context.

(3.8) a) $\lambda x \forall P[[P \in C \wedge P(x) \rightarrow P = [\![VP]\!]^o]\!]$

    b) $[_S$ Mary only VP$]$

    c) $\forall P[[P \in C \wedge P(mary) \rightarrow P = [\![VP]\!]^o]\!]$

    d) $\forall P[[P \in C \wedge P(mary) \rightarrow P = \{\lambda x[introduce(x, bill, sue)]\}]\!]$

Equating the set variable C with the full focus value of the *VP* would be unsustainable, instead we would need to recover the set of relevant properties from the context. Thus, the set C would actually be considerably smaller than the whole set of focus alternatives. However, we do still need to constrain the set C to be a subset of the focus semantic value: $C \subseteq [\![VP]\!]^f$.

As a rule, we do not need to consider the full focus semantic value when interpreting focus in a context: we only need a subset of the focus value that consists of contextually relevant alternatives. The alternative set has to minimally contain the ordinary semantic value of the focused phrase and at least one other element. This constraint is formalised in Example 3.9. According to 3.9, the ordinary semantic value $[\![\alpha]\!]^o$ of an expression α has to belong to the alternative set Γ. The set has to contain at least one more element γ which has to be distinct from $[\![\alpha]\!]^o$. The constraint further states that the set of alternatives Γ has to be a subset of the focus semantic value $[\![\alpha]\!]^f$ of the expression.

(3.9) $[\![\alpha]\!]^o \in \Gamma \wedge \gamma \in \Gamma \wedge [\![\alpha]\!]^o \neq \gamma \wedge \Gamma \subseteq [\![\alpha]\!]^f$

In Rooth 1985 and 1992 the Alternative Semantics approach is applied to the domains of questions and answers, focusing adverbs, scalar implicatures, contrastive configurations and bare remnant ellipsis. Rooth succeeds in accounting for a variety of focus effects in these domains. In explaining the different phenomena, focus always has a uniform semantic import: it is a presupposition that is defined in terms of an ordinary and a focus semantic value.

3.1.3   The Meaning of Topic

Büring (1995) develops a model theoretic approach to topic[4] in the lines of Rooth's theory of Alternative Semantics (Rooth, 1985). He argues that topic, similarly to focus, is capable of inducing alternatives. While the focus semantic value is a set of propositions, the topic semantic value is a set of sets of propositions. Büring explains the role played by topics by first discussing question semantics and answer relevance.

Büring maintains that the ultimate contribution of an utterance is that it maps one *Common Ground* into another. In other words, an utterance is a function from Common Grounds to Common Grounds. However, not every

---

[4]When speaking about topic, or *S-Topic*, as he calls it, Büring really means "the element bearing the topic accent". Some people use the term *contrastive topic* to refer to such topics.

utterance has the potential of achieving this. Only utterances that are appropriate in a given context can update the common ground.

The simplest way of observing an utterance in context is by presenting it as an answer to a question. According to Hamblin (1973), the semantic value of a question corresponds to the set of potential answers to it. Rooth (1985) presents the ordinary semantic value of a question as a subset of the focus value of the answer, on the assumption that a question word further restricts the set of focus semantic value of the answer (e.g. *who → people, what → things, etc.*). Büring equates the ordinary semantic value of a question with the focus value of the answer (see Example 3.10). He formulates the first version of his *Question-Answer Condition* as follows (Büring, 1995, p. 35):

> Sentence S can be uttered as an answer to a question Q given a Common Ground CG if $[\![S]\!]^f = [\![Q]\!]^o$.

(3.10) Who threw the baseball?
$[\![S]\!]^f = [\![Q]\!]^o$: $\lambda P.\forall x[person(x) \wedge P = threw(x, \iota z.baseball(z))]^5$

The predictions of this condition are only partly correct, since it turns out to be too restrictive. According to this condition only B1 counts as an adequate answer to the question of A in Example 3.11. However, in reality B2 is considered to be an acceptable answer[6] to the question, too.

(3.11) A: Which book would Fritz buy?
B1: Fritz would buy ['The Hotel New HAMPSHIRE']$_F$
B2: Well, [I]$_T$ would buy ['The Hotel New HAMPSHIRE']$_F$.

The answer B2 differs from B1 in one major respect: namely, the person *'Fritz'* in B1 is replaced by the first person pronoun in B2. This replacement is permitted on one condition: the expression that is substituted for the original has to carry a pitch accent.[7] The element that B1 and B2 differ in is the

---

[5] By using the universal quantifier in the formula, Büring probably intended to represent the set of "all the persons who threw the baseball". However, I believe that the use of an existential quantifier would be more appropriate, and the set of propositions would be obtained by substituting the variable x by each contextually relevant focus alternative in turn.

[6] To a certain degree, the answer B2 is a less adequate response to the question than the answer B2, and therefore it comes with a package of implicatures. It implicates more or less: "I don't know which book Fritz would buy, but I would buy 'The Hotel New HAMPSHIRE'. And therefore I believe, Fritz might buy it too." Answer B2 signals that the question is still under consideration after B2 has been uttered. For more information about S-Topic implicatures see Büring 1995, pp. 60-64.

[7] To be more precise this needs to be a topic/theme pitch accent.

topic of the sentence. Büring uses the term *S-Topic* to denote a sentence topic. He defines S-Topic as "an (improper) part of the non-Focus". He uses the term similarly to what has been called the *aboutness topic*[8] elsewhere (cf. e.g. Hajičová and Sgall 2004): it is "what the rest of the sentence is about" or "the entity anchoring the sentence to the previous discourse".

Besides S-Topic, Büring speaks of a different kind of topic which he calls *discourse topic* or simply *D-Topic*. As its name implies, D-Topic is established by the discourse. Questions achieve establishing the D-Topic in a very direct way. Answers to questions must be evaluated relative to D-Topic.

Returning to Example 3.11 above, the reason why the answer B2 is accepted as contextually relevant resides in the fact that S-Topic induces alternatives, in a very similar manner to focus. In fact, topic semantic value $[\![S]\!]^t$ can be viewed as "typed up" focus semantic value (see Example 3.12): whilst focus semantic value is a set of propositions, topic semantic value is a set of sets of propositions (see Example 3.13). Note that each subset of propositions in topic semantic value has an alternative S-Topic. We can adjust Rooth's informal definition for focus semantic value from Section 3.1.2 to Büring's topic semantic value:

> The topic semantic value for a phrase of category S is the set of propositions obtainable from the focus semantic value by making a substitution in the position corresponding to the S-Topic.

(3.12) $[\![[I]_T \text{ would buy } ['War and Peace']_F]\!]^f =$
   {I would buy 'War and Peace',
   I would buy 'The Hotel New Hampshire',
   I would buy 'The World According to Garp', ...}

(3.13) $[\![[I]_T \text{ would buy } ['War and Peace']_F]\!]^t =$
   {{I would buy 'War and Peace', I would buy 'The Hotel New Hampshire', I would buy 'The World According to Garp', ...},
   {Bolle would buy 'War and Peace', Bolle would buy 'The Hotel New Hampshire', Bolle would buy 'The World According to Garp', ...},
   {Fritz would buy 'War and Peace', Fritz would buy 'The Hotel New Hampshire', Fritz would buy 'The World According to Garp', ...},

---

[8]The standard test for this kind of topic is the phrase 'as for ...'.

{Fritz's brother would buy 'War and Peace', Fritz's brother would buy 'The Hotel New Hampshire', Fritz's brother would buy 'The World According to Garp', ...}}

Since focus semantic value of an answer was equated with the ordinary semantic value of its corresponding question above, there is an alternative way to represent topic semantic value: it can be viewed as a set of questions (see 3.14).

(3.14) $[\![[I]_T \text{ would buy ['War and Peace']}_F]\!]^t =$
{which book would you/I buy?,
which book would Bolle buy?,
which book would Fritz buy?,
which book would Fritz's brother buy?, ...}

Having defined the notion of topic semantic value, Büring is able to account for why answers like B2 to question A in Example 3.11 are seen as contextually relevant, redefining his Question-Answer Condition as follows (Büring, 1995, p. 58):

The meaning of the question must match one element in the Topic value of the answer.

So far nothing has been said about the semantics of sentences which do not contain an S-Topic. The semantics of topicless sentences is simpler: the topic semantic value of such sentences is a singleton set containing the focus value of the sentence.

3.1.4 Discussion

This section gave a brief overview of the two principal approaches to model theoretic interpretation of focus and an approach to model theoretic interpretation of topic. Since to my knowledge no competing model theoretic approach to topic exists, there is not much to add about this issue. However, we can try to compare the two approaches to focus to each other.

There do not seem to be any major controversies between the approaches. In essence, their differences boil down to representational and terminological matters. For example, Stechow uses the term *topic* for all the rest of the sentence after the abstraction of its focus, Rooth makes no reference to topic, and for Büring the topic is the element of the sentence which carries a topic accent. As for focus alternatives, Stechow mentions them in his 1981 paper (p. 115). Klein and von Stechow (1982, pp. 47-51) explain how adding content to the common ground restricts the *open alternatives*. By "open alternatives" they refer to the other expressions that could have been used in the position of the focus of the utterance, rather than to the whole propositions. However, this difference is also only of a minor consequence.

Von Stechow (1991) claims that the Alternative Semantics theory cannot account for the use of two focusing operators one after another (e.g. *'even only'*), while the Structured Meanings approach can. Hence, the Alternative Semantics theory has less expressive power than the Structured Meanings approach. However, the basis of this claim has not been explained exhaustively.

3.2 Information Structure in Discourse Representation Theory

In this section I give a brief overview of the three previous approaches to semantics with information structure formulated in the framework of Discourse Representation Theory (Kamp and Reyle, 1993): TF-DRSs (Kruijff-Korbayová, 1998), Focus Frame-Focus Structures (Kamp, 2004; Bende-Farkas et al., 2003) and New Information approach (Poesio et al., 2000). I start by making some general remarks about the representation of information structure in semantics, then I present a short summary of the main features of DRT, and finally I provide an outline of each of the three approaches to semantics which combine information structure with DRT.

3.2.1 Semantic Representation with Information Structure

Most approaches to information structure divide it into two main parts (except e.g. Vallduví 1990) which can be referred to by a variety of names as was outlined in Chapter 2. A standard way of relating these two parts to each other is by viewing them as being in a functor-argument relation. It is not important which part of the dichotomy is made the functor and which the argument. However, since it is easier to make the longer part the functor and the shorter part the argument, that is the prevailing trend. Thus, in approaches using topic-focus articulation, like the Praguian *Functional Generative Description* (FGD) framework, it is more convenient to apply the focus to the topic, giving us the formula, $S=F(T)$, for the representation (Peregrin, 1996; Buráňová et al., 2000). On the other hand, in theme-rheme (θ/ρ) approaches, like Steedman's (2000b) it seems more natural to apply the theme to the rheme, and therefore the preferred formula is $S=\theta(\rho)$, but neither is $S=\rho(\theta)$ wrong by any means. In order to present the two parts of the dichotomy independently, the argument is usually lambda-abstracted from the formula (see Example 3.15).

(3.15)

[Mary loves]$_T$ [PETER]$_F$.
Topic: λx[love(mary,x)]
Focus: peter

Information structure is a discourse phenomenon rather than being a property of a single sentence, since it crucially depends on the preceding context. As such, it makes sense to incorporate it in a dynamic semantic framework. Therefore, I omit further discussion of information structure in semantic frameworks that do not provide any means for handling inter-sentential dependencies. Instead, we move directly to looking at previous approaches to information structure in DRT.

3.2.2 Discourse Representation Theory

Discourse Representation Theory (DRT; Kamp and Reyle 1993) is a dynamic approach to semantics. It can be used to interpret a single sentence as well as a sequence of sentences. In the case of a sequence of sentences the incoming new information is interpreted in the light of the information already present in the semantic representation. Therefore, DRT is especially suited for addressing problems that have to do with inter- and intra-sentential cross-reference, like anaphora resolution.

DRT overcomes one of the biggest shortcomings of first-order predicate logic as far as representing natural language is concerned: in first-order logic, acces-

sibility of discourse referents is determined by the logical scope of quantifiers
(Blackburn et al., 1998). This is insufficient for modelling anaphoric references
so widely used in natural language. See the discourse in Example 3.16: 3.16a
and 3.16b present the sentences of the discourse along with their corresponding
first-order representations. The representation we would actually like to obtain
for our discourse is the one in 3.16c. However, if we join 3.16a and 3.16b conjunctively, we obtain 3.16d, which is different from 3.16c. If we translated 3.16d
back into English, we would obtain something like '*A girl walks and somebody
sings*'. We can enhance our representation by including the fact that the person doing the singing is female. However, we still lack the means to resolve the
reference to the girl from the first sentence: we would need a way to somehow
extend the scope of the existential quantifier to include the conjunct '$sing(y)$'.
To sum up, we cannot derive the desired meaning compositionally from first
order formulae if we process the discourse on a sentence by sentence basis.

(3.16) a) A girl walks.

$$\exists x(girl(x) \land walk(x))$$

b) She sings.

$$sing(y)$$

c) $\exists x(girl(x) \land walk(x) \land sing(x))$

d) $\exists x(girl(x) \land walk(x)) \land sing(y)$

In DRT the semantic content of sentences is represented by Discourse Representation Structures (DRSs). The two main components of a DRS are the
universe of the DRS and a set of *DRS-conditions*. The universe of the DRS
is inhabited by *discourse referents*. The DRS-conditions in the main body of
the DRS formalise the claims made about the discourse referents. When a new
utterance is added to the discourse which contains information about an old
referent, there are two possibilities: either a) following the original approach of
Kamp and Reyle (1993), to introduce a new discourse referent together with an
equality condition which expresses the link to the previous discourse referent,
and the DRS-conditions about the new referent, or b) to directly introduce the
new DRS-conditions about the old referent.

In (Geurts, 1999) the DRS language is defined as follows:

1. A DRS φ is a pair $\langle U(\varphi), Con(\varphi) \rangle$, where $U(\varphi)$ is a set of reference mark-

ers[9], and $\mathrm{Con}(\varphi)$ is a set of DRS-conditions.

2. If P is an n-place predicate, and $u_1,...,u_n$ are reference markers, then $Pu_1,...,u_n$ is a DRS-condition.

3. If u and v are reference markers, then $u = v$ is a DRS-condition.

4. If φ and ψ are DRSs, then $\neg\varphi$, $\varphi \vee \psi$ and $\varphi \Rightarrow \psi$ are DRS-conditions.

Thus, equality is already included in the above definition of the DRS language. The DRS language that is used in this book is further extended with the modal operators $\square$ and $\Diamond$, and a special kind of DRS-condition of the form u:φ, where u is a reference marker and φ is a DRS. Hence, we can add two further clauses to the above definition of the DRS language:

5 If φ is a DRS, then $\square\varphi$ and $\Diamond\varphi$ are DRS-conditions.

6 If u is a reference marker and φ is a DRS, then u:φ is a DRS-condition.

The non-standard construct u:φ requires some further explanation. Generally, a discourse referent denotes either an individual or a possible world. The referent u in this construct picks out a specific possible world, and the information denoted by the DRS φ is claimed to hold in this particular world u.

DRSs are represented as boxes which are divided into two parts: the upper part represents the DRS universe, and the lower part holds the DRS-conditions (see Example 3.17). DRSs are recursive structures: they may contain subordinate DRSs in their "conditions" part. In fact, according to points 4,5 and 6 in the above definition, a subordinate DRS together with an operator is a DRS-condition of the super-ordinate DRS. This is the case if our discourse involves negation ($\neg$) (see Example 3.18a) or implication ($\Rightarrow$) (see Example 3.18b). The outermost DRS is referred to as the *main DRS*.

(3.17) Mary walks.

x
mary(x)   walk(x)

---

[9]The same as discourse referents above

(3.18) a) Mary does not walk. b) Every man walks.

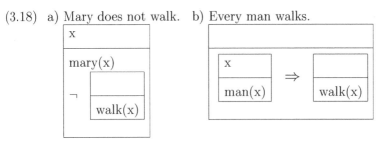

Two DRSs can be combined into a single DRS by the *merge* operation. I use the symbol $\otimes$ for the merge operator. When the information in two DRSs is combined, their universes are merged into a single universe and their sets of DRS-conditions are merged into a single set of DRS-conditions. A more formal definition can be worded as follows:

> If the pairs $\langle U(\varphi), \text{Con}(\varphi) \rangle$ and $\langle U(\psi), \text{Con}(\psi) \rangle$ are DRSs, then their merge is defined as the union of sets:
>
> $\langle U(\varphi), \text{Con}(\varphi) \rangle \otimes \langle U(\psi), \text{Con}(\psi) \rangle \Rightarrow \langle U(\varphi) \cup U(\psi), \text{Con}(\varphi) \cup \text{Con}(\psi) \rangle$

Example 3.19 demonstrates how the information that corresponds to the discourse in Example 3.16 gets dynamically incorporated in the emerging DRS. I assume that at the time of the merge, the reference of *'she'* has already been successfully resolved to the discourse referent x in the universe of the first DRS.[10]

(3.19)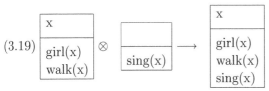

The merge operation sounds more straightforward than it really is. Actually, there are a number of technical problems associated with it. For example, a serious problem arises if two distinct discourse referents are denoted by the same variable in the two DRSs that are part of a merge. Several solutions have been offered, but probably the most convenient way to prevent clashes among variable names is to rename (all the occurrences of) one of them before the merge-reduction is performed.

---

[10]Here I diverge from the original approach of Kamp and Reyle (1993): I only add new DRS-conditions to existing referents, rather than introducing a new referent along with an equality condition. I chose to only add new conditions to old referents, since this approach is easier to implement in a unification-based framework.

3.2.3   Information Structure in DRT: Previous Approaches

TF-DRSs

Kruijff-Korbayová (1998) adopts a representation for information structure, where distinct information-structural units are represented by individual DRSs. She works in the Praguian *Functional Generative Description* (FGD) framework (Sgall et al., 1986; Hajičová, 1993; Hajičová et al., 1998, etc.) where information structure is analysed in terms of *topic and focus articulation* (TFA). Following Peregrin's (1996) proposal, she represents the topic and focus of an utterance as λ-expressions. Therefore, rather than using the standard DRS representation as laid out in (Kamp and Reyle, 1993), Kruijff-Korbayová adopts the λ-DRS in the spirit of (Kuschert, 1996). She uses the term *Topic-DRS* to refer to the λ-DRS corresponding to the topic part of an utterance and *Focus-DRS* to refer to the λ-DRS corresponding to the focus part. The two parts of information structure are combined by an infix operator: the "cookie-operator" ($\bowtie$). The cookie operator that represents the boundary between topic and focus, technically stands for "suspended" functional application of topic part to the focus part, or the other way round. The whole structure consisting of a Topic-DRS, a Focus-DRS and a cookie-operator is called a *TF-DRS*. A schematic representation of a TF-DRS can be seen in Example 3.20, while Example 3.21 illustrates a TF-DRS representation for an actual input sentence. Note, that the TFA notion in FGD is recursive, thus each Topic-DRS and Focus-DRS can contain further topic- and focus-sub-DRSs.

(3.20) | TOPIC | $\bowtie$ | FOCUS |

(3.21) [The man]$_{top}$ [met a GIRL in a park.]$_{foc}$

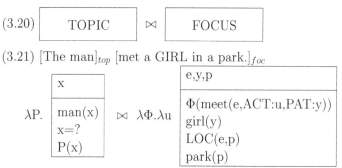

Utterances can also be "topicless". These are the so-called "out-of-the-blue" sentences that can be conceived of as answers to a question *What happened?* In the case of such sentences the Topic-DRS of the TF-DRS is empty (see 3.22).

Since the whole utterance is represented in the Focus-DRS, no λs are needed.

(3.22) [Jane met Paula.]*foc*

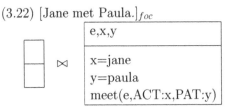

e,x,y
x=jane
y=paula
meet(e,ACT:x,PAT:y)

In Kruijff-Korbayová's approach a TF-DRS is constructed as a translation of a sentence's *tectogrammatical representation* (TR), which is the level of meaning in FGD framework. Since information structure is explicitly represented in the TR, her method is effectively a translation of one semantic representation with IS into another semantic representation with IS.

Example 3.23 illustrates the tectogrammatical representation of the sentence in Example 3.21. The nodes in the TR are marked with their dependency type. When using Kruijff-Korbayová's method, each node of the tectogrammatical representation is translated into the corresponding λ-DRS. It is regrettable that during this translation information about the syntactic category of the item represented by the TR node is needed (Kruijff-Korbayová, 1998, pages 92-112), rather than formulating the translation based solely on the dependency type of the node and the number of its direct dependants. It seems unnatural that while performing a semantics to semantics translation, which should mean operating with meaning units, one has to have recourse to surface syntax or a lexicon with syntactic categories.

(3.23) [[ACT:man^{cb}] ROOT:meet^{nb} [LOC:park^{nb}] [PAT:girl^{nb}]]

Each node in a TR is marked as *contextually bound* (CB), or *non-bound* (NB). FGD notions of *topic* and *focus* are defined based on these notions of contextual boundness and non-boundness. Roughly, the topic part of a sentence corresponds to the CB nodes in a TR, while the focus part corresponds to the NB nodes (for the exact algorithm see (Sgall et al., 1986, page 74)). During the translation of a TR into a TF-DRS, the λ-DRSs corresponding to the topic in the TR are combined by functional application. The same happens to the focus nodes in the TR. Functional application stops at the topic-focus boundary, where subsequently a cookie operator (⋈), denoting "suspended" functional application, is placed. The process of translating the TR in 3.23

into a TF-DRS can be seen in Example 3.24. The translation is performed in a linearised form. We previously saw the λ-DRS corresponding to the final result in Example 3.21 above.

(3.24) $(\theta(\text{ACT:man}^{cb})) \bowtie (\theta(\text{ROOT:meet}^{nb}) @^{11} \theta(\text{LOC:park}^{nb}) @$
$\theta(\text{PAT:girl}^{nb})) \longrightarrow (\lambda P.x;\text{man}(x);x=?;P(x)) \bowtie$
$(\lambda\Phi_u.\lambda u.\Phi_u(\lambda\Phi_v.\lambda v.\Phi_v(\lambda\Phi_w.\lambda w.(e;\text{meet}(e,\text{ACT:u,PAT:v});\phi(e);$
$\Phi_w(\text{LOC}(e,w)))) @ \lambda Q.(z;\text{park}(z);Q(z))) @ \theta(\text{PAT:girl}^{nb})) \longrightarrow$
$(\lambda P.x;\text{man}(x);x=?;P(x)) \bowtie$
$(\lambda\Phi_u.\lambda u.\Phi_u(\lambda\Phi_v.\lambda v.\Phi_v(e;\text{meet}(e,\text{ACT:u,PAT:v});\phi(e);z;\text{park}(z);\text{LOC}(e,z)))$
$@ \theta(\text{PAT:girl}^{nb})) \longrightarrow (\lambda P.x;\text{man}(x);x=?;P(x)) \bowtie$
$(\lambda\Phi_u.\lambda u.\Phi_u(\lambda\Phi_v.\lambda v.\Phi_v(e;\text{meet}(e,\text{ACT:u,PAT:v});\phi(e);z;\text{park}(z);\text{LOC}(e,z)))$
$@ \lambda R.y;\text{girl}(y);R(y)) \longrightarrow$
$(\lambda P.x;\text{man}(x);x=?;P(x)) \bowtie (\lambda\Phi_u.\lambda u.\Phi_u(\lambda v.(\lambda R.y;\text{girl}(y);R(y))$
$(e;\text{meet}(e,\text{ACT:u,PAT:v});\phi(e);z;\text{park}(z);\text{LOC}(e,z))))$

In the final part of her dissertation, Kruijff-Korbayová demonstrates how her framework can be used in connection with van der Sandt's (van der Sandt, 1992) treatment of presupposition to make predictions about presuppositions of sentences. However, due to the terse presentation and some unfortunate typos in her examples, I cannot fully understand what she means, while for the same reason I am unable to refute her claims.

Focus Frame-Focus Divisions

Kamp (Kamp, 2004; Bende-Farkas et al., 2003) develops a DRT approach that is based on Alternative Semantics (Rooth, 1985, 1992). For information structure he uses the background-focus division. Focus stands for the constituent carrying the focal pitch accent, while the rest of the utterance forms the background. The background-focus division is illustrated in Example 3.25.

(3.25)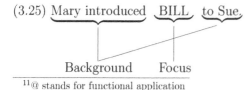

---

[11] @ stands for functional application

Besides representing the meaning of the proposition at hand, which Kamp
calls the *'Focus' proposition* (c.f. the ordinary semantic value of Rooth), he
also includes the semantics of the alternatives to the 'Focus' proposition in
his representation. He calls his representations *focus frame-focus divisions* (ff-f
divisions). A ff-f division is a three-tuple, consisting of a *restrictor*, a *focus
frame* and a *focus constituent*. Example 3.26 illustrates a ff-f division for the
sentence *'Mary introduced Bill to Sue'*.[12]

(3.26)
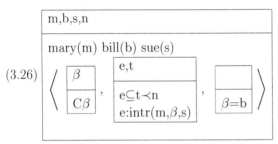

The first element in the triple in Example 3.26 is the restrictor of the given ff-f
division. β stands for the focus variable of the ff-f division. It replaces the focus
marked constituent, which is λ-abstracted from the semantic representation of
the sentence. The logical type of the focus variable is always the same as that
of the replaced focus constituent. Since in Example 3.26 the focus variable
replaces the discourse referent b that stands for Bill, the type of the focus
variable in the present case is that of an individual. The possible values for a
focus variable are restricted by the context of the utterance. Predicate C in
the restrictor expresses this constraint.

The second element of the ff-f division is the focus frame itself. The focus
frame is derived from the semantic representation of the particular utterance
by replacing its focused constituent by a focus variable.[13]

Finally, the third element of the ff-f division is the focus constituent. The
condition in the focus constituent DRS narrows the set of contextually appropriate alternatives down to the actual focus of the given utterance.

---

[12]The discourse referents m,b,s and n and the conditions $mary(m), bill(b)$ and $sue(s)$ appear outside
of the focus frame, due to their presuppositional status (these discourse referents correspond to proper
names, i.e. definite descriptions), and in the given example it is assumed that the presuppositions
associated with these referents have already been resolved.

[13]The condition $e \subseteq t \prec n$ in the focus frame says that the event e took place at a time t that was
before now (n), i.e. that the event happened in the past.

As mentioned previously, the predicate C in the restrictor of the ff-f division represents the contextual constraint on the set of focus alternatives. Since the value of C has to be determined from the context, it can be treated as an "anaphoric" presupposition (van der Sandt, 1992). This presupposition can be explicitly represented in the ff-f division (See Example 3.27).

(3.27)

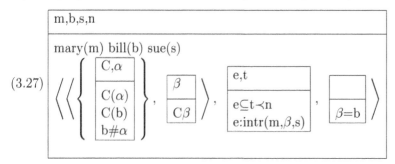

In Example 3.27 the presupposition associated with the contextual variable C is represented between the curly brackets. According to (Rooth, 1992) a set of focus alternatives has to minimally contain the focus value itself and at least one other element. In 3.27, the reference marker b stands for the actual value of the focus of the utterance, while the variable α stands for some alternative to it. It is not specified whether α stands for an individual or for a set of individuals. The condition $b\#\alpha$ captures the fact that α has to be disjoint from b.

In order to resolve the presupposition associated with the contextual variable C, one has to look into the preceding context.[14] Kamp (2004) assumes that the utterance in 3.25 was uttered in the context of Example 3.28.

(3.28) A: I know that Carl, Bill and Fred were in the room and I saw that Mary introduced one of them to Sue. But who was it?

    B: Mary introduced [Bill]$_F$ to Sue.

In the context of Example 3.28 there are three individuals, Carl, Bill and Fred, each of whom might have been introduced by Mary to Sue. Thus, the alternative set consists of three propositions where the focus variable slot in the focus frame is filled by Carl, Bill or Fred respectively. Kamp (2004) suggests that the presupposition introduced by the contextual variable C can be

---

[14]This is a simplification, as things may be contextually given without having been explicitly verbalized.

solved as the predicate $\lambda\beta.\beta \in \{c,b,f\}$, where c,b and f represent the three focus alternatives present in the context. This method allows us to convert the representation in Example 3.28 into the one in Example 3.29.

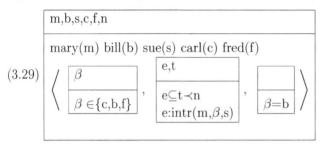

According to Alternative Semantics (Rooth, 1985, 1992) the semantic value of an utterance is a pair <Q,P>, where Q is a set of propositions and P is a proposition or set of propositions belonging to Q.[15] In terms of ff-f division the restrictor combined with the focus frame yield the alternative set Q. If all three parts of the division, the restrictor, the focus frame, and the focus constituent, are combined, the result is the actual 'Focus' proposition, which corresponds to Rooth's ordinary semantic value. Kamp (2004) calls P *focus selection.*

In Kamp et al. 2003, the representation is expanded to envelop the notion of *contrastive topic* as well. The authors assume a great similarity between the information structures induced by focus and contrastive topic (for more details please refer to Kamp et al. 2003, pp. 13-15).

The ff-f division allows Kamp (2004) to account for the behaviour of focus-sensitive operators like *'only'.* He assumes that such operators take ff-f structures as their arguments.

New information in DRT

A different approach to including information structure in DRT was taken in Poesio et al. 2000. They rely on the distinction between new and old information. In order to represent this distinction in DRSs, they mark the DRS-conditions that represent new information as new, the remaining conditions are then viewed as old or given information.

---

[15]Turning the second member of the pair into a set is an addition of Kamp (2004). He argues that there are cases where the focus value is not necessarily a singleton.

The main motivation behind the approach developed was to improve the quality of prosody of context-to-speech generation in dialogue systems. It has been observed that in natural speech the focal accent is usually placed on new information, while given information tends to be deaccented. Therefore, a semantic representation was needed that would have newness/givenness information readily available. From such a representation surface strings could be generated where words would be marked as new or given, so that they could receive appropriate accentuation from the speech synthesizer.

In order to mark new information in DRSs an addition was made to the DRS language. The addition only applied to basic DRS-conditions. It took the following form: if C is a basic DRS-condition, then $NEW(C)$ is a basic DRS-condition with the addition that it represents new information. The NEW tag was only used when deciding the placement of accents: the semantic interpretation function treated conditions of the type $NEW(C)$ as if they were of the type C.

Discussion

My aim in this book is to find a representation for semantics that reflects information structure, and is suitable both for natural language generation and automatic inference. According to Blackburn and Bos (2003a,b, 2005), it is sensible to use a representation for natural language semantics that is easy to translate into first order logic, because a wide range of first-order model builders, theorem provers and other automatic inference tools are available "off-the-shelf". Therefore, our representation language should not be more complicated than first order logic. Regarding natural language generation: not only do we want to be able to generate strings of text, but also to determine the intonation contour of the generated strings. This means that we need a semantic representation which enables inferring information related to accent placement. In what follows, we will examine the traditional Montague-style lambda-approaches with information structure and the three previously discussed approaches of information structure in DRT from the vantage point of the above requirements.

Regarding the traditional lambda-calculus-based approaches with information structure, to my knowledge the most advanced one is the approach presented by Steedman (2000b,a, 2003) (see Section 3.3.1 for a brief introduction). His semantic representation fares very well as far as being able to specify intonation from semantics is concerned. However, it performs less well when considered from the generation and inference perspective. First, the requirement of Montague-style grammar that arguments be presented in a fixed order, makes equality checks difficult. Neither is this semantics easily decomposable. From the inference perspective: in order to acquire a first order representation from the semantics with information structure, an additional step of β-reduction needs to be performed. However, in this step we lose the details about information structure. This means that we do not have a representation that simultaneously reflects information structure and is suitable for first-order inference.

Above I reviewed three approaches to representing information structure in DRT: TF-DRSs (Kruijff-Korbayová, 1998), Focus Frame-Focus Divisions (Bende-Farkas et al., 2003; Kamp, 2004) and New Information approach (Poesio et al., 2000). These approaches differ from each other considerably. This is mainly due to the difference in their objectives. The principal goal of Focus Frame-Focus Structures (Kamp, 2004; Bende-Farkas et al., 2003) was to provide a DRT representation for the model theoretic approach of Rooth (1985, 1992). TF-DRSs (Kruijff-Korbayová, 1998) aimed at giving a DRT account of Peregrin's (1996) formal treatment of information structure. On the other hand the implementation of (Poesio et al., 2000) was driven by a practical goal of using the representation in speech generation in order to improve the accuracy of accent placement.

From the inference point of view, there is the same problem with TF-DRSs (Kruijff-Korbayová, 1998) as I described above about lambda-calculus: we cannot have a representation that simultaneously conveys information structure and is compatible with the first order logic language. A step of β-reduction has to be performed in order to obtain from TF-DRSs a DRS that is suitable for inference. Note that this would be a DRS and not a TF-DRS any more: it would be stripped from the information-structural details. This DRS can then be translated into first order logic by standard algorithms (e.g. in Kamp and Reyle 1993). TF-DRSs add an additional level of recursivity to DRT, and as such they do not conform very well with the widely accepted view that for natural language generation semantic representation with minimal recursion is best suited. Finally, TF-DRSs only reflect the topic-focus partitioning, but they do not say anything about accent placement inside these partitionings. As such TF-DRSs are not too well suited for intonation generation either.

The approach of Focus Frame-Focus Divisions (Bende-Farkas et al., 2003; Kamp, 2004) uses higher order representations. No algorithm has been defined for these structures to translate them into first order logic. This means that they are not easily adaptable for first-order inference. Higher order reasoning would be needed for such structures.

Besides the above, there is another reason why ff-f divisions and TF-DRSs do not comply with my aims: I plan to embed my semantic representation in a unification-based grammar framework; however, since both ff-f divisions and TF-DRSs manipulate the inner structure of DRSs, there does not seem to be a straightforward way of incorporating them in such a framework.

All in all, my objectives are more in line with the approach presented in Poesio et al. 2000, although their representation of information structure is too "bare-bones" for my aims. I will take the approach of Poesio et al. (2000) as my point of departure and mark the DRS-conditions for information structure. However, I will considerably enrich the representation of information structure. My proposal for how to represent information structure in DRT will be outlined in Section 3.3.

3.3 IS-DRS: Discourse Representation Structure with Information Structure

In this section I will implement Steedman's prosodic account of information structure (Steedman, 2000b,a, 2003) in DRT. His approach was summarised in Section 2.2. Here, we will first take a quick look at how Steedman represents information structure in semantics. Then, as a preparatory step towards introducing my representation, we will discuss neo-Davidsonian event semantics. Finally, in 3.3.3, I will propose my own representation of information structure in DRT, where I use information-structural flags on DRS-conditions. I call this represention an *IS-DRS*. To start with, I will present a simple "bare-bones" version of the semantic representation, which only makes use of the notions

of theme and rheme, and theme- and rheme-focus. I will gradually develop
the original representation adding detail to provide a richer representation of
information structure.

As noted earlier, my aims are practical in nature: I am foremost concerned with identifying the information-structural elements in order to allow
for the generation of more natural, context-appropriate intonation. Therefore, I presently assume that the automatic inference tools *de facto* ignore the
information structure in their computations. However, since all the relevant
information about information-structural partitionings will be present in my
representation, I anticipate that in the future computations can be specified
that take information structure into account.

Due to my practical orientation, IS-DRSs do not share many common properties with either TF-DRSs (Kruijff-Korbayová, 2004), or Focus Frame-Focus
Divisions (Kamp, 2004; Bende-Farkas et al., 2003). In the case of these two previous approaches the main interest lay in the impact of information structure
on semantic computations. Kruijff-Korbayová endeavoured to demonstrate in
her framework how information structure influences the place where information gets accommodated in a DRS (i.e. global vs. local accommodation). Kamp
on the other hand sought to provide a DRT account for Alternative Semantics (Rooth, 1985), and model certain semantically interesting aspects of focus
(e.g. focus sensitive adverbs). Of the previous approaches, my approach is the
closest to the "new information" approach of Poesio et al. (2000), both with
regard to its aims and the actual representation.

3.3.1   Another Look at the Prosodic Account of Infor-
mation Structure

Leaving the precise technicalities aside, the general idea behind Steedman's
(2000b; 2000a; 2003) proposal is that lexical items which carry a pitch accent
are marked by a theme (θ) or a rheme (ρ) feature, according to the type of
the pitch accent that occurs on them. Boundary tones are independent lexical
units and serve to delimit the intonational phrases. Via the combinatorial
process the lexical items in each intonational phrase are combined with each
other. During the combinations the resulting phrases inherit their information-

structural marking from the lexical item which carries the pitch accent. At the pre-final stage of the combinatory process we are presented with full theme and rheme intonational phrases. The type of information-structural unit is also reflected in the corresponding semantics (see Example 3.30[16]). During the final step of the combinatory process the full intonational phrases are combined with each other and the whole is marked as a phrase, whereby the specifics of the information-structural partitioning are lost. Examples of the actual CCG derivations including information structure will be provided in Section 6.1 in Chapter 6.

(3.30) Harry admires   Louise.

     L+H*   LH%   H* LL%

     $\theta'(\lambda x.admire'x\ ^*harry')$ $\rho'(\lambda p.p\ ^*louise')$

In Section 2.2 in Chapter 2 we discussed the semantics that Steedman (2003) attributes to the pitch accents and boundary tones in English. His full system of pitch accents and boundary tones was illustrated in Tables 2.1 and 2.2 in Section 2.2. Example 3.31 shows the semantics for the sentence in 3.30 with the additional semantics of boundary tones (speaker commitment: $[S]$, hearer commitment: $[H]$) and pitch accents ($\pm AGREED$).

(3.31) $[H^+]\theta'(\lambda x.admire'x\ ^*harry')\ [S^+]\rho'(\lambda p.p\ ^*louise')$

I am going to implement his general ideas. However, the set of pitch accents and boundary tones that I will implement is more constrained than his, since I prefer not to include pitch accents or boundary tones which are semantically synonymous. That is not to say that I negate the existence in English of the remainder of the pitch accents and boundary tones that Steedman uses. However, I do believe that more research needs to be done into the semantics of prosody, before a fuller system can be implemented. If needed, it is easy to extend my system with additional information-structural flags. Table 3.1 illustrates the set of the pitch accents and boundary tones currently included in the system.

---

[16]The asterisk (*) in the example means that the item following it is focused, i.e. carries a pitch accent.

Table 3.1: The Meanings of the Pitch Accents and Boundary Tones

	+	−
θ	L+H*	L*+H
ρ	H*	L*

$[S]$	LL%
$[H]$	LH%

3.3.2   Neo-Davidsonian Event-Semantics

In their use of language people constantly make reference to time – through the use of tensed verbs as well as time adverbials. There have been several proposals about how to deal with temporal reference inside logical formulae.

It is important to be able to locate a sentence in time when assigning a truth value to it. But the two most natural ways of viewing time – "time as instants" and "time as intervals" pose problems of their own (see Kamp and Reyle 1993, pp. 500-504). Davidson (1967) found a way around the problem by describing actions as events, which can precede each other, follow each other, or happen simultaneously. The only problem with this semantics is that it is not easy to define events, and their general properties.

Davidson used an explicit event variable in logical forms (see Example 3.32). The great significance of this little addition to semantics lies in the fact that this little variable made it possible to speak about properties of events in the language of first order logic. Davidson proposed the representation of verbs in action sentences as multi-place relations, their arguments being a special event variable e, and their nominal argument(s). Thus, according to his approach, a transitive verb would be a three place relation.

(3.32) Fred met Mary in the street at noon.
   $\exists e \exists s \exists t (meeting(e, Fred, Mary) \,\&\, street(s) \,\&\, noon(t) \,\&\, in(e, s) \,\&\, at(e, t))$

Davidsonian theory was developed further by the so-called neo-Davidsonian approaches. In this book I implement the "Parsonian" variety of the neo-Davidsonian theory (Parsons, 1990). A more recent account of this approach is provided in Landman 2000.

There are basically two innovations: a) according to this theory all verbs, statives as well as non-statives, have an implicit event argument, b) the original arguments of the verb are now presented as separate conjuncts, by means of θ-roles. The second innovation means that in this approach verbs are no longer relations – instead, they are one-place predicates with the respective event variable as their sole argument, and the nominal arguments of the verb are added to the semantic form conjunctively as two-place predicates (see Example 3.33).

(3.33) Fred met Mary in the street at noon.

$\exists e \exists s \exists t (meeting(e) \ \& \ experiencer(e, Fred) \ \& \ patient(e, Mary) \ \& \ street(s)$
$\& \ noon(t) \ \& \ in(e, s) \ \& \ at(e, t))$

In this book I combine neo-Davidsonian event semantics with DRT. Translating the first-order formula in Example 3.33 into DRT is straightforward: in essence, I introduce the variables bound by existential quantifiers into the universe of the DRS, and the conjuncts expressing relations and properties go into the bottom part of the DRS. However, there are other two discourse referents present for which the original formula did not use variables, namely, the referent of the name *'Fred'* and the referent of the name *'Mary'*. For these I introduce two new variables (x and y) into the universe of the DRS, while the corresponding DRS-conditions (*fred(y)* and *mary(x)*) go into the bottom part of the DRS together with the rest of the conditions. Example 3.34 shows the DRS version of the formula in 3.33.

(3.34)

e,x,y,s,t	
fred(y)	mary(x)
meeting(e)	experiencer(e,y)
patient(e,x)	street(s)
noon(t)	in(e,s)
at(e,t)	

3.3.3 IS-DRS

In this section we will gradually develop the representation for DRSs with information structure that we will use in the rest of the book. I call this representation an *IS-DRS*. At first we will only include theme and rheme flags in our representation. This representation is rather general and, as such, it is compatible with any grammar system operating with the notions of theme and rheme, or topic and focus, or any other major division of information structure. Then we will specify the "kind" of theme/rheme by introducing Steedman's $\pm AGREED$ feature (Steedman, 2003) in the system. Finally, we will incorporate the semantics of boundary tones into our representation.

IS-DRS with Theme and Rheme

In contrast to the approaches of TF-DRS (Kruijff-Korbayová, 2004) and Focus Frame-Focus Divisions (Kamp, 2004; Bende-Farkas et al., 2003), which we discussed in Section 3.2.3, I do not introduce any explicit graphical partitioning of theme and rheme in the DRS. I prefer to stay as close to the original version of DRT as possible. As mentioned previously, I incorporate information structure in DRT in the form of flags on DRS conditions. In this sense my approach is similar to the "new information" approach of Poesio et al. (2000, see Section 3.2.3) where *NEW*-tags were used on DRS-conditions which corresponded to new information. However, our information-structural labels will reflect a much richer variety of semantic aspects of information structure.

Following Steedman's example (Steedman, 2000b,a, 2003) we use the Greek letters θ and ρ to denote theme and rheme respectively. We also mark the placement of pitch accents in semantics. We use '+' in the case the lexical exponent of the DRS-condition carries a pitch accent and '−' if it does not.

I will already introduce the DRS syntax here that we will adhere to in the remainder of the book: similarly to the convention of the Prolog programming language we use upper-case characters to denote variables while lower case characters are reserved for constants.

(3.35) a) Who did Aristotle teach?

[Aristotle taught]$_\theta$ [young ALEXANDER the GREAT]$_\rho$.

b) Who taught young Alexander the Great?

[ARISTOTLE]$_\rho$ [taught young Alexander the Great]$_\theta$.

c) I know Plato taught young Callippus, but who did Aristotle teach?

[ARISTOTLE taught]$_\theta$ [young ALEXANDER the GREAT]$_\rho$.

a°)

X,Y,E	
aristotle(X)	$\theta-$
alexander_the_great(Y)	$\rho+$
young(Y)	$\rho-$
teach(E)	$\theta-$
time(E,past)	
agent(E,X)	
patient(E,Y)	

b°)

X,Y,E	
aristotle(X)	$\rho+$
alexander_the_great(Y)	$\theta-$
young(Y)	$\theta-$
teach(E)	$\theta-$
time(E,past)	
agent(E,X)	
patient(E,Y)	

c°)

X,Y,E	
aristotle(X)	$\theta+$
alexander_the_great(Y)	$\rho+$
young(Y)	$\rho-$
teach(E)	$\theta-$
time(E,past)	
agent(E,X)	
patient(E,Y)	

Example 3.35 above illustrates this simple version of IS-DRS. Each of the sentences, a, b and c, have their corresponding IS-DRS, a°, b° and c°, below. Let's take a closer look at 3.35c, which contains a marked theme. The theme of the sentence '*ARISTOTLE taught*' gives rise to five DRS-conditions. I only chose to use information-structural flags on the "lexical" DRS-conditions, i.e. the ones that have a direct lexical exponent. '*ARISTOTLE*' which carries a theme pitch accent is labeled as theme and focus, i.e. $\theta+$. The other lexical item in the theme '*taught*' is unstressed and is therefore marked as an un-focused part of the theme: $\theta-$. The verb introduces three other DRS-conditions *time* and the semantic roles *agent* and *patient*. These conditions represent relations rather than having a direct lexical exponent.[17] In the case of such conditions I chose not to use any information-structural labelling. This is not the only possible choice: for example, these conditions could inherit their marking from the verb. However, this issue is not of great importance, being foremost a

---

[17] The status of the DRS-condition *time* is questionable though. Especially seen that in the case of composite verb forms like 'has taught', it is not uncommon in the least that the auxiliary carries a (contrastive) pitch accent, while the main verb does not. However, this problem is out of the scope of the present book and is left for future work.

matter of personal preference. The remaining part of the sentence, *'young ALEXANDER the GREAT'*, forms the rheme, and the two DRS-conditions introduced by it are marked as such. *'ALEXANDER the GREAT'* is marked by a pitch accent, and therefore the corresponding DRS condition is marked by '+', i.e. as a focus. The word *'young'* is unstressed and, therefore, marked as unfocused.

The Semantics of Boundary Tones

The boundary tones that we will include in our system are LL% and LH%. There is another boundary tone that Steedman (Steedman, 2000b,a, 2003) frequently uses in his examples, namely a short L boundary. This boundary only occurs in sentence internal positions, and never at the end of a sentence. Since the semantics that Steedman proposes for the L boundary is the same as the one he proposes for the LL%, I view the L boundary as a sentence internal variant of the LL% boundary. In our system these two boundaries are identical, and we always mark them by LL%. It is simply the case that sentence internally the LL% is realised with a shorter duration.

Steedman (2003) explained the difference in the meaning of the LL% and the LH% boundary by referring to the notion of "commitment" or "responsibility". Thus, by using the LL% boundary at the end of a prosodic phrase, the speaker indicates that s/he is committed to the given information unit, while by using the LH% s/he delegates the responsibility to the hearer.

Steedman marked this dimension of the speaker/hearer commitment added by boundary tones by S and H in the semantics. Due to the constraints of the DRS syntax that was specified above, we cannot use upper case letters for these values, since those are used for variables. We will keep close to Steedman's notation, but will use lower case characters instead: the letter s on a DRS-condition to indicate speaker and h to indicate hearer responsibility.

Example 3.36 re-analyses the sentence from Example 3.35c. Rather than using explicit bracketing, we show the information-structural partitioning by intonational marking. Hence, the boundary tones LH% and LL% serve to delimit the intonational phrases and the pitch accents L+H* and H* contribute the themeness/rhemeness property respectively. In addition, the LH% boundary tone indicates that the theme is the hearer's responsibility, whilst the final

LL% boundary tone attributes the rheme to the speaker. Owing to the boundary tones, the DRS conditions that the theme gives rise to are flagged by h, and the ones corresponding to the rheme are marked by s.

(3.36) I know Plato taught young Callippus, but who did Aristotle teach?

ARISTOTLE taught   young ALEXANDER the GREAT.

   L+H*   LH%   H*   H* LL%

X,Y,E
aristotle(X) $\theta + h$
alexander_the_great(Y) $\rho + s$
young(Y) $\rho - s$
teach(E) $\theta - h$
time(E,past)
agent(E,X)
patient(E,Y)

Adding the $\pm AGREED$ Dimension

Finally, we are going to add the $\pm AGREED$ dimension of pitch accents to our representation. Table 3.2 displays once more the subset of Steedman's (2003) pitch accents that we incorporate in our system. As a quick reminder: the $+AGREED$ feature marks the information-structural unit as uncontentious, while the $-AGREED$ signals that the speaker does not exactly expect the hearer to share his/her opinion. We are going to mark the $\pm AGREED$ dimension as '+' and '−' flags on DRS conditions.[18]

Example 3.37 illustrates the $\pm AGREED$ flags. Checking in Table 3.2 we see that both of the pitch accents used in 3.37a, L+H* and H*, belong to the $+AGREED$ column. Hence, the DRS-conditions introduced by both the theme and the rheme of the utterance are marked by the final '+' flags. There is nothing contentious about 3.37a: speaker B simply answers speaker A's question. On the other hand, in 3.37b, speaker B corrects speaker A's mistake. Speaker A might not agree with speaker B. Speaker B signals this by the use of an L*+H accent on *'Aristotle'*, which has the feature $-AGREED$. At the same time speaker B is sure that he is correct: he indicates his conviction by

---

[18]Note that we use the same flags for focus marking. The flags of $\pm AGREED$ dimension are distinguished form the focus flags by their final position in the array of the flags.

using the LL% boundary tone. 3.37b is an all-theme utterance, and all the DRS-conditions of the corresponding DRS are marked by the final '$-$' flags signalling the presence of the $-AGREED$ feature.

Table 3.2: The Meanings of the Pitch Accents

	+	$-$
θ	L+H*	L*+H
ρ	H*	L*

(3.37) a) A: I know Plato taught young Callippus, but who did Aristotle teach?
    B: ARISTOTLE taught   young ALEXANDER the GREAT.
         L+H*   LH%   H*   H* LL%
    b) A: Plato taught young Alexander the Great, but ...
    B: ARISTOTLE taught   young Alexander the Great.
         L*+H   LL%

X,Y,E	
aristotle(X)	$\theta+$ $h+$
alexander_the_great(Y)	$\rho+$ $s+$
young(Y)	$\rho-$ $s+$
teach(E)	$\theta-$ $h+$
time(E,past)	
agent(E,X)	
patient(E,Y)	

a°)

X,Y,E	
aristotle(X)	$\theta+$ $s-$
alexander_the_great(Y)	$\theta-$ $s-$
young(Y)	$\theta-$ $s-$
teach(E)	$\theta-$ $s-$
time(E,past)	
agent(E,X)	
patient(E,Y)	

b°)

Unmarked Themes

Besides marked themes, that contain a pitch accent, there are also unmarked themes. In fact, unmarked themes are much more common than marked themes. We already briefly touched upon the issue of unmarked themes in Section 2.2 of Chapter 2. However, I have not explained, as yet, the standing of unmarked themes in our system of representation. One option would be to flag them as regular themes: the absence of focus would then indicate that we are dealing with an unmarked theme. Another possibility would be to introduce a new flag specific to unmarked themes. However, we take a third approach of marking these information-structural phrases as underspecified: we use a variable for the themeness/rhemeness value of unmarked themes. The main motivation for this choice lies in the kind of grammar formalism I want to combine our semantic representation with. The reasons of my decision will become much clearer in Chapter 6 where the interaction between the syntax, semantics and information structure of the grammar framework will be explained. By using the literary device of foreshadowing I can reveal at this point that all the information-structural flags on DRS-conditions start up as variables, and only acquire constant values via unification during the process of syntactic combination.

Marked themes and rhemes inherit their themeness/rhemeness from the pitch accent in the intonational phrase. They also inherit their $\pm AGREED$ feature from the pitch accent. That's why in the case of unmarked themes the value of both of these DRS flags is a variable. Example 3.38 illustrates the representation for unmarked themes. The theme of the utterance, '*Aristotle taught*', does not contain any pitch accents, therefore the themeness/rhemeness and the $\pm AGREED$ feature flags are represented by variables I and A. Now one might ask how we can tell from the DRS representation that we are dealing with an unmarked theme if the value of the flag is a variable? The answer is as simple as that: "Unmarked rhemes do not exist." Rhemes always contain a pitch accent. Thus, if we have an intonational phrase which does not have its themeness/rhemeness value specified, then it can only be an unmarked theme.

(3.38) Who did Aristotle teach?

Aristotle taught young Alexander the Great.
     LL%   H*   H* LL%

X,Y,E	
aristotle(X)	$I-$ sA
alexander_the_great(Y)	$\rho+$ $s+$
young(Y)	$\rho-$ $s+$
teach(E)	$I-$ sA
time(E,past)	
agent(E,X)	
patient(E,Y)	

3.4   Conclusion

In this chapter we examined various issues pertaining to the semantics of information structure. We started by exploring the model theoretic meaning which has been attributed to information-structure partitionings. I briefly reviewed the Structured Meanings approach (von Stechow, 1981) and Alternative Semantics (Rooth, 1992; Büring, 1995) which provide a model theoretic account of focus and topic.

We briefly studied the previous representations that have been proposed for semantics with information structure. As approaches that are set in the framework of DRT (Kamp and Reyle, 1993) are especially relevant to the approach that is being developed in this book, these approaches received particular attention. We reviewed three such approaches: TF-DRSs (Kruijff-Korbayová, 1998), Focus Frame-Focus Divisions (Bende-Farkas et al., 2003; Kamp, 2004) and New Information approach (Poesio et al., 2000). The conclusion was that neither TF-DRSs nor Focus Frame-Focus Divisions were well suited for use in content-to-speech generation. For our objectives, the approach taken in Poesio et al. 2000 seemed the most promising, although in the need of considerable refinement.

I proceeded by presenting my own representation for information structure in DRT. We incorporated information structure in DRT in the form of flags on DRS-conditions. First we developed a rather simple version of the semantic representation which only included the theme, rheme and focus flags. Then we gradually added detail, such as boundary tone semantics and the contribution to meaning made by different pitch accents.

The semantic representation with information structure I presented in this chapter is well suited for the use in the analysis of natural language, since it is set in the dynamic framework of DRT. It is well-suited for the use in content-to-speech generation, because it is relatively simple, and not encumbered with excessive semantic detail. It can also be easily used in combination with natural language inference tools like first-order theorem provers and model checkers.

Chapter 4

Unification-based Combinatory Categorial Grammar

In the next three chapters we will develop the grammar formalism which will ultimately provide the link between the IS-DRSs and intonationally annotated text. I call the new formalism *Unification-based Combinatory Categorial Grammar* (UCCG). UCCG belongs to the family of *Categorial Grammars*. It employs feature structures called *signs* in its linguistic representation. Signs can be combined according to *combinatory rules* to form other signs. The operation of unification is the heart of the formalism: values are passed along between different features and different sub-parts of signs via variable unification.

The present chapter provides a general introduction to UCCG. It explains the representations and the machinery of operations available in the formalism. The main focus of the chapter is on working out the syntactic categories, and the basic features to be used in the UCCG feature structures. I also explicate my approach of closely coupling the syntax and semantics of the representations by means of variable unification. In this chapter for the sake of simplicity we use predicate calculus for semantic representation. This will be replaced by a more advanced representation at a later stage.

Section 4.1 begins by explaining the main characteristics of Categorial Grammars. Of these, *Combinatory Categorial Grammar* (CCG) and *Unification Categorial Grammar* (UCG) are the ones most closely related to UCCG. Therefore Section 4.1.1 gives an overview of CCG, whilst Section 4.1.2 provides a brief account of UCG. Section 4.2 discusses the aspects that UCCG has in common with CCG and UCG, and the ways it differs from them. The rest of the chapter is devoted to the basics of UCCG. Section 4.3 introduces the major terminology and the representations used in UCCG. Section 4.4 introduces the basic building blocks of UCCG signs. Section 4.5 introduces the machinery of combinatory rules, elaborates on the material of Section 4.4 and presents more complex structures for particular word classes.

4.1   Categorial Grammars

The term *Categorial Grammar* (CG) refers to a group of grammar theories that share some important features. Most significantly all of them make use of the notion of *category*, a functional type associated with each linguistic expression. Among the theories belonging to this group are Classical Categorial Grammar or Lambek Calculus, Categorial Unification Grammar (CUG), Unification Categorial Grammar (UCG), Combinatory Categorial Grammar (CCG) with its offsprings Multiset-CCG and Multi-Modal CCG, and Unification Combinatory Categorial Grammar (UCCG) proposed in the present book. The origin of CGs can be traced back to three principal sources: the philosophy of Frege (1891, 1892), the logic of Ajdukiewicz (1935) and the algebraic calculus of Lambek (1958).

CGs are lexicalised theories of grammar: each entry in the lexicon is associated with a category. The category of a lexical item fully determines its combinatorial capabilities: how and with which kinds of items the given item can be combined. Generally speaking, there are two types of categories: functor categories and argument categories. Since the grammar is fully specified by categories, there is no need for specific phrase structure rules. Instead, a small set of general syntactico-semantic operations is specified that, in principle, can be performed on any category the only restriction being that the given category be compatible with the particular operation. Another characteristic trait of CGs is their relaxed attitude towards the notion of traditional syntactic constituency. (For more information on CGs see Wood 1993, 2000 and Steedman 1999).

4.1.1   Combinatory Categorial Grammar

Combinatory Categorial Grammar (CCG) (Steedman, 1996, 2000b) is a gen-

eralisation of CG. The pure CG, or the classical Categorial Grammar, only involved two rules for combining categories: forward and backward application. CCG introduces several additional combinatory rules. In total it has a machinery of thirteen combinatory rules.

Unlike its predecessors, CCG uses directional slash notation. Steedman introduced this specific "result-leftmost" notation in his 1987 paper. The main motivation for this notation was the "need for consistent argument-result order for readability and cross-linguistic generalisation" (Steedman, personal communication). There was also a practical reason to choose the slash notation over a graphically more complex one: it was comfortable to use the slash notation on a typewriter, which those days was more than a minor advantage. In this notation, a forward slash means that the category is looking for an argument of the appropriate type on its right, while a backward slash means that the argument has to be found on the left.

CCG has three basic categories, which do not contain any slashes. These are: sentence (S), noun (N) and noun phrase (NP). All other categories are constructed from the three basic categories using the slash operators. For example, the CCG syntactic category for a typical transitive verb looks like follows:

(4.1) loves := (S\NP)/NP

The category in Example 4.1 means that *'loves'* is a transitive verb which first looks for an object noun phrase to its right, and then for a subject noun phrase to its left.[1]

In addition to forward and backward application, CCG incorporates rules for forward composition, backward composition, forward crossed composition, backward crossed composition, and four substitution rules: forward, backward, forward crossed and backward crossed substitution. Besides the above, it also has two rules for type-raising, which are not combinatory in the sense that they only involve an operation on a single category. And finally, it has a rule for coordination, which allows two categories with the same syntactic type, but different semantics, to be combined into a single category. The full set of CCG's combinatory rules can be seen in Table 4.1. The variables X, Y, Z and T stand

---

[1]As we will see shortly CCG also provides means that allow a transitive verb to first combine with its subject.

for any CCG category, either basic or complex. Examples 4.2a, 4.2b and 4.3 demonstrate how combinatory rules are used to analyse English sentences. In CCG analysis, usually the upside-down tree representation is used, with a line below the constituents that are being combined. This line has the notation seen in the brackets in Table 4.1 either at the right hand end or the left hand end, depending on whether the combinatory rule that it stands for involves a forward or a backward combination. The result category is recorded below the "rule" line.

Table 4.1: The Combinatory Rules of CCG

Forward application (>)	X/Y Y → X
Backward application (<)	Y X\Y → X
Forward composition (>**B**)	X/Y Y/Z →**B** X/Z
Backward composition (<**B**)	Y\Z X\Y →**B** X\Z
Forward crossed composition (>**B**×)	X/Y Y\Z →**B** X\Z
Backward crossed composition (<**B**×)	Y/Z X\Y →**B** X/Z
Forward substitution (>**S**)	(X/Y)/Z Y/Z →**s** X/Z
Backward substitution (<**S**)	Y\Z (X\Y)\Z →**s** X\Z
Forward crossed substitution (>**S**×)	(X/Y)\Z Y\Z →**s** X\Z
Backward crossed substitution (<**S**×)	Y/X (X\Y)/Z →**s** X/Z
Type-raising A (>**T**)	X →**T** T/(T\X)
Type-raising B (<**T**)	X →**T** T\(T/X)
Coordination rule (<Φ>)	X and X′ →**Φ** X″

In Example 4.2a the sentence *'Anna married Manny'* is analysed according to the "traditional" phrase structure. First, the transitive verb *'married'* is combined with its object *'Manny'* via forward application to form a verb phrase with the CCG category $S \backslash NP$. Then the verb phrase is combined with

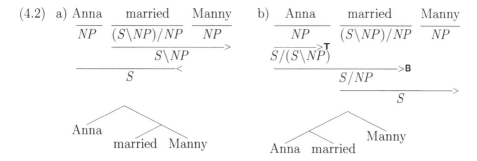

its subject using the rule of backward application. The result of this operation is the CCG category S. However, there is also an alternative analysis for the same sentence, which can be seen in Example 4.2b. According to the second analysis, the subject and the transitive verb are combined first. In order for this combination to be possible the subject NP first needs to be type-raised (type-raising rule A), which gives us the category $S/(S \backslash NP)$. The combination of the type-raised subject and the transitive verb results in the category S/NP. According to the majority of grammar theories this is not an acceptable syntactic constituent, and such combinations are not permitted. (However, as it will soon turn out this peculiarity of CCG is in many ways a virtue rather than a vice.) Finally, in 4.2b the "subject+transitive verb" category is combined with the object. Similarly to the analysis in 4.2a, the final result is the category S. Below each analysis there is a more conventionally shaped phrase structure tree which illustrates the constituent structure of the sentence according to the two different analyses.

One occasion where the non-standard constituents of CCG come very handy is that of coordination. It is equally common to have coordination between standard constituents (*NPs*, *VPs*, sentences) and non-standard constituents (subject+*TVs*, argument clusters). "Non-constituent" coordination poses big problems for theories which do not recognise such constituents. However, for CCG this is no problem at all: non-constituent coordination comes as a bonus with the package. Example 4.3 demonstrates a CCG analysis of a sentence that involves coordination between two subject+*TV* constituents.

(4.3)

Keats	steals	and	Chapman	eats	apples
NP	$(S\backslash NP)/NP$	$CONJ$	NP	$(S\backslash NP)/NP$	NP

$$\frac{NP}{S/(S\backslash NP)}\text{>}\mathbf{T}$$

$$\frac{S/(S\backslash NP)}{S/NP}\text{>}\mathbf{B}$$

$$\frac{NP}{S/(S\backslash NP)}\text{>}\mathbf{T}$$

$$\frac{S/(S\backslash NP)}{S/NP}\text{>}\mathbf{B}$$

$$\frac{}{S/NP}\text{<}\Phi\text{>}$$

$$\frac{S/NP}{S}\text{>}$$

So far I have said nothing about semantics in CCG. In essence, each syntactic category has a semantic description associated with it, and for each combinatory rule a corresponding operation on the semantics is defined, or as Steedman puts it (2000b, page 37): a syntactic rule is simply a translation of its semantic counterpart. He formulates the following principle to govern the relationship between syntax and semantics:

> *The Principle of Combinatory Type Transparency*
> All syntactic combinatory rules are type-transparent versions of one of a small number of simple semantic operations over functions.

Most commonly, the lambda calculus is used to represent semantics in the CCG tradition.[2] Example 4.4 presents the category for the transitive verb *'loves'* once more, this time with its corresponding semantics, and Example 4.5 displays the full analysis of the sentence *'Keats steals and Chapman eats apples'* including semantics.

(4.4) loves := (S\NP)/NP : $\lambda x \lambda y.\text{love}(y,x)$

(4.5)

Keats	steals	and	Chapman	eats	apples
NP	$(S\backslash NP)/NP$	$CONJ$	NP	$(S\backslash NP)/NP$	NP
$: keats'$	$: \lambda x.\lambda y.steal'xy$	$: and'$	$: chapman'$	$: \lambda x.\lambda y.eat'xy$	$: apples'$

$$\frac{S/(S\backslash NP)}{: \lambda f.f\, keats'}\text{>}\mathbf{T}$$

$$\frac{S/NP : \lambda x.steal'x\, keats'}{}\text{>}\mathbf{B}$$

$$\frac{S/(S\backslash NP)}{: \lambda f.f\, chapman'}\text{>}\mathbf{T}$$

$$\frac{S/NP : \lambda x.eat'x\, chapman'}{}\text{>}\mathbf{B}$$

$$S/NP : \lambda x.and'(eat'x\, chapman')(steal'x\, keats')\quad\text{<}\Phi\text{>}$$

$$S : and'(eat'apples'chapman')(steal'apples'keats')\quad\text{>}$$

---

[2] Steedman (1990), and Baldridge and Kruijff (2002) proposed a unification-based treatment of semantics in CCG. White and Baldridge (2003) implemented the approach proposed by Baldridge and Kruijff with some modifications in their CCG chart realizer. However, they achieve the simultaneous construction of syntax and semantics by coindexing syntactic categories with semantic representations, which in my opinion is an unnecessary complication.

Here I end the brief overview of CCG. For more information on the topic, the interested reader is kindly referred to Steedman 2000b and Steedman 1996, or see other papers by Steedman cited in this section.

4.1.2 Unification Categorial Grammar

Unification has been widely used in grammar formalisms since Kay's seminal paper (Kay, 1979). To mention but a few formalisms that have since come into existence and that this operation as the main mechanism for linguistic analysis: Generalised Phrase Structure Grammar, Head-driven Phrase Structure Grammar, Functional Unification Grammar and Unification Categorial Grammar all belong to this list.

In his 1979 paper Kay introduced the representation of linguistic expressions as *feature structures*. Feature structures are complex objects which consist of a number of *attribute value pairs*. Kay called this representation "functional description". Even more momentously, Kay (1979) exported the mathematical notion of unification into linguistic analysis. In his 1985 paper he informally defines unification as follows:

> This is an operation that compares a pair of expressions and determines whether they could be descriptions of the same object or state of affairs. If they could not, it declares as much and this is its only result. If they could, it constructs a new expression, in general more specific than either of the originals, because it contains all the details from both of them.

Unification Categorial Grammar (UCG) (Zeevat et al., 1987; Calder et al., 1988; Zeevat, 1988) is a Categorial Grammar that incorporates several insights from Head-Driven Phrase Structure Grammar (HPSG) (Pollard, 1988; Flickinger et al., 1985; Pollard and Sag, 1994) and PATR-II (Shieber, 1986). Similarly to HPSG and PATR-II, it uses feature structures for syntactic representation and the operation of unification for combining them.

The feature structures of UCG are called *signs*. There is a sign corresponding to each syntactic category. UCG makes use of three primitive categories: nouns *(noun)*, sentences *(sent)* and noun phrases *(np)*. Accordingly, there are also three basic signs in UCG: each of them corresponds to one of the aforementioned primitive categories. Although, UCG includes a primitive sign for noun phrases, in reality the type-raised version of the category is used in connection with actual noun phrases. Complex UCG signs have other signs recursively embedded inside them. In actual fact, the border between categories and signs is fairly blurred in UCG. The following definition is provided for categories (Zeevat et al., 1987, page 196):

a. Any primitive category (together with a syntactic feature specification) is a category.

b. If A is a category, and B is a sign, then A/B is a category.

Each UCG sign has four main components: phonology (W), syntactic category (C), semantics (S) and order (O). These are usually presented as a vertical list (see Example 4.6 a and b). An alternative representation as a horizontal list (see Example 4.6 c and d) is preferred in case the sign is an active part of a complex sign.

(4.6)   a) W   b) student   c) W:C:S:O
        C   noun
        S   STUDENT(x)   d) student:noun:STUDENT(x):O
        O   O

The feature values can be either constants or variables. If the feature value is a variable, it may be omitted from the list. (For example, it is not necessary to write 'O' in 4.6 b and d.) Variables, which stand for incomplete information, can be further specified by unification. Unification is defined as follows (Zeevat et al., 1987, page 196):

... the unification of two variables is a variable, the unification of a variable and a constant is that constant, and the unification of two distinct constants always fails.

The reason why having a single representation for a linguistic expression with a number of features, rather than several separate representations, is particularly attractive resides in the fact that the variables at one level of a sign can be reused at another level. This allows, for example, phonology and semantics to be built up simultaneously.

Unlike CCG, which records the linear ordering of the arguments in respect to their functor by using directional slashes, UCG uses a special ordering feature. The ordering feature can take two values: *pre* and *post*. Zeevat et al. define the meaning of these feature values as follows:

> *Post* says, on a sign: "if I am an argument in a functional application, my functor follows me." *Pre* says: "if I am an argument in a functional application, my functor precedes me."

Example 4.7 illustrates a typical UCG sign for a transitive verb. The rightmost argument has the ordering feature value *post*, and thus it linearly precedes the verb *'love'*, while the other argument, with the ordering feature value *pre*, follows the verb.[3]

(4.7) love

sent[fin]/W_1:np:x:pre/W_2:np:y:post

[e]LOVE(e,x,y)

O

Similarly to Classical CG, UCG employs two rules for combining signs: those of forward and backward application. In order to account for the different values of the ordering feature the application rules are redefined as follows (Zeevat et al., 1987, page 202):[4]

(4.8) Forward application: W_1W_2:C:S → W_1:C/E:S E(W_2:pre)

Backward application: W_2W_1:C:S → E(W_2:post) W_1:C/E:S

In UCG terminology, if a category has the form A/B, then the sign B is referred to as the *active part* of the category: this is the part that needs to be unified with the argument in order for a combination to be successful. Functional application can be divided into two consecutive steps. During the first part, *instantiation*, the active part of the sign is unified with the argument of the appropriate type. The second step, *stripping*, involves deleting the unified active part: the sign is stripped of its active part.

For semantic representation UCG uses Indexed Language (InL). InL is closely related to DRT, but differs in some ways. Besides the less consequential differences from DRT, like the linear layout of InL and the fact that it does not

---

[3]I personally find the meaning of the ordering feature values counterintuitive. Moreover, there seems to be some confusion as for how they are used in the examples provided.

[4]The variable E in the rules stands for a whole sign.

involve an explicit division of semantics into a set of discourse referents and a set of conditions on these referents, there is also a more significant difference: the notion of an *index*. An index is a designated variable of a formula: it specifies the type of the expression. Some of the types used for expressions are as follows: event, an unspecified eventuality, object, quantity of mass, etc. The types can be further specified: for example, the type of a singular object is distinct from that of a plural object. The same holds for a male and a female object. As an illustration: the index of the semantic formula in 4.7 is the variable e and its type is that of event. The use of semantic indices means that some combinations of signs can correctly be blocked by their semantics (see Example 4.9).

(4.9) a) *The boys walks.

b) *Mary likes to wash himself.

Examples 4.10-4.13 (from Zeevat et al., 1987, pp. 200-201) demonstrate how signs are combined in UCG. Example 4.10 shows the two signs we are going to combine: the sign for the proper name *'John'* and that for the verb *'walks'*. Remember that for actual noun phrases their type-raised version is used rather than the primitive category *np*. The two signs will be combined by forward application, the noun phrase acting as the functor and the verb as its argument. Example 4.11 and Example 4.12 deal with the instantiation part of the combination. Example 4.11 shows the result of the unification of the active part of the noun phrase (i.e. C/(np:JOHN:O):S:O) with the category of the verb. Example 4.12 displays the full instantiation of the functor sign with the values from its argument. Finally, Example 4.13 displays the end-result of the combination, where the instantiated functor sign is stripped down to the category *sent[fin]*.

(4.10) john   walks

   C/(C/(np:JOHN:O):S:O)   sent[fin]/np[nom]:x:pre

   S   [e]WALK(e,x)

(4.11) walks

   sent[fin]/np[nom]:JOHN:pre

   [e]WALK(e,JOHN)

   pre

(4.12) john

   sent[fin]/(walks:sent[fin]/(np[nom]:JOHN:pre):[e]WALK(e,JOHN):pre)

   [e]WALK(e,JOHN)

(4.13) john walks

   sent[fin]

   [e]WALK(e,JOHN)

In what follows, I will expose some critical remarks I have in store for UCG. Firstly, I do not find the UCG definition of category particularly helpful. This definition blurs the boundary between the notion of syntactic category and that of sign. Secondly, alternating between the modes of vertical versus horizontal layout (the main sign is usually represented vertically, while the recursively embedded signs of the active part are depicted horizontally) unnecessarily complicates the picture and inhibits comprehension. Thirdly, the ordering features *pre* and *post* are used counter-intuitively. Fourthly, unification was said to be the only permitted operation on signs, but in that case it is not clear how the cooperation between the ordering features and the phonology element of the sign (which results in the correct order of the values in the phonology element) functions. Finally, the semantic treatment of agreement features is of dubious merit. The authors themselves admit that the issue is controversial referring to the distinction between "natural" and "grammatical" gender and number. Grammatical gender in languages with a rich gender system does not necessarily reflect semantic gender. Number agreement poses a similar problem: grammatically plural objects can refer to semantically singular objects and vice versa. For example, the word *'hair'* is grammatically singular in English, while in many other languages a plural form is used. Assuming that the language of semantics is universal, how would it be possible to make semantics accountable for the difference in the number agreement in different languages in the case at hand? In addition, there are grammatically plural objects, like *'scissors'* and *'trousers'*, the semantic treatment of which as singular objects seems far more credible.

4.2   From UCG and CCG to UCCG

Unification-based Combinatory Categorial Grammar (UCCG) aims to marry
the best parts of CCG and UCG, whilst also enhancing the framework with
new features. From CCG it inherits the directional slash notation and a rich
machinery of combinatory rules: forward and backward application, forward
and backward composition, type-raising, coordination, etc. Similarly to UCG,
UCCG employs feature structures to represent linguistic data. In contrast to
UCG, there is no recursive embedding in UCCG signs and a uniform vertical
layout of features is used throughout. I believe that this makes the signs of
UCCG much more readable than those of UCG. In UCG the terms *category* and
sign are used in a sloppy manner. UCCG makes a clear distinction between the
meaning of these two terms. The most important characteristic UCCG shares
with UCG is that they both build up semantics and syntax simultaneously by
means of unification.

The categories used in UCCG slightly differ from those used in CCG and
UCG. The atomic categories UCCG operates with are sentence (s), noun (n)
and verb phrase (vp). Both CCG and UCG use sentence, noun, and noun
phrase as their primitive categories. Noun phrases in UCCG are always complex categories. This requirement was caused by the need to account for the
quantificational scope of determiners. Intransitive verbs, which are complex
categories both in UCG and CCG (s\np), are collapsed into a basic category
in UCCG. Due to the use of different building blocks, the complex categories
of UCCG also differ from those of CCG and UCG.

In its mature form, UCCG will incorporate the DRT semantics. Combining
CCG with DRT has never been attempted: CCG has mainly used some version
of predicate calculus for its semantic representation.[5] UCG's way of representing semantics is more akin to that of UCCG. Moreover, both of them build the
semantics up compositionally, each sign and sub-sign making its own semantic
contribution. However, I claim that the use of the traditional version of DRT,
rather than any modification, has clear advantages. Simply the fact that it is
widely known and used in computational natural language applications makes
it an attractive choice. Besides, the representation adopted in DRT is very clear

---

[5]See the footnote on page 70.

and readable. Furthermore, DRT is particularly well suited for accounting for linguistic phenomena which cross sentence boundaries, like anaphora resolution. Despite this, for the sake of simplicity we will use predicate calculus for the UCCG semantic representations in this chapter. This way, as I assume the readers' general familiarity with predicate calculus, I can concentrate on explaining other features of UCCG here.

Incorporating intonation and information structure in CCG was first proposed by Steedman (2000b). These issues have not been discussed in UCG. The approach to information structure adopted in UCCG is very similar to that of CCG in its theoretical aspects. However, the representations UCCG provides for information structure, as well as its unification-based construction mechanisms differ from those employed by CCG. Also unlike CCG, information-structural marking is retained in the semantics of the result of the complete syntactic analysis.

4.3 Signs and Categories

UCCG uses feature structures called *signs* in its linguistic description. There are two types of signs: *basic* and *complex signs*. A UCCG basic sign is a list of attributes or features that describe the syntactic and semantic characteristics of a linguistic expression. A UCCG basic sign can have a varied number of features, depending on the syntactic category of the linguistic expression the sign is characterising. There are three obligatory features any sign must have, namely the phonological form (PHO), the syntactic category (CAT) and the semantic representation (SEM). Besides the above three, a sign can also incorporate the feature VAR for a variable which stands for a discourse referent and AGR to mark the inflectional characteristics of a verb (e.g. finite or non-finite). Example 4.14 illustrates the notion of a basic sign. This sign describes the linguistic expression with the phonology *'child'*, which belongs to the category of noun. The value of the VAR feature is the variable X that also appears in the SEM feature.

$$(4.14) \begin{bmatrix} \text{PHO: child} \\ \text{CAT: n} \\ \text{VAR: X} \\ \text{SEM: child(X)} \end{bmatrix}$$

Depending on the needs of a specific application and the properties of a particular language many more features can be introduced in each basic sign. Quoting Martin Kay (1985; 1979):

> There is no notion of a completely specified functional description just as, in everyday life, there is no notion of a complete description of an object – it is always possible to add more detail.

> Intuitively, a description is a set of properties. The objects it describes are those that share just those properties. Generally speaking, to add new properties to a description is to reduce the number of objects in the set described.

There are three kinds of basic signs in UCCG corresponding to the basic categories of UCCG: those with the CAT feature sentence (s), those with the CAT feature noun (n) and those with verb phrase (vp). The three types of signs can be seen in Example 4.15. At the moment it seems that we could arrange the basic signs into a hierarchy: the basic sign with the CAT feature "sentence" has the minimum number of features, the noun sign has an additional feature as compared to the sentence sign, and the vp sign has an extra feature as compared to the noun sign. However, we need to bear in mind that adding or deleting features would instantly change the position of the sign in the hierarchy.

$$(4.15) \begin{bmatrix} \text{PHO: P} \\ \text{CAT: s} \\ \text{SEM: S} \end{bmatrix} \qquad \begin{bmatrix} \text{PHO: P} \\ \text{CAT: n} \\ \text{VAR: X} \\ \text{SEM: S} \end{bmatrix} \qquad \begin{bmatrix} \text{PHO: P} \\ \text{CAT: vp} \\ \text{AGR: A} \\ \text{VAR: X} \\ \text{SEM: S} \end{bmatrix}$$

Besides the basic signs, UCCG makes use of complex signs. Complex signs are formed from basic signs by the use of CCG style slashes. For example a sign characterising a noun phrase is a complex sign (see Example 4.16). The process of forming complex signs is recursive in the sense that complex signs can be combined to form even more complex signs. Example 4.17 illustrates a complex sign for the ditransitive verb *'gives'*. The ditransitive verb sign can be said to consist of a transitive verb sign and a noun phrase sign, both of which are complex signs themselves. More formally, the set of UCCG signs can be defined as follows:

> - *If A and B are signs then A/B is a complex sign.*
> - *If A and B are signs then A\B is a complex sign.*
> - *All basic and complex signs are UCCG signs.*

$$(4.16) \quad \begin{bmatrix} \text{PHO: } \text{a+child+W} \\ \text{CAT: } \text{s} \\ \text{SEM: } \exists X(\text{child}(X)\wedge S) \end{bmatrix} \Big/ \begin{bmatrix} \text{PHO: } W \\ \text{CAT: } \text{vp} \\ \text{VAR: } X \\ \text{SEM: } S \end{bmatrix}$$

In order to be able to refer to sub-parts of complex signs, I have to introduce some more terminology (illustrated in Example 4.17):

> - *X is the* **result** *of a sign X/Y or X\Y.*
> - *Y is the* **active part** *of a sign X/Y or X\Y.*
> - *A basic sign Z is the* **result head** *of the sign Z/$ or Z\$.[6]*

(4.17)

$$\overset{\longleftarrow \text{ result } \longrightarrow}{\underset{\longleftarrow \text{ result head } \longrightarrow}{}} \qquad \longleftarrow \text{ active part } \longrightarrow$$

$$\left(\begin{bmatrix} \text{PHO: } \text{gives+W+W1} \\ \text{CAT: } \text{vp} \\ \text{AGR: } \text{fin} \\ \text{VAR: } X \\ \text{SEM: } S \end{bmatrix} \Big/ \left(\begin{bmatrix} \text{PHO: } \text{W+W2} \\ \text{CAT: } \text{s} \\ \text{SEM: } S \end{bmatrix} \Big/ \begin{bmatrix} \text{PHO: } \text{W2} \\ \text{CAT: } \text{vp} \\ \text{AGR: } A \\ \text{VAR: } Y \\ \text{SEM: } S1 \end{bmatrix} \right) \right) \Big/ \left(\begin{bmatrix} \text{PHO: } \text{W1+W3} \\ \text{CAT: } \text{s} \\ \text{SEM: } S1 \end{bmatrix} \Big/ \begin{bmatrix} \text{PHO: } \text{W3} \\ \text{CAT: } \text{vp} \\ \text{AGR: } A1 \\ \text{VAR: } Z \\ \text{SEM: } \text{give}(X,Z,Y) \end{bmatrix} \right)$$

Each sign has a syntactic category. In the case of basic signs their category corresponds to their CAT feature, in the case of complex signs it is made up of the CAT features of all the component parts of the complex sign, separated by the slashes and brackets present in the given complex sign. For example the syntactic categories of the complex signs in Examples 4.16 and 4.17 are s/vp and (vp/(s/vp))/(s/vp).

---

[6]This definition uses the so-called "$ convention" from Steedman 2000b, which is defined in the source as follows: "For a category α, $\{\alpha\$\}$ (respectively, $\{\alpha/\$\}$, $\{\alpha\backslash\$\}$) denotes the set containing α and all functions (respectively, leftward functions, rightward functions) into a category in $\{\alpha\$\}$ (respectively, $\{\alpha/\$\}$, $\{\alpha\backslash\$\}$)." To adapt this definition for our purposes we need to replace all the occurrences of *category* in the definition with the word *sign*.

Similarly to basic and complex signs we can speak about basic and complex categories. Thus, we use three basic categories in UCCG: sentence (s), noun (n) and verb phrase (vp), while all other categories, e.g. noun phrases, adjectives, transitive verbs, etc., are formed by combining the above three, using backward and forward slashes.

In our notation we follow the convention of the Prolog programming language in that constants are represented by lower case letters, whilst upper case letters are used for variables. The feature names are printed in small capitals. To make the feature structures more easily readable I narrow the choice of possible variable names for each type of variable:

- Variables used inside the phonology feature (PHO) are of the form W, W1, W2, etc. (W stands for "word".)

- The CAT feature uses variables of the form C, C1, C2, etc.

- The agreement feature (AGR) uses variables of the form A, A1, A2, etc.

- The semantic feature (SEM) uses variables of the form S, S1, S2, etc.

- Discourse referents (VAR) can be represented by any other capital letter with the preference for the characters towards the end of the alphabet: X, Y, Z, etc.

The same variable can be used in different locations inside a UCCG sign. For example, the variables standing for discourse referents serve as a link between syntax and semantics: the variable in the VAR feature in the feature structure fits into its corresponding slot in the predicate logic formula in the SEM feature. All the occurrences of the same variable get replaced simultaneously via unification when signs are combined.

Besides being a variable, the features in the signs can have several constant values. For example, the CAT feature can have the values s, n, or vp. However, the value of the VAR feature is always a variable.

PHO feature holds the string value of the linguistic expression represented by the given feature structure. In basic signs the PHO feature is filled by lexical items, in complex signs it also contains variables, which acquire constant values when the functor sign is combined with its argument signs. The PHO feature in the result head of complex signs is of the form: $\ldots + W1 + word + W2 + \ldots,$

where *word* is a lexical item, and W1 and W2 are variables that get constant values through unification in the categorial combination process. This form of representation also encodes the linear order of the lexical items. Thus, the item unifying with W1 will precede and the one unifying with W2 will follow the lexical item *word*. Note that a variable can correspond to more than one word. The exact number and order of the variables that the PHO feature contains depends on the category of the given sign.

The AGR feature is used in connection with verb phrases. The constant values it takes (for example, *fin* (finite) and *non-fin* (non finite)) describe the inflectional properties of verbs. In Chapter 5 I will introduce additional agreement features NUM (number) and PER (person) which will be employed in both noun and verb signs.

The SEM feature, if it is not a variable itself, holds the predicate logic formula which corresponds to the semantics of the lexical item(s) characterised by the given sign. The predicate logic formula recycles the variables from the VAR feature of the sign. This way a direct link is established between syntax and semantics, and semantics gets built up spontaneously during the syntactic combinations. An illustration of the use of VAR variables inside the formula in the SEM feature can be seen in examples 4.14, 4.16 and 4.17 above. The important role of these variables will become clearer once I introduce the combinatory rules and illustrate them with examples in Section 4.5.2 .

4.4   Basic Signs

As mentioned previously, there are three basic signs in UCCG, which correspond to the three basic categories: nouns (CAT:n), verb phrases (CAT:vp), and sentences(CAT:s). The first two of these categories are largely lexical categories, the third one is mostly a non-lexical category, although depending on the choice of the lexicographer it can be present in the lexicon as the category for some idiomatic phrases, and single word sentences like "okay".

The lexical sign for nouns is very straightforward and its category directly corresponds to the CCG category n:

$$(4.18) \begin{bmatrix} \text{PHO: child} \\ \text{CAT: n} \\ \text{VAR: X} \\ \text{SEM: child(X)} \end{bmatrix}$$

UCCG introduces intransitive verbs, and verb phrases in general, among atomic signs. The vp category corresponds to the CCG category s\np. In UCCG it turned out to be more practical (due to the way UCCG represents noun phrases, see Section 4.5.1) to view it as an atomic category, which serves as a building block for several other categories, e.g. noun phrases, transitive verbs, etc. Example 4.19 illustrates a vp sign for the intransitive verb *'walks'*. In the case of a verb phrase like *'gives Mary an ice-cream'* the sign would be very similar: only the PHO and the SEM features would contain more information.

$$(4.19) \begin{bmatrix} \text{PHO: walks} \\ \text{CAT: vp} \\ \text{AGR: fin} \\ \text{VAR: X} \\ \text{SEM: walk(X)} \end{bmatrix}$$

Example 4.20 presents a simple non-lexical sentence sign. In Section 4.5.2 we will see more examples of sentence signs, and we will also learn how such signs come into existence.

$$(4.20) \begin{bmatrix} \text{PHO: john + walks} \\ \text{CAT: s} \\ \text{SEM: } \exists X(\text{john}(X) \wedge \text{walk}(X)) \end{bmatrix}$$

4.5   Complex Signs and Combinatory Rules

Complex signs are constructed from basic signs and slash operators. Similarly to CCG a forward slash in some sign X/Y means that the sign is looking for a sign of type Y on its right, while a backslash means that a sign of type W\Z is expecting an argument that can unify with its active part on its left. Sometimes brackets are used to show the associativity of the basic signs making up a complex sign. Some complex signs are lexical, others are the product of combinations with other signs.

4.5.1 Lexical Complex Signs

This Section gives a brief overview of the main types of complex signs present in a UCCG lexicon. The list is incomplete: the goal of the section is to explicate the general idea of what a UCCG complex sign is.

Determiners. The complex signs for determiners are lexical complex signs. The most straightforward category for a determiner would seem to be np/n. However, there is a problem with this category: it does not provide the means for specifying the scope of the determiner. Therefore, UCCG does not use the simple CCG np category for noun phrases, but rather its type-raised counterpart s/(s\np) (see Section 5.2 about type-raising). In order to make the complex sign for noun phrases slightly more compact, I chose to represent s\np, that stands for verb phrases, as vp in UCCG. Thus, the category for noun phrases in UCCG is s/vp, and that for determiners accordingly (s/vp)/n.

There are multiple signs for determiners. This is due to the different semantics that different determiners introduce into a noun phrase. The sign for the indefinite article can be seen in Example 4.21. The determiner *'every'* (and *'all'* if we ignore the difference in number agreement) is represented by the sign in Example 4.22. Notice the different value of the SEM feature in the result head of these two signs.

$$(4.21) \; (\; \begin{bmatrix} \text{PHO: a+W1+W2} \\ \text{CAT: s} \\ \text{SEM: } \exists X(S1 \wedge S2) \end{bmatrix} / \begin{bmatrix} \text{PHO: W2} \\ \text{CAT: vp} \\ \text{AGR: fin} \\ \text{VAR: X} \\ \text{SEM: S2} \end{bmatrix})/ \begin{bmatrix} \text{PHO: W1} \\ \text{CAT: n} \\ \text{VAR: X} \\ \text{SEM: S1} \end{bmatrix}$$

$$(4.22) \; (\; \begin{bmatrix} \text{PHO: every+W1+W2} \\ \text{CAT: s} \\ \text{SEM: } \forall X(S1 \rightarrow S2) \end{bmatrix} / \begin{bmatrix} \text{PHO: W2} \\ \text{CAT: vp} \\ \text{AGR: fin} \\ \text{VAR: X} \\ \text{SEM: S2} \end{bmatrix})/ \begin{bmatrix} \text{PHO: W1} \\ \text{CAT: n} \\ \text{VAR: X} \\ \text{SEM: S1} \end{bmatrix}$$

Adjectives. The category of adjectives is derived from that of nouns: the adjectival category is that of a noun looking for a noun on its right: n/n. Example 4.23 shows the sign for the adjective *'cute'.*

$$(4.23) \quad \begin{bmatrix} \text{PHO: cute+W} \\ \text{CAT: n} \\ \text{VAR: X} \\ \text{SEM: S$\wedge$cute(X)} \end{bmatrix} \Big/ \begin{bmatrix} \text{PHO: W} \\ \text{CAT: n} \\ \text{VAR: X} \\ \text{SEM: S} \end{bmatrix}$$

Noun phrases. Most noun phrases are non-lexical: they are constructed from other signs (e.g. the lexical signs of a determiner and a noun) by the combinatory rules. However, there are certain groups of lexical noun phrases: proper nouns, mass nouns, plural nouns (unless we assume the combination with a null determiner), etc. As already hinted above while speaking about determiners, the category for noun phrases is s/vp. Example 4.24 illustrates the sign for the proper name *'Mary'*.

$$(4.24) \quad \begin{bmatrix} \text{PHO: mary+W} \\ \text{CAT: s} \\ \text{AGR: A} \\ \text{SEM: $\exists$X(mary(X)$\wedge$S)} \end{bmatrix} \Big/ \begin{bmatrix} \text{PHO: W} \\ \text{CAT: vp} \\ \text{AGR: fin} \\ \text{VAR: X} \\ \text{SEM: S} \end{bmatrix}$$

Verbs. We already encountered intransitive verbs among the basic signs. While the category of an intransitive verb or a complete verb phrase is just vp, that of a transitive verb is vp/(s/vp), where s/vp stands for the direct object of the verb. Accordingly, the sign for a ditransitive verb is (vp/(s/vp))/(s/vp), where the rightmost noun phrase stands for the indirect object of the verb, and the one next to the vp stands for the direct object. A sign for a transitive verb is illustrated in Example 4.25, while we saw a ditransitive verb above in Example 4.17.

$$(4.25) \quad \begin{bmatrix} \text{PHO: loves+W1} \\ \text{CAT: vp} \\ \text{AGR: fin} \\ \text{VAR: X} \\ \text{SEM: S} \end{bmatrix} \Big/ \Big(\begin{bmatrix} \text{PHO: W1+W2} \\ \text{CAT: s} \\ \text{SEM: S} \end{bmatrix} \Big/ \begin{bmatrix} \text{PHO: W2} \\ \text{CAT: vp} \\ \text{VAR: Y} \\ \text{SEM: love(X,Y)} \end{bmatrix} \Big)$$

Auxiliary verbs. The category for auxiliary verbs is vp/vp. However, the actual signs differ in the agreement feature in the active part: some auxiliary verbs combine with the base form of a verb, some with the present participle, and some with the past participle. Example 4.26 shows the sign for the auxiliary *'does'*, which combines with a verb to its right that is in the base form. As exemplified by the sign for *'does'*, in this simple approach to auxiliary verbs, they just copy the semantics of the main verb.

$$(4.26) \quad \begin{bmatrix} \text{PHO: } \text{does}+\text{W} \\ \text{CAT: } \text{vp} \\ \text{AGR: } \text{fin} \\ \text{VAR: } \text{X} \\ \text{DRS: } \text{S} \end{bmatrix} \Big/ \begin{bmatrix} \text{PHO: } \text{W} \\ \text{CAT: } \text{vp} \\ \text{AGR: } \text{non-fin-base} \\ \text{VAR: } \text{X} \\ \text{DRS: } \text{S} \end{bmatrix}$$

Prepositions. Prepositional phrases can post-modify either nouns (e.g. *'child in the park'*) or verb phrases (e.g. *'walks in the park'*). The category for prepositions in prepositional phrases that post-modify nouns is $(n\backslash n)/(s/vp)$. If the prepositional phrase post-modifies a verb phrase, its category is $(vp\backslash vp)/(s/vp)$.[7] Both of these categories state that after having combined with a noun phrase to their right, they will have the category of a post-modifier – that of a noun or a verb phrase accordingly. Example 4.27 shows the sign for the preposition *'in'* when it modifies a noun.

(4.27)

$$\left(\begin{bmatrix} \text{PHO: } \text{W1}+\text{in}+\text{W2} \\ \text{CAT: } \text{n} \\ \text{VAR: } \text{X} \\ \text{SEM: } \text{S1}\wedge\text{S2} \end{bmatrix} \Big\backslash \begin{bmatrix} \text{PHO: } \text{W1} \\ \text{CAT: } \text{n} \\ \text{VAR: } \text{X} \\ \text{SEM: } \text{S1} \end{bmatrix} \right) / \left(\begin{bmatrix} \text{PHO: } \text{W2}+\text{W3} \\ \text{CAT: } \text{s} \\ \text{SEM: } \text{S2} \end{bmatrix} \Big/ \begin{bmatrix} \text{PHO: } \text{W3} \\ \text{CAT: } \text{vp} \\ \text{AGR: } \text{A} \\ \text{VAR: } \text{Y} \\ \text{SEM: } \text{in(X,Y)} \end{bmatrix} \right)$$

Relativisers. There are two kinds of finite relative clause: subject relative clauses and object relative clauses. The two types are illustrated in Example 4.28: the sentence in 4.28a contains a subject relative clause, whilst the one in 4.28b contains an object relative clause. Depending on the different relative clause types the relativisers need to have two different categories and signs. The category for the subject relativiser is $(n\backslash n)/vp$ and the corresponding sign can be seen in Example 4.29. The category for the object relativiser is somewhat more complicated: $(n\backslash n)/(s/(s/vp))$. Example 4.30 illustrates the sign which corresponds to the object relativiser.

---

[7]I will only provide the sign for prepositions in verbal post-modifiers in Section 5.1.1, where I will already have introduced neo-Davidsonian event semantics (see 3.3.2) into UCCG signs.

(4.28) a) This is the man that loves Mary.

b) This is the man that Mary loves.

$$(4.29) \; (\begin{bmatrix} \text{PHO: W1+that+W2} \\ \text{CAT: n} \\ \text{VAR: X} \\ \text{SEM: S1}\wedge\text{S2} \end{bmatrix} \backslash \begin{bmatrix} \text{PHO: W1} \\ \text{CAT: n} \\ \text{VAR: X} \\ \text{SEM: S1} \end{bmatrix})/ \begin{bmatrix} \text{PHO: W2} \\ \text{CAT: vp} \\ \text{AGR: fin} \\ \text{VAR: X} \\ \text{SEM: S2} \end{bmatrix}$$

(4.30)

$$(\begin{bmatrix} \text{PHO: W1+that+} \\ \text{W2+W3} \\ \text{CAT: n} \\ \text{VAR: X} \\ \text{SEM: S1}\wedge\text{S2} \end{bmatrix} \backslash \begin{bmatrix} \text{PHO: W1} \\ \text{CAT: n} \\ \text{VAR: X} \\ \text{SEM: S1} \end{bmatrix})/(\begin{bmatrix} \text{PHO: W2+(W3+W4)} \\ \text{CAT: s} \\ \text{SEM: S2} \end{bmatrix} /(\begin{bmatrix} \text{PHO: W4+W5} \\ \text{CAT: s} \\ \text{SEM: S3} \end{bmatrix} / \begin{bmatrix} \text{PHO: W5} \\ \text{CAT: vp} \\ \text{AGR: fin} \\ \text{VAR: X} \\ \text{SEM: S3} \end{bmatrix}))$$

Negation. There are several varieties of negation: nouns, verbs or whole propositions may be negated. First, we will look at the word *'no'*, which belongs to the class of determiners. This negation is ambiguous between nominal and propositional negation. In a sentence like *'No newborn baby walks'*, *'no'* can be seen as negating the existence of newborn babies among the walking crowd, or seen from a different perspective, it can negate the walking property of newborn babies, although they have many other admirable properties. Here we will view *'no'* as negating the whole proposition. It has a regular determiner category, (s/vp)/n, but again the semantics of the sign differs from that of other determiners. The sign for *'no'* can be seen in Example 4.31.

$$(4.31) \; (\begin{bmatrix} \text{PHO: no+W1+W2} \\ \text{CAT: s} \\ \text{SEM: } \neg\exists X(\text{S1}\wedge\text{S2}) \end{bmatrix} / \begin{bmatrix} \text{PHO: W2} \\ \text{CAT: vp} \\ \text{AGR: fin} \\ \text{VAR: X} \\ \text{SEM: S2} \end{bmatrix})/ \begin{bmatrix} \text{PHO: W1} \\ \text{CAT: n} \\ \text{VAR: X} \\ \text{SEM: S1} \end{bmatrix}$$

Another type of negation we will consider here is the verbal negation by means of the negative particle *'not'*. This kind of negation is present in the sentence *'A newborn baby does not walk'*. Again, the meaning is ambiguous, since we can get a reading that is the same as the propositional negation reading with *'no'* above. Here we view *'not'* as negating the verb, in our case the walking property. The category of *'not'* is the same as that of auxiliary verbs:

vp/vp. The corresponding sign is shown in Example 4.32. The sign differs from that of auxiliaries in that the AGR feature value stays the non-finite base verb form in the result sign, while the semantics is modified by the negation operator.

$$
(4.32) \quad
\begin{bmatrix}
\text{PHO: not+W} \\
\text{CAT: vp} \\
\text{AGR: non-fin-base} \\
\text{VAR: X} \\
\text{DRS: } \neg S
\end{bmatrix}
\Big/
\begin{bmatrix}
\text{PHO: W} \\
\text{CAT: vp} \\
\text{AGR: non-fin-base} \\
\text{VAR: X} \\
\text{DRS: S}
\end{bmatrix}
$$

4.5.2   Combinatory Rules and Combined Signs

When introducing complex categories and signs in Section 4.5.1, I frequently mentioned some sign expecting a sign of a certain type on its left or its right. However, I have not revealed yet what happens when it finds it. The answer is given by combinatory rules. At present, I have introduced the following seven CCG combinatory rules into UCCG: forward application, backward application, forward composition, backward composition, type-raising (two rules) and coordination. I am confident that other CCG combinatory rules can be introduced into UCCG with equal ease when the need for them arises.

Table 4.2 presents the formal definitions of the combinatory rules of UCCG. In the first column of the table, there are the names of the rules, in the second, the rules themselves, and in the third, the corresponding notation that will be used in derivations. The variables X, Y, Z and T stand for signs, which can be either basic or complex. The same holds about X', Y' and Z'. The sign X' is similar to the sign X: most importantly, it has the same syntactic category as X does.[8] With the exception of the type-raising rules, the rules in Table 4.2 all involve the operation of unification. For example, the forward application rule says that if a sign X/Y has a sign Y' to its right, and the feature structures Y and Y' can be successfully unified, then the result is X', which is similar to X, except that its features have been updated with the values resulting from the unification of Y and Y'.

---

[8]This is a slight simplification: later in the book we will encounter signs where the CAT feature value is a variable. Therefore, it would be more correct to say that the category of the sign X needs to be unifiable with that of the sign X'.

Examples of the use of application and composition rules will be provided below. The phenomena of coordination (that CCG is so well-known for handling successfully) as well as the operation of type-raising will be addressed in Section 5.2 of Chapter 5, where the UCCG formalism is presented complete with DRT semantics.

Table 4.2: UCCG combinatory rules

Forward application	$X/Y\ Y' \to X'$	———————>
Backward application	$Y\ X\backslash Y' \to X'$	<———————
Forward composition	$X/Y\ Y'/Z \to_{\mathbf{c}} X'/Z'$	————$C>$
Backward composition	$Y\backslash Z\ X\backslash Y' \to_{\mathbf{c}} X'\backslash Z'$	$<C$————
Type-raising A	$X \to_{\mathbf{T}} T/(T\backslash X)$	————$T>$
Type-raising B	$X \to_{\mathbf{T}} T\backslash(T/X)$	$<T$————
Coordination	X and $X' \to_{\&} X''$	————$<\&>$

Noun phrases. The simplest noun phrases are formed by combining a determiner and a noun by forward application. Example 4.33 demonstrates forming a noun phrase from the indefinite article *'a'* and the noun *'child'*.

(4.33)

$$
\left(
\begin{bmatrix}
\text{PHO: a+W1+W2} \\
\text{CAT: s} \\
\text{SEM: } \exists X(S1 \wedge S2)
\end{bmatrix}
/
\begin{bmatrix}
\text{PHO: W2} \\
\text{CAT: vp} \\
\text{AGR: fin} \\
\text{VAR: X} \\
\text{SEM: S2}
\end{bmatrix}
\right)
/
\begin{bmatrix}
\text{PHO: W1} \\
\text{CAT: n} \\
\text{VAR: X} \\
\text{SEM: S1}
\end{bmatrix}
\begin{bmatrix}
\text{PHO: child} \\
\text{CAT: n} \\
\text{VAR: Y} \\
\text{SEM: child(Y)}
\end{bmatrix}
$$

———>

$$
\begin{bmatrix}
\text{PHO: a+child+W2} \\
\text{CAT: s} \\
\text{SEM: } \exists X(\text{child}(X) \wedge S2)
\end{bmatrix}
/
\begin{bmatrix}
\text{PHO: W2} \\
\text{CAT: vp} \\
\text{AGR: fin} \\
\text{VAR: X} \\
\text{SEM: S2}
\end{bmatrix}
$$

In Example 4.33 the determiner *'a'* is combined with the noun *'child'* via forward application. The following effects are achieved by unification:

1) The variable $W1$ in the PHO feature in the active part of the determiner sign unifies with the value *'child'* in the PHO feature of the noun sign. Through unification this value is also introduced in the appropriate location in the value of the PHO feature in the result head of the determiner sign.

2) The CAT feature values in the active part of the determiner sign and in the noun sign unify, since they have the same constant value n.

3) Variable X in the VAR feature of the active part of the functor sign is unified with the variable Y in the argument sign; via unification also the semantics of the noun sign gets updated with the new unified variable value.

4) The variable $S1$ in the SEM feature of the active part of the determiner sign unifies with the corresponding value in the SEM feature in the noun sign. Due to the use of the same variable the new value of the variable $S1$ is introduced in the semantics of the result head.

When combining the same noun *'child'* with the determiner *'every'* the resulting noun phrase is slightly different: it has a different semantics inherited from the determiner the noun is combined with (see Example 4.34).

(4.34)

$$
\left(\begin{bmatrix} \text{PHO: every+W1+W2} \\ \text{CAT: s} \\ \text{SEM: } \forall X(S1 \rightarrow S2) \end{bmatrix} \bigg/ \begin{bmatrix} \text{PHO: W2} \\ \text{CAT: vp} \\ \text{AGR: fin} \\ \text{VAR: X} \\ \text{SEM: S2} \end{bmatrix} \right) \bigg/ \begin{bmatrix} \text{PHO: W1} \\ \text{CAT: n} \\ \text{VAR: X} \\ \text{SEM: S1} \end{bmatrix} \begin{bmatrix} \text{PHO: child} \\ \text{CAT: n} \\ \text{VAR: Y} \\ \text{SEM: child(Y)} \end{bmatrix}
$$

$$
\begin{bmatrix} \text{PHO: every+child+W2} \\ \text{CAT: s} \\ \text{SEM: } \forall X(\text{child}(X) \rightarrow S2) \end{bmatrix} \bigg/ \begin{bmatrix} \text{PHO: W2} \\ \text{CAT: vp} \\ \text{AGR: fin} \\ \text{VAR: X} \\ \text{SEM: S2} \end{bmatrix}
$$

Noun phrases can be much more complicated than the ones in Examples 4.33 and 4.34. The formation of a slightly more complex noun phrase can be seen in steps a and b of Example 4.35 below. This noun phrase consists of a determiner, an adjective, and a noun.

Combinatory rules at work. Example 4.35 is a slightly longer example of how combinatory rules work in UCCG. We parse the sentence *'a cute child walks quickly'*. UCCG allows variability in the order in which the neighbouring constituents are combined. In our example, first the signs for the determiner *'a'* and the adjective *'cute'* are combined by forward composition. Thereafter, the outcome of step a is combined with the noun *'child'* using forward application. In step c the sign for the verb *'walks'* is combined with the adverb *'quickly'* by backward application. Finally, in step d the product of step b is combined with that of step c, again by forward application.

(4.35)

a)
$$
\left(\begin{bmatrix} \text{PHO: a+W1+W2} \\ \text{CAT: s} \\ \text{SEM: } \exists X(S1{\wedge}S2) \end{bmatrix} / \begin{bmatrix} \text{PHO: W2} \\ \text{CAT: vp} \\ \text{AGR: fin} \\ \text{VAR: X} \\ \text{SEM: S2} \end{bmatrix} \right)/ \begin{bmatrix} \text{PHO: W1} \\ \text{CAT: n} \\ \text{VAR: X} \\ \text{SEM: S1} \end{bmatrix} \quad \begin{bmatrix} \text{PHO: cute+W3} \\ \text{CAT: n} \\ \text{VAR: Y} \\ \text{SEM: S3{\wedge}cute(Y)} \end{bmatrix} / \begin{bmatrix} \text{PHO: W3} \\ \text{CAT: n} \\ \text{VAR: Y} \\ \text{SEM: S3} \end{bmatrix}
$$

$$
\rule{10cm}{0.4pt} \;_{C>}
$$

$$
\left(\begin{bmatrix} \text{PHO: a+(cute+W3)+W2} \\ \text{CAT: s} \\ \text{SEM: } \exists X(S3{\wedge}cute(X){\wedge}S2) \end{bmatrix} / \begin{bmatrix} \text{PHO: W2} \\ \text{CAT: vp} \\ \text{AGR: fin} \\ \text{VAR: X} \\ \text{SEM: S2} \end{bmatrix} \right)/ \begin{bmatrix} \text{PHO: W3} \\ \text{CAT: n} \\ \text{VAR: X} \\ \text{SEM: S3} \end{bmatrix}
$$

b)
$$
\left(\begin{bmatrix} \text{PHO: a+(cute+W1)+W2} \\ \text{CAT: s} \\ \text{SEM: } \exists X(S1{\wedge}cute(X){\wedge}S2) \end{bmatrix} / \begin{bmatrix} \text{PHO: W2} \\ \text{CAT: vp} \\ \text{AGR: fin} \\ \text{VAR: X} \\ \text{SEM: S2} \end{bmatrix} \right)/ \begin{bmatrix} \text{PHO: W1} \\ \text{CAT: n} \\ \text{VAR: X} \\ \text{SEM: S1} \end{bmatrix} \quad \begin{bmatrix} \text{PHO: child} \\ \text{CAT: n} \\ \text{VAR: Z} \\ \text{SEM: child(Z)} \end{bmatrix}
$$

$$
\rule{10cm}{0.4pt} \;_{>}
$$

$$
\begin{bmatrix} \text{PHO: a+(cute+child)+W2} \\ \text{CAT: s} \\ \text{SEM: } \exists X(child(X){\wedge}cute(X){\wedge}S2) \end{bmatrix} / \begin{bmatrix} \text{PHO: W2} \\ \text{CAT: vp} \\ \text{AGR: fin} \\ \text{VAR: X} \\ \text{SEM: S2} \end{bmatrix}
$$

c)
$$
\left\{
\begin{array}{l}
\begin{bmatrix}
\text{PHO: walks} \\
\text{CAT: vp} \\
\text{AGR: fin} \\
\text{VAR: X} \\
\text{SEM: walk(X)}
\end{bmatrix}
\begin{bmatrix}
\text{PHO: W+quickly} \\
\text{CAT: vp} \\
\text{AGR: A} \\
\text{VAR: V} \\
\text{SEM: quickly(S)}
\end{bmatrix}
\ \backslash \
\begin{bmatrix}
\text{PHO: W} \\
\text{CAT: vp} \\
\text{AGR: A} \\
\text{VAR: V} \\
\text{SEM: S}
\end{bmatrix} \\[2em]
< \overline{\qquad\qquad\qquad\qquad\qquad\qquad\qquad\qquad} \\
\begin{bmatrix}
\text{PHO: walks+quickly} \\
\text{CAT: vp} \\
\text{AGR: fin} \\
\text{VAR: X} \\
\text{SEM: quickly(walk(X))}
\end{bmatrix}
\end{array}
\right.
$$

d)
$$
\left\{
\begin{array}{l}
\begin{bmatrix}
\text{PHO: a+(cute+child)+W4} \\
\text{CAT: s} \\
\text{VAR: X} \\
\text{SEM: } \exists X(child(X) \wedge cute(X) \wedge S2)
\end{bmatrix}
\ / \
\begin{bmatrix}
\text{PHO: W4} \\
\text{CAT: vp} \\
\text{AGR: fin} \\
\text{VAR: X} \\
\text{SEM: S2}
\end{bmatrix}
\begin{bmatrix}
\text{PHO: walks+quickly} \\
\text{CAT: vp} \\
\text{AGR: fin} \\
\text{VAR: T} \\
\text{SEM: quickly(walk(T))}
\end{bmatrix} \\[2em]
\overline{\qquad\qquad\qquad\qquad\qquad\qquad\qquad\qquad\qquad\qquad} > \\
\begin{bmatrix}
\text{PHO: a+(cute+child)+(walks+quickly)} \\
\text{CAT: s} \\
\text{VAR: X} \\
\text{SEM: } \exists X(child(X) \wedge cute(X) \wedge quickly(walk(X)))
\end{bmatrix}
\end{array}
\right.
$$

4.6 Conclusion

This chapter introduced the basic notions of the UCCG formalism, which is the second main contribution of this book. We saw that UCCG has several things in common with its close relatives CCG and UCG. Most importantly, it uses the directional slash notation similarly to CCG, as well as a rich machinery of combinatory rules. Like UCG, UCCG employs feature structures called signs in its linguistic representation. However, UCCG signs differ from those of UCG in several respects.

UCCG has three basic categories: noun (n), verb phrase (vp) and sentence (s). Its sign system includes three basic signs, which correspond to the three simple categories. All other UCCG signs are complex signs. Complex signs are made up of basic signs and slash operators. Some UCCG signs are lexical, while others are produced by combinatory rules. Sections 4.4 and 4.5 presented several examples of UCCG signs corresponding to different word classes and sentential constituents.

At present UCCG includes seven combinatory rules: forward application, backward application, forward composition, backward composition, two rules of type-raising and a rule for coordination. However, I believe that there are no obstacles to introducing the rest of the CCG rules into UCCG if the need arises.

Unification plays a crucial role in UCCG. The same variables can be used in different features and different sub-parts of UCCG signs. During the combinations all the occurrences of the same variable are replaced simultaneously. In this way syntactic combinations naturally build up the phonological and semantic representations.

In this chapter we used predicate calculus to represent the semantics of linguistic expressions. However this was a simplification, and in Chapter 5 we will replace this representation by Discourse Representation Structures.

Chapter 5

Adding DRT Semantics

This chapter serves as the necessary link between Chapter 4, which outlined the basics of UCCG, and Chapter 6, where we will combine UCCG and IS-DRS. The most important contribution of this chapter is the combining of UCCG with the DRT framework, but we elaborate also other improvements to the formalism, like the inclusion of the neo-Davidsonian semantics and enhancing the signs with additional agreement features. In this chapter, the formalism is extended to a non-trivial fragment of English.

DRT semantics is a very practical choice for semantic representation, because DRT is widely used in computational text analysis and generation. Furthermore, I believe that among current theories of semantics, the DRT model has potential for covering the widest range of linguistic phenomena, whilst retaining the simple first order property. Furthermore, DRT is particularly attractive for discourse processing, because it provides tools for the analysis of cross-sentential phenomena such as anaphora and presupposition, among others.

As mentioned above, the second important improvement that we make to UCCG in this chaper involves the inclusion of neo-Davidsonian semantics in the formalism. Neo-Davidsonian semantics provides us with a concise and uniform way of referring to events, and offers a way of analysing phenomena such as verb modification in first order logic.

In Section 5.1 we will introduce DRT into UCCG signs, and I will elaborate several other useful additions and modifications to UCCG. We will discuss how these improvements affect different basic and complex signs. The material will be illustrated with abundant examples, which involve combining signs by means of various combinatory rules. Section 5.2 focuses on the complex issues of coordination and type-raising.

5.1 UCCG with DRT

The first change we make in UCCG signs in this section is replacing the feature SEM that was present in the signs in Chapter 4 with a new feature: DRS. The feature value can either be a full discourse representation structure, or it can be filled by a variable or several variables of the form D, D1, D2, D3, etc. The convention we use for variables and constants in the DRSs is the same as introduced in Section 3.3 of Chapter 3: variables are printed in upper case and constants in lower case. According to that convention discourse referents are represented by upper case characters, while predicates in the DRS-conditions are in lower case (see 5.1a, b and c).

(5.1)

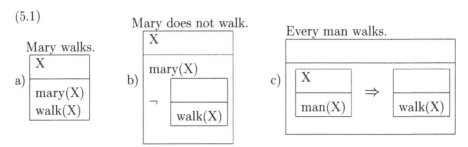

Example 5.2 demonstrates the complete sign for the noun *'child'* with the newly added DRS feature. We retain the close relationship between syntax and semantics discussed in Chapter 4: the same variable X appears in the VAR feature of the sign and inside the DRS in the condition *child(X)*.

(5.2)

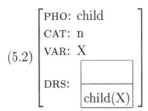

The second enhancement that we make to UCCG is to introduce the neo-Davidsonian semantics (see Section 3.3.2, Chapter 3) into DRSs. Instead of being a multi-argument relation the semantics of verbs now introduces several simpler DRS-conditions: a one-place predicate that describes the type of the event, and several two-place relations between the event and its participants. The number of conditions that a verb introduces depends on the type of the verb, i.e. on how many participants the particular event involves. Thus, an intransitive verb introduces only two conditions, a transitive verb introduces three conditions, and a ditransitive verb introduces four conditions.

In order to accommodate the neo-Davidsonian event semantics, besides the changes in the DRSs, we also need to modify the feature structures of verb phrases and sentences:[1] we add a new feature, SIT, to represent the event variable. The event variable, similar to the variable in the VAR feature, serves as an important link between the syntax and the semantics. The full significance of this will become clear when we discuss how signs are combined.

We also introduce two more agreement features into vp and n signs: number (NUM) and person (PER). NUM can take the constant values singular (sg) and plural (pl). If the number agreement is not relevant (for example in the active part of a transitive verb sign which corresponds to the direct object), a variable is used. The feature PER can have the values 1, 2 or 3, or it can be a variable. The sign for the verb *'walks'* now looks like that in Example 5.3b.

5.1.1 UCCG Signs Revisited

Basic signs. The three basic signs, those with the categories n, vp and s, now have the representations seen in Example 5.3a, b, and c. As compared to the basic signs presented in Chapter 4, the signs in 5.3a, b, and c have undergone several modifications. The sentence sign (5.3c) has been changed the least: the previously used SEM feature has been replaced by the DRS feature and a new SIT feature has been added. The modifications in the noun sign (5.3a) involve replacing the old semantics feature with the DRS feature, and the addition of two new agreement features: NUM and PER. The vp sign (5.3b) has been modified the most: besides the update of the semantics feature, three new features NUM, PER and SIT have been added.

---

[1]We need event variables in sentence signs in order to analyze sentence initial adverbials, such as *'yesterday'* in the sentence *'Yesterday Fred met Mary in the street.'*

(5.3)

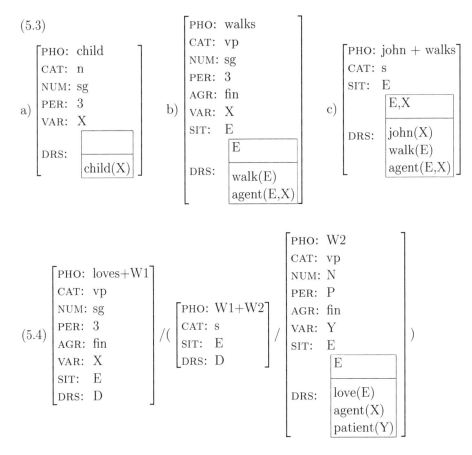

Verbs. I begin my review of complex signs with the discussion of transitive and ditransitive verbs. As we saw above, the introduction of neo-Davidsonian event semantics caused several changes in vp signs. The biggest changes occur inside the DRSs. However, the feature structures themselves, too, are modified by the addition of the new SIT feature, which holds the event variable. While the semantics of intransitive verbs only included one participant, in the case of transitive verbs there are two participants involved in the event. For example, the event described by the verb *'loves'* includes an agent and a patient. The sign corresponding to this verb can be seen above in Example 5.4. In the case of ditransitive verbs (e.g. *'give'*) the number of participants would be three. The NUM and PER features in the result part of the transitive verb sign in Example 5.4 are fixed to constant values that the subject (actor) has to agree with. However, the number and person feature values in the vp sign in the active part have been left open, since the verb does not pose restrictions on these properties of its direct object (patient) (e.g. *'loves you'*, *'loves Mary'*, *'loves children'*, *'loves ice-cream'*, etc.).

Figure 5.1 shows the combination of a transitive verb with its object (See Figure 5.10 for the combination of a transitive verb with its subject.). The following unifications take place:

- The PHO variables W and $W2$ of the two signs unify. The PHO variable $W1$ in the active part of the sign for *'loves'* unifies with the constant value *'Mary'*. It also introduces the new value in the result.

- The constant values of the CAT and AGR features of the sign for *'Mary'* and of the active part of the transitive verb unify.

- The number and person feature variables N and P in the active part of the transitive verb sign assume constant values by unifying with the corresponding values sg and 3 of the noun phrase sign.

- The discourse referent variable Y in the active part of the transitive verb sign is unified with the variable Z of the noun phrase sign. The new unified value is also introduced in the DRS in the result part of the noun phrase sign.

- The event variables E and $E1$ are unified, and the new unified value is introduced in the DRS in the active part of the transitive verb sign.

- The DRS variable $D1$ in the active part of the sign for *'Mary'* is unified with the DRS in the vp sub-sign of the active part of the sign for *'loves'*. The new value is introduced in the result part of the noun phrase sign, where it is merged with the DRS already present. The combined DRS is unified with the DRS variable D in the active part of the transitive verb sign, and simultaneously introduced in the DRS feature of the result.

Note the use of the operator $\otimes$ in the result part of the sign of the proper name *'Mary'*. The symbol $\otimes$ stands for the *merge* operation (previously discussed in Section 3.2.2, Chapter 3). Once the DRSs on both sides of the operator are instantiated, the merge operator joins them together to form a single DRS. More precisely, the merge operation consists of two steps. First, the sets of the discourse referents of the two DRSs are combined together resulting in the universe of the new DRS. The second step involves joining the DRS-conditions of the two original DRSs to provide the set of the DRS-conditions of the result DRS. The associativity of the ⊗-operator does not play any significant role: the result is the same irrespective of the order in which the DRSs are merged. The meaning of the ⊗-operator is similar to ∧ in predicate calculus.

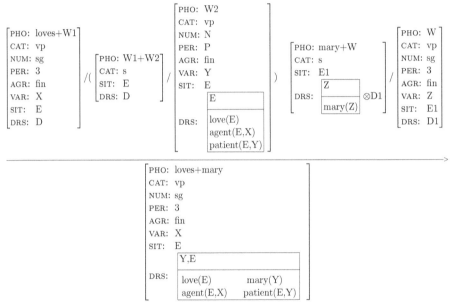

Figure 5.1: Combining the transitive verb *'loves'* with its object *'Mary'*

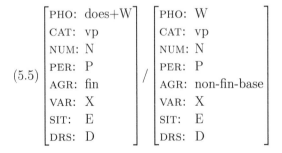

Auxiliary verbs. The signs for auxiliary verbs remain very similar to that introduced in Chapter 4. The modifications consist in the introduction of event variables into the feature structure, and the additional agreement features NUM and PER. As the semantic values in the sub-signs of auxiliary verbs are uninstantiated, the replacement of the SEM feature by the DRS feature is only a nominal change. Example 5.5 illustrates the sign for the auxiliary *'does'*.

Verbal negation The modifications of the sign for *'not'* are similar to the ones made to the auxiliary verb sign. In addition, now the DRS feature of the result of the sign introduces a negated sub-DRS into the main DRS.

$$
(5.6) \quad
\begin{bmatrix}
\text{PHO:} & \text{not+W} \\
\text{CAT:} & \text{vp} \\
\text{NUM:} & \text{N} \\
\text{PER:} & \text{P} \\
\text{AGR:} & \text{non-fin} \\
\text{VAR:} & \text{X} \\
\text{SIT:} & \text{E} \\
\text{DRS:} & \boxed{\begin{array}{c} \\ \hline \neg D \end{array}}
\end{bmatrix}
\Big/
\begin{bmatrix}
\text{PHO:} & \text{W} \\
\text{CAT:} & \text{vp} \\
\text{NUM:} & \text{N} \\
\text{PER:} & \text{P} \\
\text{AGR:} & \text{non-fin} \\
\text{VAR:} & \text{X} \\
\text{SIT:} & \text{E} \\
\text{DRS:} & \text{D}
\end{bmatrix}
$$

Determiners. Although the signs of the three determiners we viewed in Section 4.5 of Chapter 4 are alike in other respects, each of them introduces a very different DRT semantics. Thus, the indefinite article takes the form seen in Example 5.7. The DRS in the result head of the universal quantifier contains two sub-DRSs which stand in an implicational relation (see 5.8). The negative determiner, too, introduces a sub-DRS in the main DRS of its result head: the whole sub-DRS is under the scope of the negation operator (see 5.9).

$$
(5.7) \; (
\begin{bmatrix}
\text{PHO:} & \text{a+W1+W2} \\
\text{CAT:} & \text{s} \\
\text{SIT:} & \text{E} \\
\text{DRS:} & \boxed{\begin{array}{c} X \\ \hline \end{array}} \otimes D1 \otimes D2
\end{bmatrix}
\Big/
\begin{bmatrix}
\text{PHO:} & \text{W2} \\
\text{CAT:} & \text{vp} \\
\text{NUM:} & \text{sg} \\
\text{PER:} & \text{3} \\
\text{AGR:} & \text{fin} \\
\text{VAR:} & \text{X} \\
\text{SIT:} & \text{E} \\
\text{DRS:} & \text{D2}
\end{bmatrix}
) \Big/
\begin{bmatrix}
\text{PHO:} & \text{W1} \\
\text{CAT:} & \text{n} \\
\text{NUM:} & \text{sg} \\
\text{PER:} & \text{3} \\
\text{VAR:} & \text{X} \\
\text{DRS:} & \text{D1}
\end{bmatrix}
$$

(5.8) (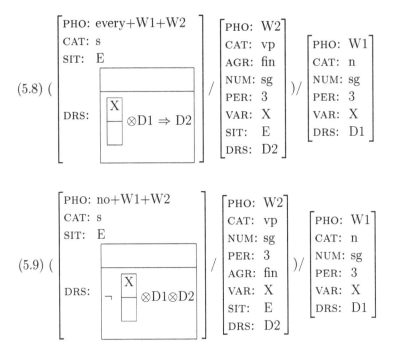

(5.9) (

Adjectives.   As before, the sign of prenominal adjectives is derived from the sign of nouns: if an adjective is combined with a noun to its right, the result is a "noun". Example 5.10 shows the sign for the adjective *'cute'*. When an adjective is combined with a noun, the noun's DRS is merged with the DRS found in the result of the adjective. The number of the active part of an adjective is unspecified: therefore an adjective sign can combine with either singular or plural nouns.

(5.10)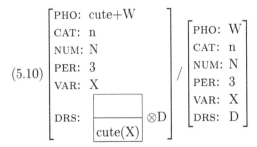

Prenominal position is not the only place where adjectives can be found, there are also the so-called "predicative adjectives" that follow a copula, for example *'tall'* in the sentence *'John is tall'.* I would like the semantic import of predicative adjectives to be similar to what is outlined in Parsons 1990 (pages 186-194). In his approach such adjectives (and adjectives in general) introduce states. In our representation we do not distinguish between states and events. Therefore, we require predicative adjectives to introduce an event variable E in the DRS. However, rather than specifying a new category for adjectives in a post-copular position, I delegate the task of introducing the event variable in semantics to the sign of the copula. The details of this are provided below when discussing the UCCG representation of the copula.

Noun phrases. The sign of lexical noun phrases can be seen in Example 5.11. The agreement features NUM, PER and AGR in the active part of the sign indicate that if the sign is the subject of the sentence then the verb it combines with has to be the third person singular finite verb form.

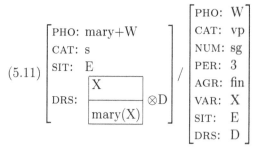

The category of combined noun phrases is the same as that of lexical noun phrases. However, the DRSs in the signs exhibit some variability. The exact form of the DRS in the result part of combined noun phrases depends on the signs combined to form the noun phrase. Examples 5.2 and 5.3 show how the sign of a noun phrase *'every cute child'* is constructed. There are two possible orders in which the signs forming this noun phrase can be combined. In our example, first the determiner is combined with the adjective via forward composition (5.2), and then the resultant sign is combined with the noun via forward application (5.3).

During the step of forward composition illustrated in Figure 5.2 the following is achieved:

1) The active part of the sign for *'every'* is unified with the result part of the

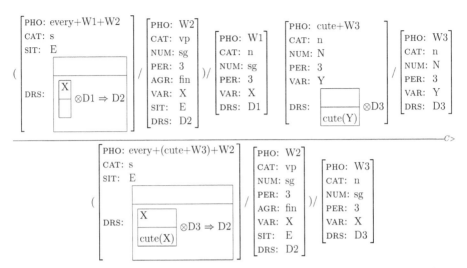

Figure 5.2: Combining the determiner *'every'* with the adjective *'cute'* via forward composition

sign for *'cute'*. For simplicity, in what follows, I will refer to the signs to be combined as sign A (the left-hand sign) and sign B (the right-hand sign).

- The PHO features of the active part of sign A and the result part of sign B unify, whereby the value of variable $W1$ becomes $cute+W3$. Via unification this value is also substituted for $W1$ in the PHO feature of the result of sign A.

- The CAT features of the active part of sign A and the result of sign B, which both have the constant value n, unify. The same happens to the corresponding PER features, which hold the constant value 3.

- As for the NUM features of the active part of sign A and the result part of sign B: due to unification, the variable N in the latter is instantiated to the constant value sg from the former.

- The VAR features of the argument of sign A and the result of sign B unify. I refer to this unified variable value by X. Via unification, the unified value X also finds its way into the DRSs of the results of both signs A and B.

- $D1$, a variable in the DRS feature of the active part of sign A, is assigned

the value in Example 5.12a. This value is also entered in the place of *D1* in the result of sign A. Subsequently, the two sub-DRSs with constant value on the left side of the implication in the main DRS of the result of sign A (see Example 5.12b) are merged into a single DRS. The final value of the DRS feature of the result of sign A in illustrated in Example 5.12c.

2) According to the forward composition rule $X/Y \ Y/Z \Rightarrow X/Z$ the active part of sign A and the result of sign B (the noun portions of each complex sign) are removed, and the result of sign A and the active part of sign B are joined together.

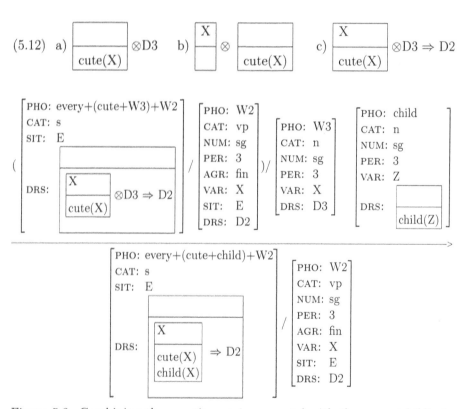

Figure 5.3: Combining the constituent *'every cute'* with the noun *'child'* via forward application

During the step of forward application illustrated in Figure 5.3 the following operations are performed:

1) The argument of the left-hand sign (A) is unified with the right-hand sign (B).

- The PHO feature of the active part of sign A is unified with the PHO feature of sign B, whereby the value of the variable $W3$ is replaced by the constant value *child*. This substitution also takes place in the PHO feature of the result of A.

- The constant values n, 3 and sg of the CAT, NUM and PER features of the active part of sign A and the corresponding features of sign B unify.

- The VAR feature value of the active part of sign A and the VAR feature value of sign B unify. The unified variable value is also introduced in the DRS of the result of sign A and in the DRS of sign B.

- $D3$, the variable in the DRS feature of the active part of sign A, assumes the value in Example 5.13a. This new value is also introduced in the appropriate place in the main DRS of the result of sign A. Then once more, the two sub-DRSs on the left side of the implication (see 5.13b) are merged together into a single DRS. The final value of the DRS feature of the result of sign A is illustrated in Example 5.13c.

2) According to the forward application rule $X/Y\ Y \Rightarrow X$ the outcome of this combination is sign A (with its new unified values) with its argument part removed.

(5.13) a)
$$\boxed{\begin{array}{c} \\ \hline \text{child}(X) \end{array}}$$
b)
$$\boxed{\begin{array}{c} X \\ \hline \text{cute}(X) \end{array}} \otimes \boxed{\begin{array}{c} \\ \hline \text{child}(X) \end{array}}$$
c)
$$\boxed{\begin{array}{c} X \\ \hline \text{cute}(X) \\ \text{child}(X) \end{array}} \Rightarrow \text{D2}$$

Copula. The copula fulfills several different functions in English. First, it is an auxiliary verb. As an auxiliary it can be followed by a present or a past participle (see Example 5.14). In this role the copula has a sign very similar to other auxiliary signs (see Example 5.5 above). It only differs from the sign in Example 5.5 by the value of the AGR feature of its active part, which is either *ppl* (present participle) or *pspl* (past participle).

(5.14) a) My uncle is building a house.
        b) The house is built.

Another important function that the copula fulfills in English is that of predication. The copula predicates some property of a noun phrase. The predicated property can be expressed either by a noun phrase or an adjective (see Example 5.15). Two distinct categories/signs need to be provided for the copula to cover these two distinct instances.

(5.15) a) John is a man.

b) John is tall.

If the predicated property is expressed by a noun phrase, then the category of the copula is similar to that of a transitive verb. However, the semantics provided is different. More specifically, there are three things to note about the semantics of the copula (see Example 5.16): first, the copula introduces an equality relation between the referents of the noun phrases on its either side; second, the copula introduces an event variable E the value of which is a sub-DRS; third, the contents of this sub-DRS are made up of the equality relation and the semantics of the second noun phrase. Placing the semantics of the second DRS into a sub-DRS rather than in the main DRS is motivated by the fact that direct anaphoric reference to that noun phrase is not possible. Figures 5.4 and 5.5 show the formation of the sentence *'John is a man'* in two consecutive steps of forward application. The precise details of the feature unifications are omitted.

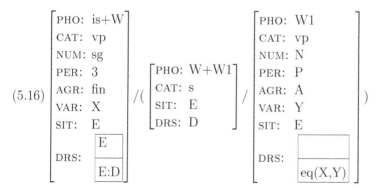

As mentioned above the predicated property may be expressed by an adjective. We only introduced a single sign for adjectives to be used irrespective of whether the adjective is used prenominally or predicatively. Since the category for the adjective sign is n/n, the category for a copula taking an adjective on its

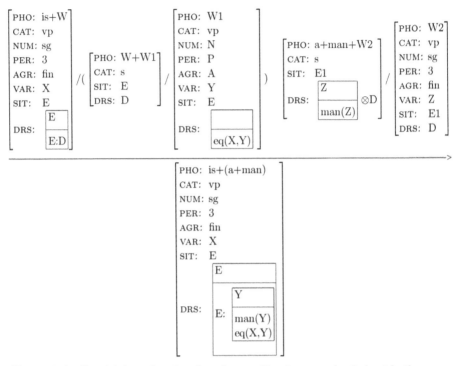

Figure 5.4: Combining the sign for the predicative copula *'is'* with the noun phrase *'a man'*

right assumes the form vp/(n/n). However, when discussing adjectives, I also said that predicative adjectives should introduce states. Since we only have a single sign for adjectives, the actual burden of introducing the event variable lies on the copula. Example 5.17 illustrates the sign for the copula predicating an adjective. This sign is similar to the copula sign in Example 5.16 in that it introduces an event variable E in the domain of the DRS and a sub-DRS in the DRS-conditions part which describes the event E. However, in contrast to the sign for the copula predicating a noun phrase, the sign predicating an adjective introduces no equality condition. Figure 5.6 illustrates the combination of the copula with the adjective *'tall'*. If we further combine the sign for *'is tall'* (see Fig. 5.6) with the sign for the proper name *'John'*, then the DRS of the result takes the form seen in Example 5.18.

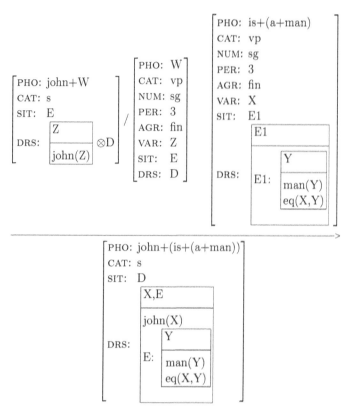

Figure 5.5: Combining the sign for the proper name *'John'* with the sign for *'is a man'*

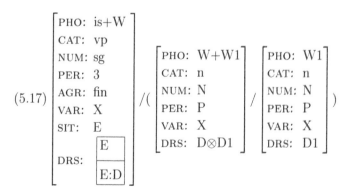

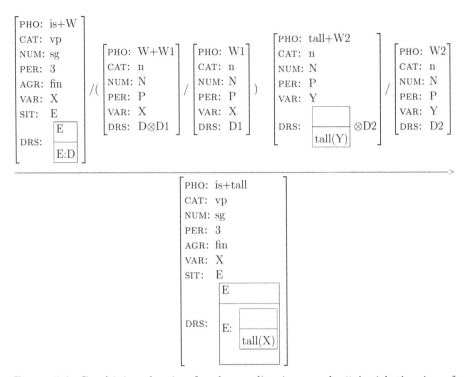

Figure 5.6: Combining the sign for the predicative copula *'is'* with the sign of the adjective *'tall'*

(5.18)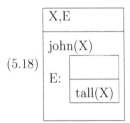

Prepositions. Remember that prepositions have two different categories: one that allows them to form prepositional phrases that post-modify nouns ((n\n)/(s/vp)), and another which allows them to form the ones that post-modify verb phrases ((vp\vp)/(s/vp)). The sign for prepositions participating in prepositional phrases that post-modify nouns can be seen in Example 5.19.

The sign for prepositions which follow verb phrases is illustrated in Example 5.20. Note that in both of these signs the agreement features share variables only in the result part; the values of the same features in the active part are independent from those in the result. This way the same "post-noun" preposition sign can participate in the formation of any of the following noun phrases: *'a child in the park', 'children in the park', 'the water in the parks'*, etc. Similarly, the "post-vp" preposition sign would allow *'walks in the park', '[we] walk in the park', 'walk in the parks'*, etc. In the post-vp preposition sign the same event variable is used throughout. In the case of the vp *'walks in the park'* this enables us to convey the fact that the walking event and the event taking place in the park are one and the same, or in other words, that the event in this vp is a "walking in the park" event. The formation of a preposition phrase to post-modify a vp is shown in Figure 5.14.

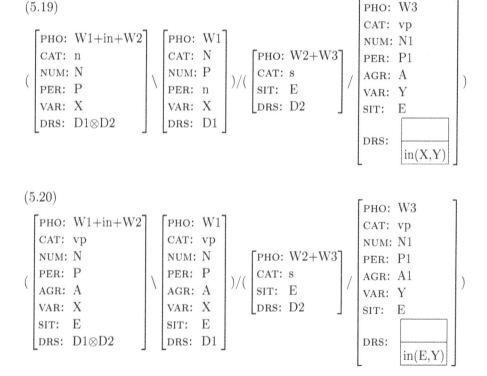

(5.19)

(5.20)

Relativisers. The sign for the subject relativiser can be seen in Example 5.21 and that for the object relativiser is illustrated in Example 5.22. Their signs are very similar to those that were introduced in Chapter 4. However, note the agreement features: in the subject relativiser sign the NUM and PER feature values must be the same in the result and the active part (to allow *'the child who walks'* but not *'the children who walks'*), while in the object relativiser sign these values can be different, since no agreement is required between a direct object an a verb (e.g. *'the book she reads'*, *'the books she reads'*). Figure 5.7 demonstrates the combination of the object relativiser *'that'* with the object relative clause *'Mary loves'*. Note that the sign resulting from this combination is very similar to the adjective sign, except the direction of the slashes: adjectives pre-modify nouns, while relative clauses post-modify them.

$$
(5.21) \ \left(
\begin{bmatrix}
\text{PHO:} & \text{W1+that+W2} \\
\text{CAT:} & \text{n} \\
\text{NUM:} & \text{N} \\
\text{PER:} & \text{P} \\
\text{VAR:} & \text{X} \\
\text{DRS:} & \text{D1}\otimes\text{D2}
\end{bmatrix}
\ \backslash \
\begin{bmatrix}
\text{PHO:} & \text{W1} \\
\text{CAT:} & \text{n} \\
\text{NUM:} & \text{N} \\
\text{PER:} & \text{P} \\
\text{VAR:} & \text{X} \\
\text{DRS:} & \text{D1}
\end{bmatrix}
\ \right)/
\begin{bmatrix}
\text{PHO:} & \text{W2} \\
\text{CAT:} & \text{vp} \\
\text{NUM:} & \text{N} \\
\text{PER:} & \text{P} \\
\text{AGR:} & \text{fin} \\
\text{VAR:} & \text{X} \\
\text{SIT:} & \text{E} \\
\text{DRS:} & \text{D2}
\end{bmatrix}
$$

$$
(5.22)
$$

$$
\left(
\begin{bmatrix}
\text{PHO:} & \text{W1+that+W2+W3} \\
\text{CAT:} & \text{n} \\
\text{NUM:} & \text{N} \\
\text{PER:} & \text{P} \\
\text{VAR:} & \text{X} \\
\text{DRS:} & \text{D1}\otimes\text{D2}
\end{bmatrix}
\ \backslash \
\begin{bmatrix}
\text{PHO:} & \text{W1} \\
\text{CAT:} & \text{n} \\
\text{NUM:} & \text{N} \\
\text{PER:} & \text{P} \\
\text{VAR:} & \text{X} \\
\text{DRS:} & \text{D1}
\end{bmatrix}
\right)/(
\begin{bmatrix}
\text{PHO:} & \text{W2+(W3+W4)} \\
\text{CAT:} & \text{s} \\
\text{SIT:} & \text{E} \\
\text{DRS:} & \text{D2}
\end{bmatrix}
/(
\begin{bmatrix}
\text{PHO:} & \text{W4+W5} \\
\text{CAT:} & \text{s} \\
\text{SIT:} & \text{E} \\
\text{DRS:} & \text{D3}
\end{bmatrix}
/
\begin{bmatrix}
\text{PHO:} & \text{W5} \\
\text{CAT:} & \text{vp} \\
\text{NUM:} & \text{N1} \\
\text{PER:} & \text{P1} \\
\text{AGR:} & \text{fin} \\
\text{VAR:} & \text{X} \\
\text{SIT:} & \text{E} \\
\text{DRS:} & \text{D3}
\end{bmatrix}
))
$$

Propositional attitude verbs. Propositional attitude verbs are the verbs like *'reckon'*, *'think'*, *'hope'*, *'believe'*, *'wish'*, etc. They share the property of taking a complement to their right in their propositional attitude use. The semantics of propositional attitude verbs is problematic and intricate, and therefore also the DRS representation is complex. I did not introduce these verbs in Chapter 4, because their semantics was not representable in first order logic

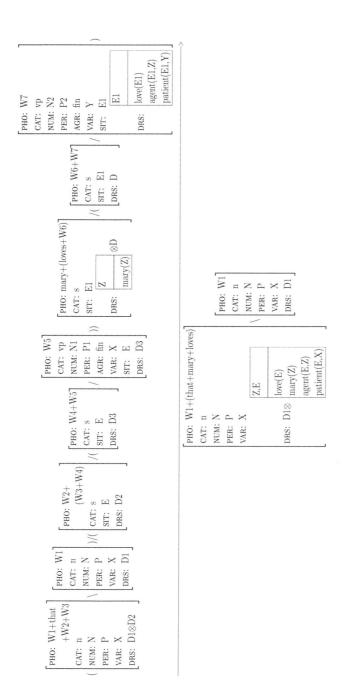

Figure 5.7. Combining the relativiser *'that'* with the relative clause *'Mary loves'*

with the tools we had at our disposal. In the case of a propositional attitude
verb like *'believe'* we are dealing with two events: the event E of believing, and
the event $E1$ of what is believed. Such verbs use two semantic roles: those of
agent and theme (not to be confused with the IS term of the same name). In
our notation, the content of the theme is specified by a special infix operator
':', that takes the theme variable as its left argument, and the DRS expressing
what is believed as its right argument. The category for such verbs is vp/s-
comp, where *s-comp* stands for a complement sentence. The corresponding sign
is shown in Example 5.23.

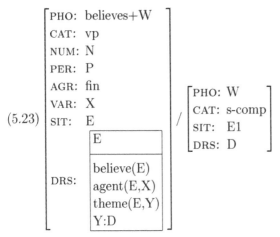

Figure 5.8 shows a combination that involves the verb *'believes'*. Here the
negated verb has already been combined with its subject forming the constituent *'Tim does not believe'*. This example demonstrates the combination
of this constituent with the complement clause *'that John hates the man that
Mary loves'*. The DRS of the complement clause unifies with the DRS variable D in the active part of the left-hand sign. The variable plugs the whole
DRS into the negation sub-DRS of the result, more precisely into the condition
which corresponds to the theme thematic role.

Complementisers. After having introduced propositional attitude verbs, I
also need to present the sign for complementisers. Some examples of English
complementisers are *'that'*, *'whether'*, *'if'*, *'who'*, *'which'*, *'where'*, etc. Example
5.24 shows some of them being used in a sentence. Different complementisers
have slightly different categories. The category of the prototypical complemen-

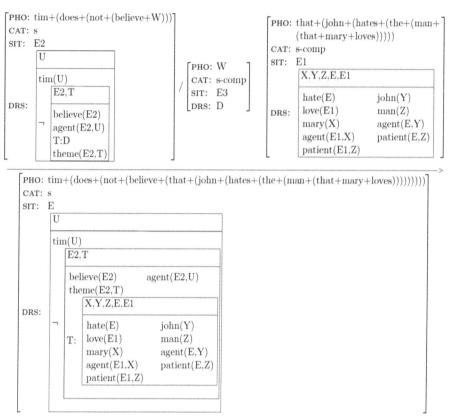

Figure 5.8: Combining the constituents *'Tim does not believe'* and *'that John hates the man that Mary loves'*

tiser *'that'* is s-comp/s: a complement sentence taking a sentence to its right. We need to use s-comp for the result category rather than the regular sentence category in order to make sure that strings like *'that he is the centre of the universe'* are not accepted as complete sentences. The sign for *'that'* in its complementiser use can be seen in Example 5.25.

(5.24) a) John thinks <u>that</u> he is the centre of the universe.

b) John knows <u>who</u> is to blame for what happened.

c) Only John knows <u>whether</u> he or somebody else is to blame for what happened.

d) Only John knows <u>which</u> is the correct answer.

$$(5.25) \quad \begin{bmatrix} \text{PHO:} & \text{that+W} \\ \text{CAT:} & \text{s-comp} \\ \text{SIT:} & \text{E} \\ \text{DRS:} & \text{D} \end{bmatrix} \Big/ \begin{bmatrix} \text{PHO:} & \text{W} \\ \text{CAT:} & \text{s} \\ \text{SIT:} & \text{E} \\ \text{DRS:} & \text{D} \end{bmatrix}$$

Adverbs.   Adverbs were not discussed in Chapter 4, since without events it is not possible to describe their semantics in the language of first order logic. Now, with neo-Davidsonian event semantics, we can view adverbs as functions over the event variable: they modify events. Adverbs are an optional element, and as such we cannot adjust the verb category to accommodate adverbs as members of the verb phrase. Rather, we give adverbs a category that takes a verb phrase as its argument. Thus the category for adverbs is vp\vp. The corresponding sign can be seen in Example 5.26.

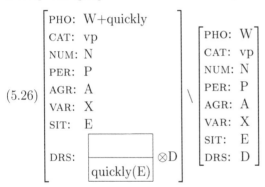

Adverbs can also appear sentence initially, modifying the whole sentence. Therefore they also have the category s/s. Semantically, the adverb still modifies the event. That is exactly the reason why we needed to introduce event variables in sentence signs.

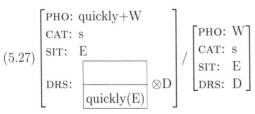

5.2 Coordination and Type-Raising

The brief introduction to UCCG in Chapter 4 did not include any discussion of coordination and type-raising. Coordination is a very interesting issue, which poses problems to grammar theories which only recognise the so-called "traditional" syntactic constituents. CCG provides a very natural treatment of the non-constituent coordination phenomena. Together with the rich machinery of combinatory rules, UCCG inherits this faculty from CCG. The operation of type-raising is needed for a variety of constructions including non-constituent coordination.

As we will see in Chapter 6, it is also indispensable in constructing certain information-structural constituents.

5.2.1 Type-Raising

In Chapter 4, I presented two rules for type-raising: rule A: $X \Rightarrow_T T/(T \backslash X)$, and rule B: $X \Rightarrow_T T \backslash (T/X)$. In these rules X stands for the sign to be type-raised, and T is a variable over signs. According to these two rules, type-raising turns a sign X either into a rightward-looking functor over a leftward looking functor over the sign X, or into a leftward-looking functor over a rightward-looking functor over the sign X. The variable T stands for a full sign, basic or complex, where all values are instantiated to variables. If we were to type-raise a vp sign into a sign where T is a basic sign, then the type-raised vp sign would look like the one in Figure 5.9. This sign differs from any sign seen so far. Until now it was the case that the result head contained the largest share of constant values in a sign (e.g. the PHO and DRS values), but in the case of type-raised signs the result part is instead a dummy. However, during combinations the constant values find their way into the result part via unification.

In UCCG, the operation of type-raising is needed less frequently than in CCG, because the noun phrases already use the type-raised category in the lexicon. However, it is still necessary in some varieties of non-constituent co-ordination (see Section 5.2.2) and in forming certain information-structural constituents (see Chapter 6).

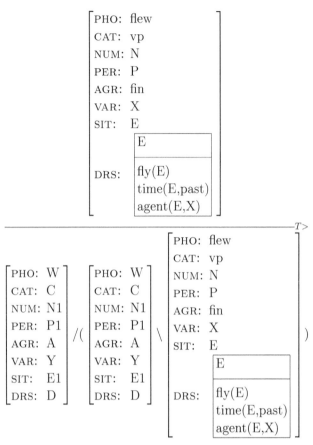

Figure 5.9: Type-raising of the vp *'flew'*

5.2.2   Coordination

In essence, the coordination rule, X and $X' \Rightarrow_\& X''$, says that conjuncts with the same syntactic category can be combined to form another sign with that syntactic category. The coordination rule was presented in the list of combinatory rules in Chapter 4 for the sake of completeness. In reality, this rule is purely representational: in actual fact the relevant combinatorial information is captured in the sign of the conjunction, and the effect of the coordination rule is achieved by the subsequent use of forward and backward application. The general shape of the conjunction sign is $(X\backslash X)/X$, where X is a sign with the category of the conjuncts. However, we need to be careful here, since a sign like that would also allow composition into it, which has undesirable effects. Therefore, we need to make use of a special kind of slash operator that only allows application. Baldridge (2002) introduced multi-modal slashes into CCG that restricted the use of combinatorial rules according to the slash type. From the set of Baldridge's multi-modal slashes we pick the slashes $/_\star$ and $\backslash_\star$ which restrict the combinatorial capabilities of a category $X/_\star Y$ or $X\backslash_\star Y$ to application only. Hence, the actual category of our conjunction sign is $(X\backslash_\star X)/_\star X$.

The purely syntactic part of coordination is very straightforward. However, getting the semantics right is a trickier business. Different kinds of coordination constructions require different modifications to the semantics. In some cases we allow the discourse referent or event variable to semantically correspond to a set. For example, in the case of a sentence like *'Mary and John walk'*, the role of the actor of the walking event E is filled by the set X which has the value $\{Y,Z\}$, where Y stands for Mary and Z for John. In the semantics, the DRS-condition for the actor role would still have the usual form: *'actor(X)'*. However, there would be an additional condition present in the DRS specifying that X corresponds to a set $\{Y,Z\}$. Similarly, in the sentence *'Mary drove and John flew to London'* the two events, driving (*E1*) and flying (*E2*), are post-modified by the same prepositional phrase which describes the goal of these events. Therefore, the conjunction sign introduces a combined event E which semantically corresponds to the set $\{E1,E2\}$. We will not discuss the issue of distributive and collective readings here, since this is outside the scope of this book.

In what follows, we will look at two examples of coordination. I assume that the sign for the conjunction is specified in the lexicon.[2]

The first example that we examine is the sentence *'Keats steals and Chapman eats apples'*. We analysed the same sentence in Example 4.3, page 69, Chapter 4, as a CCG example of coordination. This sentence contains non-constituent coordination: in order for the conjunction to be able to combine two categories together of the same type on either side, the subject and the transitive verb need to form a constituent. In the CCG example, we needed to type-raise the

---

[2]In an actual implementation which aims at wide coverage, some kind of a generalisation of the conjunction sign needs to be made. The use of recursive unification defined in Chapter 6 for prosodic signs might prove helpful here too.

subject noun phrases to allow them to combine with the transitive verbs to
their right. In UCCG no type-raising is needed in the analysis of this sentence,
because UCCG already uses the type-raised version of np categories. The
main steps of the UCCG derivation for *'Keats steals and Chapman eats apples'*
can be seen in Figures 5.10-5.13. I only present the derivation of one of the
conjuncts, since the derivation of the other is very similar.

Figure 5.10 shows the combination of the proper noun *'Chapman'* and the
transitive verb *'eats'*. The UCCG category of a proper noun is s/vp, and that
of a transitive verb is vp/(s/vp). Consequently, the two signs corresponding to
them combine via forward composition, resulting in a constituent *'Chapman
eats'* with the category s/(s/vp). The other conjunct *'Keats steals'* is formed
in a similar manner.

Figure 5.11 presents the combination of the conjunct *'Chapman eats'* with
the conjunction sign. The conjunction sign for this type of coordination has
the category $((s/(s/vp))\backslash_\star(s/(s/vp)))/_\star(s/(s/vp))$. This means that after the
conjunction has combined with a conjunct of an appropriate type to its right
via forward application and another to its left via backward application, the
category of the result sign is that of "subject+transitive verb" constituent:
s/(s/vp). By means of the unification of the DRS variables the semantic addition of the conjunct is promoted to the result part of the sign. The variable
D is unified with $D5$, and $D5$ is unified with the DRS in the vp sub-sign of
'Chapman eats'. D introduces the new constant value into the result head of
the sign of *'Chapman eats'*. The two DRSs in the result head of the conjunct
are merged together. The combined DRS is unified with the variable $D1$, which
introduces the semantics into the result part of the conjunction sign. Note also
the use of the same variable X as the VAR value throughout the conjunction
sign. This is the key to obtaining the same value for the patient semantic role
associated with the two verbs *'steals'* and *'eats'*. Note also the use of the event
variables: the value of the SIT feature in the result part of the result sign, E,
stands for a set: looking at the DRS, we see that E actually corresponds to the
set of two events $E1$ and $E2$. The motivation for this is provided by sentences
like *'Yesterday Keats stole and Chapman ate apples'* that contain sentential
adverbials. The adverbial here modifies both of the events expressed by the
conjuncts.

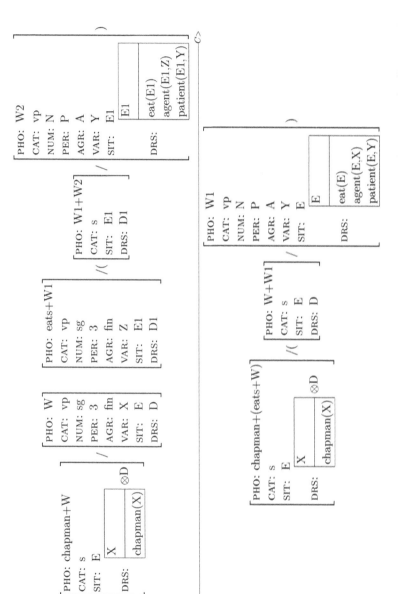

Figure 5.10. Formation of the constituent *'Chapman eats'* by combining the signs of *'Chapman'* and *'eats'* via forward composition

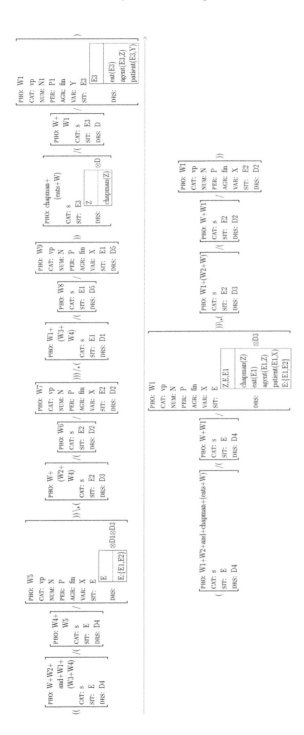

Figure 5.11. Formation of the constituent *'and Chapman eats'* by combining the signs of *'and'* and *'Chapman eats'* via forward application

Figure 5.12 shows the formation of the constituent *'Keats steals and Chapman eats'* out of *'Keats steals'* and *'and Chapman eats'*. Here, the backward application rule is used. Again the same kind of promotion of semantics to the result sign occurs as was described in association with the previous step. The DRS semantics resulting from this combination specifies that there are two events, those of stealing (*E1*) and eating (*E2*), which have different actors but are aimed at the same patient. The category of the result constituent is s/(s/vp): a sentence missing an object.

The combination in Figure 5.13 provides the syntactic constituent *'Keats steals and Chapman eats'* with its object *'apples'*, thereby completing the analysis of the sentence *'Keats steals and Chapman eats apples'*. This step is performed using forward application. Note that the final DRS specifies that the semantic value of the variable *E* in the result sign is a composite event which consists of stealing and eating.

The second example that we examine is *'Mary drove and John flew to London'*. Unless we are willing to provide multiple categories for vp modification, or furnish verbs in the lexicon with categories that include vp modification in the category, we will need to use type-raising in this example. In Section 5.1.1 we provided adverbs with the category vp\vp. This is the generic category for all vp post-modifiers. This category works fine in many cases. Example 5.28 shows a CCG style derivation with UCCG categories for the sentence *'Mary drove to London'*. Note that the modification needs to be able to directly apply to the vp sign. However, this can cause problems: for example, we are unable to obtain the reading for the sentence *'Mary drove and John flew to London'* where both Mary's and John's motion was directed towards London. Here the coordination rule would need to apply first, and after that the modification would apply to the whole coordinated constituent. With the usual noun phrase and vp categories, the conjuncts would end up having the category s (s/vp vp ⇒ s), which means that the category of the whole coordinated constituent would also be s. The vp modification vp\vp is unable to combine with the sentence category (s vp\vp ⇒).

A way around would be to provide an alternative category s\s for the vp modification. However, it is hard to find a convincing reason why in the sentence *'Mary drove to London'* the vp modification can have the category vp\vp,

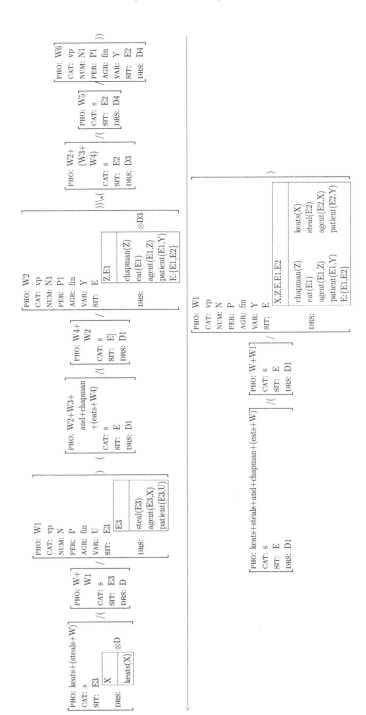

Figure 5.12. Formation of the constituent *'Keats steals and Chapman eats'* by combining the signs of *'Keats steals'* and *'and Chapman eats'* via backward application

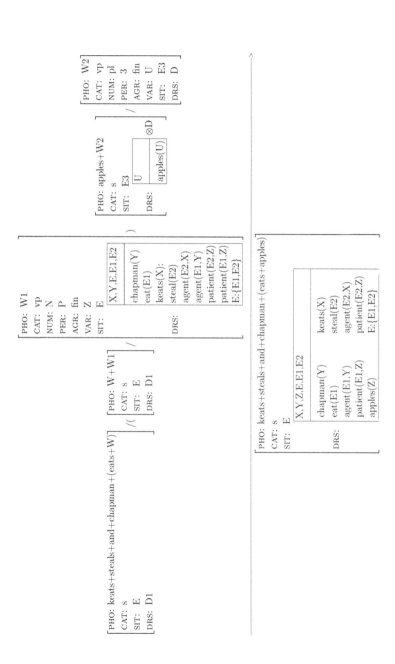

Figure 5.13. Formation of the sentence *'Keats steals and Chapman eats apples'* by combining the signs of *'Keats steals and Chapman eats'* and *'apples'* via forward application

while in *'Mary drove and John flew to London'* it must be s\s.

(5.28)

Mary	drove	to London
$\overline{s/vp}$	$\overline{vp}$	$\overline{vp\backslash vp}$

$$\frac{\qquad\qquad\qquad}{vp}<$$

$$\frac{\qquad\qquad\qquad}{s}>$$

Another solution would be to provide verbs in the lexicon with multiple categories: verbs with and without modification. However, the number of modifiers a verb can take is not fixed to any specific number. This means that we would need a separate sign for each verb with any number of modifiers. An incomplete list of lexical categories needed for intransitive verbs can be seen in Example 5.29a, and that for transitive verbs in 5.29b. Seen from this vantage point, multiple lexical categories for verbs with modification does not seem a very good idea.

(5.29) a) vp/(vp\vp)

(vp/(vp\vp))/(vp\vp)

((vp/(vp\vp))/(vp\vp))/(vp\vp)

(((vp/(vp\vp))/(vp\vp))/(vp\vp))/(vp\vp)

((((vp/(vp\vp))/(vp\vp))/(vp\vp))/(vp\vp))/(vp\vp)

. . .

b) (vp/(vp\vp))/(s/vp)

((vp/(vp\vp))/(vp\vp))/(s/vp)

(((vp/(vp\vp))/(vp\vp))/(vp\vp))/(s/vp)

((((vp/(vp\vp))/(vp\vp))/(vp\vp))/(vp\vp))/(s/vp)

(((((vp/(vp\vp))/(vp\vp))/(vp\vp))/(vp\vp))/(vp\vp))/(s/vp)

. . .

The third option would be to use type-raising for verb phrases. This works well with no need for additional lexical categories. Type-raising for a verb phrase was illustrated above in Figure 5.9. The category for a type-raised vp using the type-raising rule A is T/(T\vp). Again using CCG-style derivation representation, the desired analysis of the sentence *'Mary drove and John flew to London'* looks as seen in Example 5.30. The main steps of the UCCG derivation with complete signs is illustrated in Figures 5.14 – 5.18.

(5.30)

$$
\frac{
\begin{array}{cccccc}
\text{Mary} & \text{drove} & \text{and} & \text{John} & \text{flew} & \text{to\ London} \\
\hline
s/vp & vp & CONJ & s/vp & vp & vp\backslash vp
\end{array}
}{
}
$$

Mary drove   and   John   flew   to London
s/vp vp $CONJ$ s/vp vp $vp\backslash vp$

$\dfrac{}{T/(T\backslash vp)}\text{>T}$ $\dfrac{}{T/(T\backslash vp)}\text{>T}$

$\dfrac{}{s/(vp\backslash vp)}\text{>B}$ $\dfrac{}{s/(vp\backslash vp)}\text{>B}$

$\dfrac{}{s/(vp\backslash vp)}\text{<Φ>}$

$\dfrac{}{s}\text{>}$

5.3   Conclusion

In this chapter we took an important step towards our goal of combining UCCG and IS-DRSs: we replaced the previously used predicate calculus with the more advanced DRT semantics. Additionally, we improved the formalism in several other respects, including introducing neo-Davidsonian event semantics into it and adding several new features to the signs. The introduction of neo-Davidsonian event semantics is highly significant, because it allows us to speak about events (important for phenomena like verb modification) in first order logic. Event variables in the feature structures play and active role in building up a semantic representation parallel to syntactic combination. In this sense their function is similar to that of discourse referent variables. All of these modifications had several implications for the UCCG signs as originally presented in Chapter 4. We revised the signs of the major sentential constituents, and introduced several new signs.

This chapter extended the UCCG formalism to cover a non-trivial fragment of English. In its final sections we addressed the complex issues of type-raising and coordination. We saw that, even though type-raising is less frequently needed in UCCG than in CCG, the operation is indispensable on certain occasions. Finally, I presented a detailed analysis of some sentences with coordinated constituents.

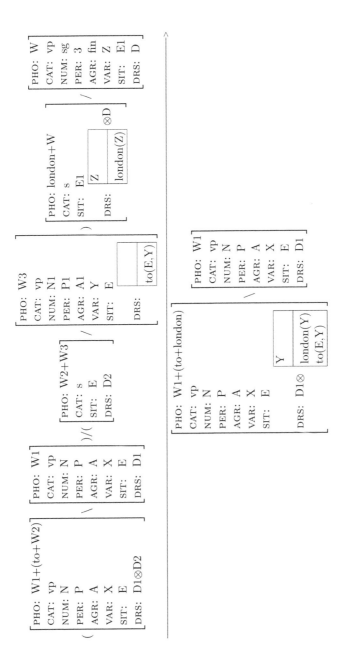

Figure 5.14. Formation of the prepositional phrase *'to London'* from the preposition *'to'* and the proper noun *'London'* using forward application

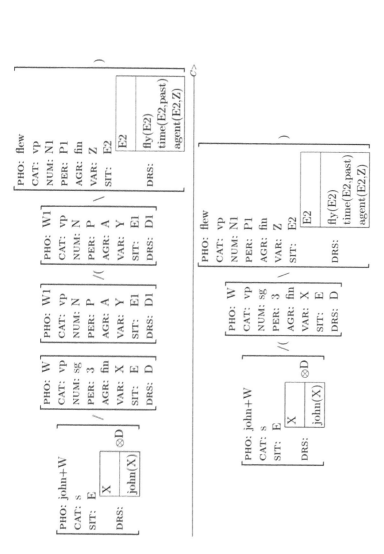

Figure 5.15. Formation of the constituent 'John flew' from the proper noun 'John' and the type-raised vp 'flew' using forward composition

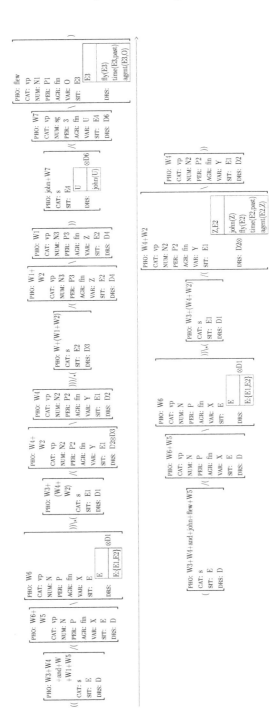

Figure 5.16. Formation of the constituent 'and John flew' from the conjunction 'and' and the conjunct 'John flew' using forward application

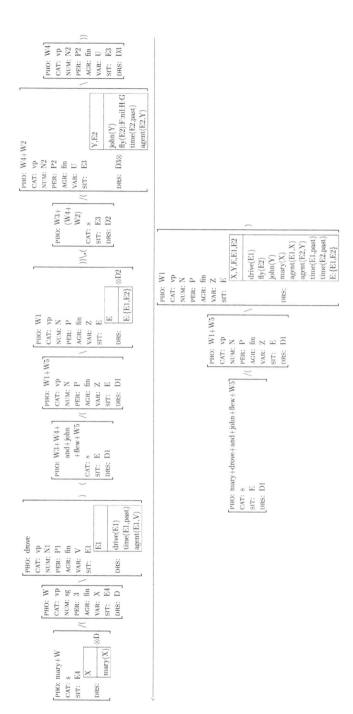

Figure 5.17. Formation of the coordinated constituent *'Mary drove and John flew'* from the conjunct *'Mary drove'* and the constituent *'and John flew'* using backward application

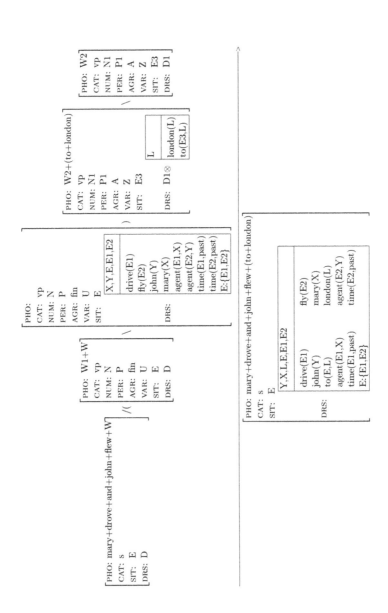

Figure 5.18. Formation of the sentence *'Mary drove and John flew to London'* from the coordinated constituent *'Mary drove and John flew'* and the prepositional phrase *'to London'* using forward application

Chapter 6

Adding Information Structure to UCCG

The present chapter constitutes the crux of the whole book. It describes an extension to UCCG whereby an account of information structure is included in the formalism. As described in Section 2.1, *information structure* stands for the way people arrange the content they want to communicate in an utterance. I use the terms *theme/rheme* and *focus/background* as used by Steedman (2000b). When introducing prosodic and information-structural features into UCCG, by and large, I followed the prosodic approach of Steedman (2000b), the basics of which were described in Section 2.2.1. In Section 3.3 we developed an approach of including his ideas in DRT semantics. Section 6.1 of this chapter will explain the part that information structure plays in CCG syntax.

Since I was simultaneously implementing a UCCG parser, I needed to specify how the unification in the signs was achieved much more precisely than presented in Steedman 2000b. Adding intonation to UCCG raised several problems. Combination of signs only via straightforward unification was not feasible any more: wherefore I introduced the concept of *recursive unification*, which will be explained below in Section 6.2.

When introducing information structure into UCCG syntax, I will follow the general structure of Section 3.3.3 (Chapter 3) where I presented my approach to the semantics of information structure, in that I first discuss the issues concerning theme/rheme and focus, then proceed to boundary tone semantics and finally add the $\pm AGREED$ property. Section 6.7 summarises how information structure, syntax and semantics work together in UCCG, and briefly touches upon some specific topics: unmarked themes, split themes, the need for type-raising induced by information structure, multiple foci in a prosodic phrase, and focus marking on function words. For brevity, I omit the agreement features in signs in the examples in this chapter, but their presence is still to be assumed.

6.1   Information Structure in CCG

We already discussed the main ideas behind Steedman's prosodic approach to information structure in Section 2.2.1 (Chapter 2) and Section 3.3.1 (Chapter 3). In this chapter we are concerned primarily with information-structural syntax: how syntactic combinations can be used in order to build up a semantic representation which is annotated for information structure. Recall that the main idea behind Steedman's (1991a; 1991b; 2000a; 2000b; 2003) theory of information structure is that information structure is transparently reflected in intonation. Hence, by knowing the location and type of pitch accents and boundary tones, it is possible to determine the information-structural partitionings of the utterance. Boundary tones serve to delimit intonational phrases which correspond to information-structural components. Themeness and rhemeness is assigned to intonational phrases by pitch accents: there is a specific set of theme pitch accents and another one of rheme pitch accents (see Fig. 2.1 on page 26).

In Section 4.1.1, Chapter 4, we witnessed that CCG provides multiple analyses for a single sentence. This "spurious" ambiguity is often seen as a major shortcoming of CCG. However, Steedman contends that allowing multiple analyses is a virtue rather than a vice: the different analyses reflect different information structure. Quoting Steedman (2000b, page 109):

> The claim is that in spoken utterances, intonation helps to determine which of the many possible bracketings permitted by the combinatory syntax of English is intended, and that the interpretations of the constituents that arise from these derivations, far from being "spurious", are related to distinctions of Information Structure and discourse focus among the topics that the speaker has in mind and the comments that the speaker has to contribute.

In the spirit of the above, the two analyses of the sentence '*Anna married Manny*' in Examples 6.1 and 6.2 correspond to two different information structure bracketings. In 6.1 '*Anna*' is the rheme, while the vp '*married Manny*' is the theme. In 6.2, '*Anna*' together with the verb '*married*' forms the theme, and '*Manny*' represents the rheme. In the grammar theories which insist on the "traditional" syntactic constituents, syntactic and prosodic/information-structural analysis causes discrepancies, but in CCG, syntax and information structure can coexist harmoniously.

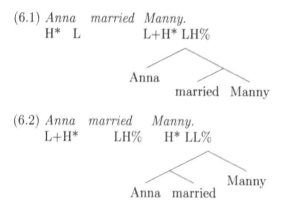

(6.1) *Anna   married   Manny.*
    H*   L   L+H* LH%

(6.2) *Anna   married   Manny.*
    L+H*   LH%   H* LL%

Steedman proves his claim about the close relationship between syntax and information structure by showing that "the rules of combinatory grammar can be made sensitive to intonation contour, which limits their application in spoken discourse" (Steedman, 2000b, page 109). His solution is to grant the pitch accents the facility of marking the syntactic category of the accented word with focus feature in the way that it "project" theme-rheme status to elements with which the word combines. The addition of information-structural features allows Steedman to formulate the *Prosodic Constituent Condition*, according to which syntactic categories are only permitted to combine via a syntactic combinatory rule if the result of their combination is a valid prosodic constituent. This condition is similar to Selkirk's *Sense Unit condition* (Selkirk, 1984, page 286). However, a major difference here is that in CCG the condition comes into existence naturally without the need for a separate stipulation.

Parsing according to intonational phrasing is accomplished in the following way in CCG: the categories of lexical items can be either theme-marked by a theme accent, rheme-marked by a rheme accent, or unmarked (i.e. unaccented).

Theme- and rheme-marked categories can freely combine with adjacent categories with the same information-structural marking, or with unmarked categories. If a theme- or rheme-marked category combines with an unmarked
category, the result category inherits the themeness or rhemeness from the
marked category that participated in the combination. While pitch accents are
seen as properties of words that carry them, boundary tones are seen as indi-
vidual lexical entries, which have their own category of the form $S\$_\phi \backslash S\$_\eta$.[1] The
boundary tone category copies the category to its left with which it combines,
and replaces its intonational marking by ϕ, which stands for "phrase". Phrase-
marked categories can only combine with other phrase-marked categories: this
way combinations over intonational phrase boundaries are avoided.

$$(6.3)$$

Anna	married		Manny	
$L+H^*$		$LH\%$	H^*	$LL\%$

$$
\cfrac{\cfrac{\cfrac{S_\theta/(S_\theta\backslash NP_\theta) \quad (S\backslash NP)/NP}{S_\theta/NP_\theta}\text{>B} \quad S\$_\phi\backslash S\$_\eta}{S_\phi/NP_\phi}< \quad \cfrac{S_\rho/(S_\rho\backslash NP_\rho) \quad S\$_\phi\backslash S\$_\eta}{S_\phi/(S_\phi\backslash NP_\phi)}<}{S_\phi}<
$$

Example 6.3 demonstrates the projection of themeness/rhemeness during
the syntactic analysis of the sentence *'Anna married Manny'* where the words
'Anna' and *'Manny'* carry pitch accents. Besides the final boundary there is
a boundary after the verb. The entry for *'Anna'* with the pitch accent $L+H^*$
is marked for themeness in the lexicon. When the category of *'Anna:L+H*'*
is combined with its neighbouring unmarked verb *'married'* via forward composition, the resulting category inherits the theme-marking of *'Anna'*. Next, the
constituent *'Anna married'* is combined with the boundary tone category via
backward application. The resulting category is marked as a phrase (ϕ). A similar operation is performed with the categories of *'Manny'* and the boundary
tone following it. At this point we have two complete intonational phrases. As
the categories of both of them bear the same information-structural marking,
they can be combined to form a sentence, again by using the rule of backward
application. Example 6.4 shows the analysis of the same sentence, but com-

---

[1]$S\$$ is a variable that stands for any category that is a function from sentence to something. η
is a variable that ranges over the syntactic features of information structure, θ and ρ. η' is the
corresponding semantic variable.

plete with semantics (the meaning of the $\pm$ and H/S marking will be explained below).

In his 2003 paper, Steedman added two new dimensions to his prosodic approach to information structure: $\pm AGREED$, and speaker/hearer commitment (see Section 2.2.1, Chapter 2). Syntactically, it is fairly straightforward to include the $\pm AGREED$ feature: it is projected from the pitch accents to the whole intonational phrase similarly to the themeness and rhemeness quality. Speaker and hearer commitment does not play an active part in syntactic combinations. It is part of the boundary tone semantics, and as such becomes part of the semantics of the complete intonational phrase. In addition, boundary tones apply the θ or ρ marking to the semantics of the category they combine with. This is done in accordance with the corresponding syntactic feature on the category that the boundary combines with. Example 6.4 once more presents the analysis of the sentence 'Anna married Manny', this time including the semantic combinations and the four features contributed by intonation: theme/rheme (θ, ρ, η), focus (the semantics of the focused word is marked by '*'), $\pm AGREED$ ($+$, $-$) and speaker/hearer commitment ($[H]$, $[S]$).

(6.4)

$$
\begin{array}{c}
\begin{array}{cccc}
\text{Anna} & \text{married} & & \text{Manny} \\
L+H^* & & LH\% & H^* & LL\% \\
\hline
S_{\theta+}/(S_{\theta+}\backslash NP_{\theta+}) & (S\backslash NP)/NP & S\$_{\phi}\backslash S\$_{\eta\pm} & S_{\rho+}/(S_{\rho+}\backslash NP_{\rho+}) & S\$_{\phi}\backslash S\$_{\eta\pm} \\
:\lambda f.f\,{}^*\!anna' & \lambda x.\lambda y.marry'xy & \lambda f.[H^{\pm}]\eta'f & \lambda p.p\,{}^*\!manny' & \lambda g.[S^{\pm}]\eta'g \\
\end{array}
\end{array}
$$

$$\overline{S_{\theta+}/NP_{\theta+} : \lambda x.marry'x\,{}^*\!anna'}^{>B}$$

$$\overline{S_{\phi}/NP_{\phi} : [H^+]\theta'(\lambda x.marry'x\,{}^*\!anna')}^{<} \qquad \overline{S_{\phi}/(S_{\phi}\backslash NP_{\phi}) : [S^+]\rho'(\lambda p.p\,{}^*\!manny')}^{<}$$

$$\overline{S_{\phi} : ([S^+]\rho'(\lambda p.p\,{}^*\!manny'))([H^+]\theta'(\lambda x.marry'x\,{}^*\!anna'))}^{<}$$

$$\overline{S : marry'\,manny'\,anna'}$$

6.2 Adding Information Structure to UCCG Signs

As we saw above, CCG treats pitch accents and boundary tones in a dissimilar manner: pitch accents are properties of words, introduced as features on the corresponding category in the lexicon, but boundary tones are separate lexical units. In CCG several lexical entries are needed for a single linguistic expression: namely, for the case it is theme-marked, when it is rheme-marked, and when it is unmarked. In UCCG pitch accents and boundary tones receive a uniform treatment: they are autonomous lexical entries. This way we avoid having to expand the lexicon. However, when accommodating pitch accents as independent signs, we need to add the special requirement that they be the first to combine with the sign of the word on which they occur. Otherwise, it would not be possible to tell at a later stage of parsing which item carried the accent, i.e. which item was focused. Without this constraint, we could first combine *'loves'* and *'Mary'* to form the unit *'loves Mary'* in Example 6.5, and only then combine this two word unit with the pitch accent. However, this is not what we want, because this way we can no longer determine which of the two words was focused. I postpone further discussion of focus marking until Section 6.4.

(6.5) loves Mary H* LL%

I assume that the category of all prosodic signs of UCCG is similar to what Steedman proposed for the boundary tones in CCG (see Section 6.1). The general shape of the sign is thus $S'\backslash S$, where S and S' stand for UCCG signs, either basic or complex. S' and S are almost identical, except for their information structure feature which may be different.[2] The sign applies to its argument on its left, and essentially copies the whole sign, supplementing it with information-structural marking.

From now on, we assume that there is an information structure value associated with each sign. Since in the case of complex word signs, all sub-signs have the same information structure value, we could attempt to take a different approach to the information structure feature than the features introduced earlier, and mark it as a single flag on a sign. Figure 6.1 shows the combining of the sign for *'loves'*, annotated with a single information-structural flag, and a stylised pitch accent sign.[3] We would need to redefine the combinatory rules in minor detail to accommodate this flag.

---

[2]In the case of pitch accent signs, S' and S are identical, including the information structure feature. Thus, the shape of pitch accent signs is actually $S\backslash S$. In the case of boundary tone signs the information structure feature values on either side of the slash are different.

[3]The righthand sign in Fig. 6.1 is a stylised pitch accent sign. The big upper case S and VP are variables standing for a whole s or vp sign correspondingly. I stands for an uninstantiated information structure variable and θ stands for theme marking.

This solution, however, does not take us a long way. Remember that in CCG the boundary tones had the function of changing the information-structural marking on the full intonational phrase, which allowed it to combine with other, similarly complete, prosodic phrases. A single flag does not provide the necessary means for achieving this goal.

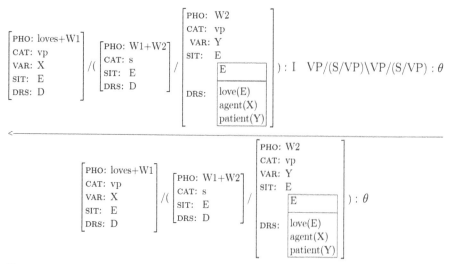

Figure 6.1: Combining the sign for *'loves'* with a pitch accent sign, the information structure value being represented as a single flag on the sign

Given the above observations, I introduced an information structure feature INF in each sub-sign as seen in Example 6.6.

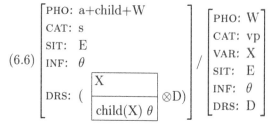

6.3   Theme/Rheme-Marking

Having decided to treat pitch accents as indipendent lexical units, we assume that entries for words in the lexicon do not include explicit marking for information structure: their information structure value is a variable. This variable gets replaced by a constant value during the process of combining the signs. The information structure variable can get a value directly from a pitch accent sign, i.e. when it combines with a pitch accent sign. Alternatively, the information structure variable of a sign can get instantiated through a combination with another sign, which has its information structure feature value already determined. Thus, even though there may be only one pitch accent in an intonational phrase, the same information structure value is projected to the whole phrase.

The variable used as the value of the information structure feature in a sign is also present among the flags on DRS-conditions (see Example 6.6 and the discussion in Section 3.3.3, Chapter 3). In this manner, once the feature variable is instantiated during syntactic combination, the DRS-condition flag, too, acquires the same constant value. The way information feature variable is related to the information-structural flags on DRS-conditions via unification is analogous to the way the discourse referent variables (see Section 4.3) and event variables (see Section 5.1) are tied to the variables in semantics.

In our system we have the following pitch accents: theme pitch accents L+H*, L*+H, and rheme accents H* and L*. Given that the general shape of the pitch accent sign is S\S, the whole sign for a theme pitch accent (L+H* or L*+H) looks like the one seen in Example 6.7 and that for a rheme pitch accent (H* or L*) is like that in Example 6.8.

$$
(6.7) \quad \begin{bmatrix} \text{PHO: W} \\ \text{CAT: C} \\ \text{VAR: X} \\ \text{SIT: E} \\ \text{INF: } \theta \\ \text{DRS: D} \end{bmatrix} *\backslash_* \begin{bmatrix} \text{PHO: W} \\ \text{CAT: C} \\ \text{VAR: X} \\ \text{SIT: E} \\ \text{INF: } \theta \\ \text{DRS: D} \end{bmatrix} * \qquad (6.8) \quad \begin{bmatrix} \text{PHO: W} \\ \text{CAT: C} \\ \text{VAR: X} \\ \text{SIT: E} \\ \text{INF: } \rho \\ \text{DRS: D} \end{bmatrix} *\backslash_* \begin{bmatrix} \text{PHO: W} \\ \text{CAT: C} \\ \text{VAR: X} \\ \text{SIT: E} \\ \text{INF: } \rho \\ \text{DRS: D} \end{bmatrix} *
$$

I need to clarify several issues about the pitch accent signs. First we discuss the INF feature. Note that we have the same constant value θ or ρ[4] in both the active part and the result part of a pitch accent sign. This allows the theme pitch accent sign to combine with either another theme-marked sign or a sign the INF feature value of which is a variable. However, unification blocks the combination of the theme accent sign with a rheme- or phrase-marked sign.

---

[4]Like before, θ stands for *theme*, and ρ for *rheme*.

Similarly, the rheme pitch accent sign can combine with another rheme-marked sign or a sign that is information-structurally unmarked, and it cannot combine with a theme- or a phrase-marked sign.

The second comment concerns the CAT feature. All the lexical non-prosodic signs had a constant value for the CAT feature. However, the prosodic signs inherit their cat feature from their argument by means of variable unification.

The third issue concerns the PHO feature. The prosodic signs do not leave a trace in the PHO feature.[5] This is so for practical reasons: it is not possible to accommodate prosody in the phonology feature using only simple variable unification, unless we make an assumption that the prosodic signs are much more specific than they are in our current approach. In order to determine the exact location of the prosodic marking in the PHO feature of the result, we would need to include multiple signs for each prosodic item in the lexicon, and both the active part and the result part of these signs would need to be spelled out such as to unify with a specific category. However, I find that in practice providing all possible categories for prosodic signs in the lexicon is inelegant and cumbersome, if tractable, given the presence of type-raised signs.

Figure 6.2 illustrates the first three points made. The sign for the vp *'walks'* is combined with a rheme pitch accent sign, say the sign for H*, by means of backward application. The category variable C of the pitch accent sign unifies with the value *vp* in the vp sign. Initially, the INF value of the vp sign is uninstantiated. The variable I unifies with the value ρ in the INF feature of the prosodic sign. Unification introduces this new information structure value also in the DRS of the vp sign. The PHO feature variable X unifies with the corresponding value *'walks'* in the phonology feature of the vp sign. The PHO feature of the result does not reflect the presence of an accent on the sign, however, we can still detect the presence of a rheme accent on the word by looking at the ρ flag on the corresponding DRS-condition.

There is a vital question which we have not addressed so far: namely that about prosodic signs combining with a complex sign. Again a way around could be found by providing multiple signs for prosodic items, which, besides basic signs, would allow them to combine with all possible complex signs. This, how-

---

[5]Hence, it would be more correct to call the PHO feature *"the feature of segmental phonology"*, since the phonology feature does not reflect suprasegmental phenomena like stress and intonation.

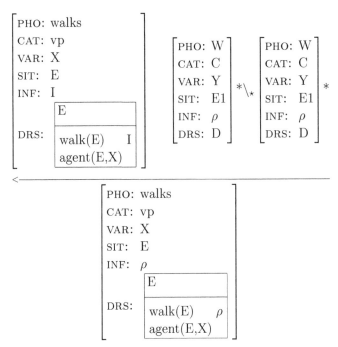

Figure 6.2: The combination of a basic vp sign with a rheme pitch accent

ever, causes an undesirable expansion of the lexicon, whilst giving no guarantee
that an appropriate prosodic sign is available to combine with each, possibly
type-raised, sign. In order to avoid these problems, I define a new kind of
unification operation for signs, called *recursive unification*. This operation can
be applied to basic (sub-)signs marked by '*'.

Let's say we have a basic sign S, which is marked by a star: thus, S*. The
meaning of the star is similar to the meaning that it has in regular expression
syntax in programming languages. However, there are differences as well. First,
in the definition we gave for a sign, we specified that all the basic sub-signs of
a complex sign had to be separated by a slash. Second, the repetitions of S in
S* are not distinct occurrences of the same object,[6] rather a new copy,[7] S', is

---

[6]Like identical twins are in fact two different persons with their own hands and feet, even though
they "share" the same genes and look very much alike.

[7]The variables in the feature values of the sign S are renamed in the copy S', however, the constant
values remain the same.

made of S at each iteration. In a nutshell, S* is the shorthand for any of the signs S, $S \mid S'$, $S \mid S' \mid S''$, $S \mid S' \mid S'' \mid S'''$, etc., where $\mid$ stands for a slash: either a forward or a backward slash. However, why call it "recursive unification" if, as a matter of fact, recursivity is the property of the sign? The reason for that lies in the fact that this ability of the sign to expand is only called for in the context where unification with another sign is attempted.

The only occasion where we use this recursive marking in our framework is in connection with prosodic signs. Therefore, we skip further abstract level discussion, and take a look at prosodic signs, and at what happens when they are combined with other signs. With the newly introduced recursivity marking, the general shape of prosodic signs is $S* \backslash S'*$. $S*$ and $S'*$ share the same set of variables, but there are some differences in the constant values that their information structure related features have. Backward application is the only type of combination that prosodic signs participate in. Therefore, we will further study recursive unification in the context of backward application. For the sake of simplicity, I have formulated a rule called *Backward Application with Recursive Unification* (BARU). The pseudocode algorithm for it can be seen in Figure 6.3. However, I want to stress that the slightly unusual behaviour of backward application is triggered by the special recursive category of prosodic signs which enables them to unify recursively, and therefore BARU is really nothing else than the good old backward application rule in disguise.

1:	*BARU:* $\mathbf{X}\ \mathbf{S*}\backslash\mathbf{S*} \rightarrow_{ru} \mathbf{X'}$
2:	*if X is a basic sign*
3:	*use standard backward application* $\mathbf{X}\ \mathbf{S}\backslash\mathbf{S'} \rightarrow \mathbf{X'}$
4:	*else*
5:	*make a copy* $S_1^*\backslash S_1'^*$
6:	*if X is of the form Y/Z*
7:	*apply BARU to Y:* $\mathbf{Y}\ \mathbf{S*}\backslash\mathbf{S*} \rightarrow_{ru} \mathbf{Y'}$
8:	*apply BARU to Z:* $\mathbf{Z}\ \mathbf{S_1^*}\backslash\mathbf{S_1'^*} \rightarrow_{ru} \mathbf{Z'}$
9:	*return Y'/Z'*
10:	*else*
11:	*apply BARU to Y:* $\mathbf{Y}\ \mathbf{S*}\backslash\mathbf{S'*} \rightarrow_{ru} \mathbf{Y'}$
12:	*apply BARU to Z:* $\mathbf{Z}\ \mathbf{S_1^*}\backslash\mathbf{S_1'^*} \rightarrow_{ru} \mathbf{Z'}$
13:	*return* $Y'\backslash Z'$

Figure 6.3: Algorithm for backward application with recursive unification

As illustrated in Figure 6.3, if a prosodic sign applies to a basic sign, then standard backward application is used (lines 2,3). If the argument to the prosodic sign turns out to have a complex category, then the prosodic sign needs to adjust its category to its argument. Therefore, a copy, $S_1^*\backslash S_1'^*$, is made of the original prosodic sign, $S^*\backslash S'^*$ (line 5).[8] The argument category X is split at its principal slash (the one that is the least embedded), and BARU is applied to both sub-signs (lines 7,8 and 11,12). If the sign only contains one slash (A/B or A\B), then the next step involves using standard backward application (lines 1,2,3) with both basic sub-signs, A (with the original $S^*\backslash S'^*$) and B (with the copy $S_1^*\backslash S_1'^*$), after which the resulting sign (A'/B' or A'\B') is stitched back together (lines 9,13). If the argument sign X is more complex than that, and contains multiple slashes, then furhter recursion is needed (lines 4-13).

The "template" sub-signs (S and S') of a pitch accent sign have every possible feature. The sign that it combines with may have fewer features. In that case the values of the features present in both signs combined are unified, whilst the superfluous features of the template are discarded. Features can only be discarded from template signs, that is signs where the CAT feature is a variable. Features can never be discarded from signs with known category.

Figure 6.4 illustrates the process of the combination of the sign for '*Anna*' with the sign for the theme accent L+H*. First, standard backward application is attempted. When this does not work, a copy is made of the pitch accent sign, and the np sign is split into its s and vp components. The original pitch accent sign combines with the result part of the np sign. Let's call the outcome of this combination s'. Now the copy of the pitch accent sign is combined with the vp portion of the np sign, resulting in vp'. As the final step, s' and vp' are joined back together by the forward slash.

For illustration purposes only, I present an expanded form of the pitch accent sign in Figure 6.5. Notice how, through unification, also the information-structural flag on the DRS condition *anna(X)* obtains the value θ.

Once a sign has received an INF value θ or ρ, it spreads this value to all

---

[8]The features in S and S' share several variables. The variables are renamed in the copy, i.e. they differ from the ones used in the original. However, if a feature A, that is used both in S and S', is renamed B in the copy, then both S_1 and S_1' share the same variable. Thus, the tight connection between the result and the active part of the prosodic sign is not lost during recursive unification.

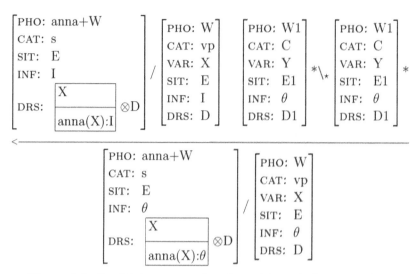

Figure 6.4: Combining a complex sign with a pitch accent sign

the signs that it combines with (see Figure 6.6). Thus, via the combination of the signs the theme or rheme property can be spread over infinitely long phrases. However, this property cannot be spread over the intonational phrase boundaries, the signs of which we are going to examine in Section 6.5.

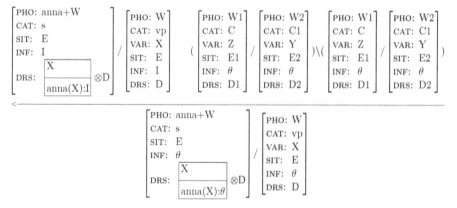

Figure 6.5: Combining a complex sign with an expanded pitch accent sign

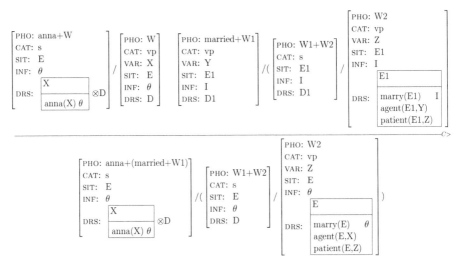

Figure 6.6: Combining the θ-marked sign for *'Anna'* with the sign for *'married'*

Finally, I make a remark about the use of the multi-modal slash[9] in prosodic signs. Remember that a slash with the modality '$\star$' only allows the use of the combinatory rule of functional application. We use this restrictive slash in order to avoid the composition of prosodic signs into adjacent signs, which would give rise to unacceptable and wrong outcomes. The function of prosodic signs is to solely alter the information structure features of their argument sign without making changes in its category. Later in this chapter I will show how allowing prosodic signs to compose into adjacent signs is a very bad solution: this produces signs where different parts of the result sign have different information structure values.

6.4   Focus

Focus-marking is rather different from theme- and rheme-marking, although it is also introduced by pitch accent signs. While theme- and rheme-marking is projected to the whole intonational phrase via unification during the combinatory process, focus-marking is a property that strictly belongs to only the word with the pitch accent.

---

[9]See Section 5.2.2 about the multi-modal slash.

A possible approach to focus-marking would be to contend that focus marking only affects the DRS. This would be easy to do, if we, similarly to Steedman (see Section 6.1), assumed that there are different lexical entries for words in the lexicon that are already marked for focus and themeness/rhemeness. However, having pitch accents as independent lexical entries we would need to introduce a special mechanism for changing specific flags on a DRS conditions when a lexical sign is combined with a pitch accent sign. This would unnecessarily complicate the system, and would be a rather ad hoc solution.

My approach is to introduce a new feature in lexical signs, called FOC, which stands for *focus* (see Example 6.9). This feature can have one of the two constant values: '+' if there is a pitch accent on the word, and '−' if there is no pitch accent present. Before receiving a constant value, the FOC feature value is a variable. The FOC feature serves as a link between the feature-structural and the focus flags on DRS-conditions: whenever a lexical sign is combined with a pitch accent sign, the corresponding focus flag on a DRS-condition assumes the value '+' via unification. However, we still seem to lack the way of stopping this feature value from spreading to other signs during the combination process. Nor is it clear where the intonationally unmarked words should obtain their "non-focus" value '−'.

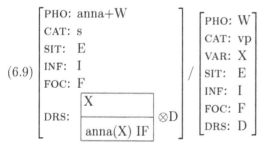

The solution is provided by a clever assignment of constant FOC values to pitch accent signs: in the active part, a pitch accent sign has the focus value '+', and in the result part, it has '−'. Remember, that pitch accent signs can only combine by backward application rule due to the use of the modal slash '\⋆'. This means that when the argument that the pitch accent sign is applied to unifies with the active part of the prosodic sign, its FOC feature value becomes '+'. Via unification, this focus value is introduced in the appropriate place in the DRS of the argument. However, the FOC value in the result part of the pitch accent sign remains '−'. Hence, non-pitch accent signs only have two possible values that can occur in their FOC feature: a variable or the constant value '−'. Examples 6.10 and 6.11 illustrate the new pitch accent signs for theme and rheme pitch accents respectively. A combination between the lexical sign for *'Anna'* and the pitch accent sign for L+H* is illustrated in Example 6.7. In the result sign the focus marking is '+' only in semantics on the DRS-condition *anna(X)*, in the FOC feature it has the value '−'.

$$(6.10) \quad \begin{bmatrix} \text{PHO:} & \text{W} \\ \text{CAT:} & \text{C} \\ \text{VAR:} & \text{X} \\ \text{SIT:} & \text{E} \\ \text{INF:} & \theta \\ \text{FOC:} & - \\ \text{DRS:} & \text{D} \end{bmatrix} *\backslash_\star \begin{bmatrix} \text{PHO:} & \text{W} \\ \text{CAT:} & \text{C} \\ \text{VAR:} & \text{X} \\ \text{SIT:} & \text{E} \\ \text{INF:} & \theta \\ \text{FOC:} & + \\ \text{DRS:} & \text{D} \end{bmatrix} * \qquad (6.11) \quad \begin{bmatrix} \text{PHO:} & \text{W} \\ \text{CAT:} & \text{C} \\ \text{VAR:} & \text{X} \\ \text{SIT:} & \text{E} \\ \text{INF:} & \rho \\ \text{FOC:} & - \\ \text{DRS:} & \text{D} \end{bmatrix} *\backslash_\star \begin{bmatrix} \text{PHO:} & \text{W} \\ \text{CAT:} & \text{C} \\ \text{VAR:} & \text{X} \\ \text{SIT:} & \text{E} \\ \text{INF:} & \rho \\ \text{FOC:} & + \\ \text{DRS:} & \text{D} \end{bmatrix} *$$

Regarding unfocused words, the focus feature value in their signs remains a variable until they combine with a sign corresponding to a focused word, or a sign that already has obtained the value '−' from another combination. If this occurs, the FOC value of the unfocused word sign becomes '−'. If the intonational phrase is an unmarked theme, and thus contains no pitch accents, the phrase gets the constant value '−' from the boundary tone sign.

Remember that we had a requirement that the combinations between pitch accents signs and their exponent signs had to take place before any other combinations. I call this part of syntactic analysis the *lexical stage*. Thus, the focus-marking is handled during the lexical stage, and plays no active part in the later stages of syntactic processing.

6.5   Boundary Tones

The set of boundary tones I implement in UCCG consists of LH% and LL%. Steedman (2003) uses a bigger set of boundary tones (see Fig. 2.2, page 28). However, semantically he divides them into two groups. I prefer not to introduce full synonyms in my system.

In essence, UCCG boundary tone signs are very similar to pitch accent signs, that were presented in the previous section. They have the general shape S′\S.

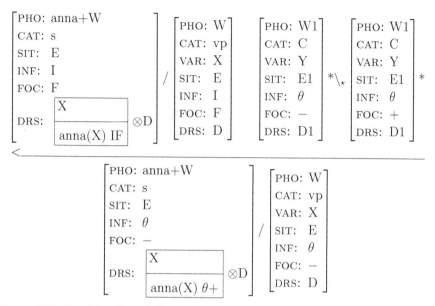

Figure 6.7: Combination of the sign for *'Anna'* with a theme pitch accent sign which includes the focus feature

Example 6.12 shows the sign for a UCCG boundary tone. The active part of boundary tone signs can unify with theme- or rheme-marked signs, or with signs the INF value of which is a variable. As with CCG (see Section 6.1), when combining with other signs, boundary tones replace the information feature of the other sign with the value *phrase* (see Figure 6.8), which I denote as ϕ. Boundary tones achieve this, because they have different INF values in the active and the result part. The FOC value of boundary tones is '−'. This means, that they can never carry a pitch accent, which, if technically allowed, would empirically be utter nonsense. However, the focus value '−' of boundary tones has another implication, too: that is where the unmarked theme phrases get their focus value from.

$$(6.12) \begin{bmatrix} \text{PHO:} & \text{W} \\ \text{CAT:} & \text{C} \\ \text{VAR:} & \text{X} \\ \text{SIT:} & \text{E} \\ \text{INF:} & \phi \\ \text{FOC:} & - \\ \text{DRS:} & \text{D} \end{bmatrix} * \backslash_* \begin{bmatrix} \text{PHO:} & \text{W} \\ \text{CAT:} & \text{C} \\ \text{VAR:} & \text{X} \\ \text{SIT:} & \text{E} \\ \text{INF:} & \text{I} \\ \text{FOC:} & - \\ \text{DRS:} & \text{D} \end{bmatrix} *$$

Similarly to pitch accents signs, when boundary tone signs are combined with other signs, the active part of the boundary tone sign recursively unifies with all sub-signs of the lexical sign. In the sign resulting from the combination, the INF feature value is ϕ.

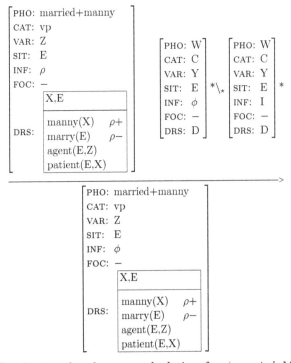

Figure 6.8: Combining the rheme marked sign for *'married Manny'* with a boundary tone sign

Boundary tones have no impact on the theme/rheme flags in semantics, because rather than unifying their INF feature value with that of another sign during the combination, boundary tones replace the previous INF value of the other sign with the new constant value ϕ. The constant value ϕ for the INF feature only serves the purpose of limiting the combinatory capabilities of full intonational phrases: it only allows them to combine with signs which are similarly phrase marked.

There is still a minor flaw in the representation of boundary tones. The problem is that at certain occasions ϕ does get introduced into the DRS feature via variable unification. This unfortunate shortcoming will get fixed in Section 6.5.1, where a detail will be added to boundary tones that makes their result so different from other signs that any combinations between phrase-marked and not phrase-marked signs becomes impossible.

The following scenario is an example where things go wrong in the case of the present representation. We will view the analysis of the second intonational phrase of the sentence *'Anna H* L married Manny LL%'*. The prosodic phrase *'married Manny LL%'* is an unmarked theme. If we started the combination of the signs in this phrase from the end, the first step (see Figure 6.9) would seem to do the right thing: even though the INF feature of the outcome of the combination is ϕ, the flag in the DRS remains a variable, and the focus feature and the corresponding DRS flag receive the value '−'. However, during the next combination (see Figure 6.10) things would go horribly wrong and the information-structural flag on the DRS-condition *marry(E)* would receive the value ϕ.

6.5.1   Boundary Tones Enhanced with Semantics

In this section we add the semantic import of boundary tones (see Section 3.3.3, Chapter 3) to the corresponding UCCG signs. The way I approach it, also solves the problem of phrase-marking entering among the DRS-flags. I introduce a new feature BND, which stands for "boundary", in the signs. This feature can have two constant values: s and h, where s stands for speaker commitment, and h stands for hearer commitment (see Section 3.3.1, Chapter 3 or Steedman (2003)). Other signs acquire these constant values from boundary tone signs: until combining with a boundary tone sign, their BND value is a variable. The boundary semantic value, similarly to theme and rheme is projected to the whole intonational phrase.

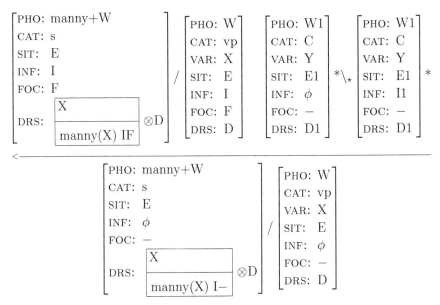

Figure 6.9: Combining a sign with an unmarked INF value with a boundary tone sign

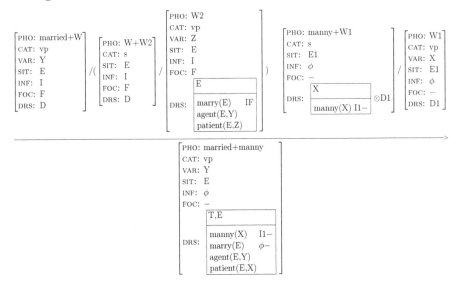

Figure 6.10: During the combination, a DRS-flag erroneously receives the value ϕ via variable unification

I introduce the BND feature in boundary tones in a rather special way: I only introduce it in the active part of the boundary tone sign. This means that whenever a sign is combined with a boundary tone sign, the sign resulting from the combination has one feature less than the input signs. This effectively eliminates the possibility that complete intonational phrases combine with incomplete ones.

$$(6.13) \quad \begin{bmatrix} \text{PHO:} & \text{W} \\ \text{CAT:} & \text{C} \\ \text{VAR:} & \text{X} \\ \text{SIT:} & \text{E} \\ \text{INF:} & \phi \\ \text{FOC:} & - \\ \text{DRS:} & \text{D} \end{bmatrix} *\backslash_* \begin{bmatrix} \text{PHO:} & \text{W} \\ \text{CAT:} & \text{C} \\ \text{VAR:} & \text{X} \\ \text{SIT:} & \text{E} \\ \text{INF:} & \text{I} \\ \text{BND:} & s \\ \text{FOC:} & - \\ \text{DRS:} & \text{D} \end{bmatrix} *$$

Figure 6.11 demonstrates the combination of the proper name *'Manny'* with the boundary tone sign for LL%. LL% signals speaker commitment: hence, the value s in the boundary feature of its active part. The BND feature variable of the sign for *'Manny'* unifies with the value s in the active part of the boundary tone sign. Via unification, this value is introduced in the appropriate location among the DRS flags. Since the result part of the boundary tone sign does not contain the BND feature, the final outcome of the combination also lacks this feature. If we were to try combining the result of the combination with another sign, say that for *'marry'*, the unification involved in the combination (e.g. between the active part of the transitive verb sign and the noun phrase sign) would fail, since the signs to be unified have a different number of features.

The above means that only one analysis is possible for the unmarked theme *'married Manny LL%'*: we first have to combine the signs for *'married'* and *'Manny'*, and only then can the sign for *'married Manny'* further combine with the boundary tone sign. This matches my intuition. The function of the boundary tone is to complete the intonational phrase: whenever a sign has combined with a boundary tone, the result stands for a complete intonational phrase. If we have an intonational phrase consisting of multiple words, all non-boundary signs in the phrase need to be combined first, and only then the boundary tone sign can complete the analysis of the phrase. Figure 6.12 demonstrates the combination of the complete unmarked theme *'married Manny'* with the

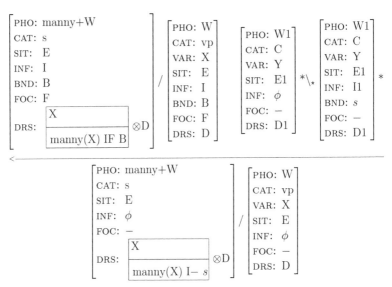

Figure 6.11: Combining a noun phrase sign with a semantically enhanced boundary tone sign

boundary tone LL%.

The approach of having a different number of features in the complete and incomplete intonational phrases also chooses the correct parse in the case of prosodical phrases which do contain pitch accents. For example, when analysing the rheme 'Anna H* married LL%' we first combine the sign for 'Anna' with the pitch accent sign. Then we have a choice between two options. The first option is to combine the sign for 'married' with the sign for 'Anna H*'. This combination is successful, and the resulting sign is rheme-marked. This sign now happily combines with the boundary tone sign, and the parse is a success. If at the choice point we chose to combine the sign for 'married' with the boundary tone sign, the first step would be successful: we would get a phrase-marked sign for the unit 'married LL%'. However, further analysis is not possible, since now we have two signs with two different constant INF values: ρ and ϕ, which cannot unify. Furthermore, the unification is blocked by the presence of the BND feature in the rheme-marked sign, while it is absent from the phrase-marked sign. The two analyses are illustrated by the parse trees (to be read bottom-up) in Example 6.14, where the edges of the

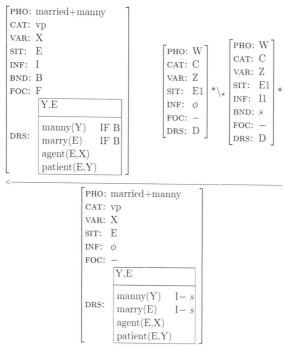

Figure 6.12: Combining the complete unmarked theme *'married Manny'* with the boundary LL%

graph show combinations, and the non-terminal nodes the INF feature value after each combination.

(6.14)

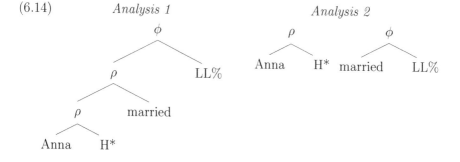

6.5.2   Do we still need multi-modal slashes?

The approach we took for adding boundary tone semantics to boundary tone signs already restricts the combinatory possibilities between the phrase-marked signs and non-phrase-marked signs. However, this is not a sufficient safeguard against obtaining unwanted constituents: we do still need to use the "application-only" modal slash. Figure 6.13 demonstrates a combination which would be allowed if boundary tones did not have the modal slash. The combination showed takes place between a complete intonational phrase and the preceding boundary tone by means of backward composition. The scenario of this example is as follows: we are analysing the sentence *'Mary drove LH% to London H* LL%'* and by the time of the combination showed in the figure, *'to London H* LL%'* has already been successfully parsed, and is marked as a complete intonational phrase by the INF value ϕ. In the figure, *'to London H* LL%'* is erroneously combined with the preceding boundary tone LH%. *'LH% to London H* LL%'* is an invalid constituent, since we only have phrase final boundaries in our system. Note that the sign for *'LH% to London H* LL%'* has a phrase-marked result part, while its active part has no information-structural marking. The analysis of the sentence would come to a halt after *'LH% to London H* LL%'* is combined with the verb *'drove'*, since the noun phrase *'Mary'* would not be able to take a phrase-marked vp as its argument due to the difference in the number of features. However, we should not allow the analysis to proceed that far: according to Steedman's *Prosodic Constituent Condition*, syntactic categories are only allowed to combine if the result of their combination is a valid prosodic constituent. In order to stop the combination in Fig. 6.13 we could either formulate a constraint or we can use a modal slash in the sign of the boundary tone which only allows the sign to participate in combinations which use an application rule. While allowing constraints would mean adding a whole new facet to the formalism, the modal slash, being a subtype of the normal slash, would not bring along any major changes. Hence I chose the latter.

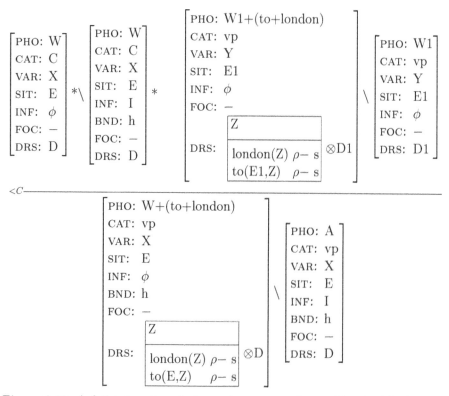

Figure 6.13: A full intonational phrase is erroneously combined with the preceding boundary tone via backward composition

6.6   Pitch Accents Revisited: ±*AGREED*

In Section 3.3.3 we included yet another aspect of Steedman's prosodic approach to information structure in the IS-DRS: namely, the ±*AGREED* feature. We still need to accommodate it in the feature structure of UCCG signs. The ±*AGREED* feature indicates whether the speaker perceives the issue talked about as contentious or uncontentious. Similarly to themeness and rhemeness, the ±*AGREED* quality is contributed by pitch accents, and projected over the whole intonational phrase. However, the feature is orthogonal to themeness and rhemeness in the sense that part of theme pitch accents and part of rheme pitch accents carry the +*AGREED*, while the remainder of theme and rheme pitch accents are marked by −*AGREED*. We implement two

+*AGREED*-marked pitch accents (L+H*, H*) and two pitch accents that are marked by −*AGREED* (L*+H, L*). In naturally occurring speech, the pitch accents marked by +*AGREED* are much more common than the ones marked by −*AGREED*. Therefore, the majority of our examples will also be using the +*AGREED*-marked pitch accents.

Since like themeness and rhemeness, the ±*AGREED* aspect is provided by pitch accents, we do not need to introduce a new feature for this aspect, but can incorporate its value, too, in the INF feature. In principle, we could combine these two values into one. However, in the IS-DRS we represented these two aspects by different non-adjacent flags. Therefore, we will need to present them in a form, from which it is easy to extract the separate values of the two aspects. From now on, the INF value will generally have the shape *I:A*, where *I* stands for themeness/rhemeness and *A* stands for the value of ±*AGREED*. However, there is one exception: for the sake of simplicity, the INF value of complete phrases is still just ϕ. The ±*AGREED* can have two constant values, either '+' or '−', or it can be a variable.

$$(6.15)\begin{bmatrix} \text{PHO:} & \text{W} \\ \text{CAT:} & \text{C} \\ \text{VAR:} & \text{X} \\ \text{SIT:} & \text{E} \\ \text{INF:} & \theta\text{:+} \\ \text{BND:} & \text{B} \\ \text{FOC:} & - \\ \text{DRS:} & \text{D} \end{bmatrix} *\backslash_* \begin{bmatrix} \text{PHO:} & \text{W} \\ \text{CAT:} & \text{C} \\ \text{VAR:} & \text{X} \\ \text{SIT:} & \text{E} \\ \text{INF:} & \theta\text{:+} \\ \text{BND:} & \text{B} \\ \text{FOC:} & + \\ \text{DRS:} & \text{D} \end{bmatrix} * \qquad (6.16)\begin{bmatrix} \text{PHO:} & \text{W} \\ \text{CAT:} & \text{C} \\ \text{VAR:} & \text{X} \\ \text{SIT:} & \text{E} \\ \text{INF:} & \phi \\ \text{FOC:} & - \\ \text{DRS:} & \text{D} \end{bmatrix} *\backslash_* \begin{bmatrix} \text{PHO:} & \text{W} \\ \text{CAT:} & \text{C} \\ \text{VAR:} & \text{X} \\ \text{SIT:} & \text{E} \\ \text{INF:} & \text{I} \\ \text{BND:} & s \\ \text{FOC:} & - \\ \text{DRS:} & \text{D} \end{bmatrix} *$$

The finalised sign for the L+H* pitch accent can be seen in Example 6.15 and the finalised sign for LL% is presented in Example 6.16. Although the prosodic items themselves are not present in the signs' phonology feature, the signs uniquely identify the prosodic items which correspond to them in our system. In the case of the pitch accent sign in Example 6.15, we can be sure that the sign stands for a pitch accent, since pitch accent signs are the only signs that can ever have the value '+' in the focus feature. Furthermore, we can be sure that the sign stands for the L+H* accent, since from the INF feature we learn that it is a theme pitch accent and that its ±*AGREED* value is '+'. We can be confident of the identity of the boundary tone sign, since only boundary tone signs have the INF value ϕ in the result part and a variable in the active part, as well a BND feature in the active part, which is absent from the result part. To further specify the identity of the boundary tone: the BND value s is specific to the boundary LL%.

Figure 6.14 illustrates the combination of the sign for the proper name *'Manny'* with the sign for the pitch accent H*. Initially, the INF feature of the sign for *'Manny'* has the value $I{:}A$, where I is the themeness/rhemeness variable, and A is the $\pm AGREED$ variable. I gets unified with the value ρ in the INF feature of the active part of the pitch accent sign. By means of unification, the new information structure value ρ replaces I among the DRS-flags in the noun phrase semantics. The variable A of the sign for *'Manny'* unifies with the corresponding value '+' in the active part of the pitch accent sign. The latter value is again introduced in the DRS of the noun phrase via unification. The focus variable F of the proper noun sign is unified with the value '+' in the active part of the pitch accent sign, and the DRS-flag F gets replaced by the new value. The DRS of the outcome of this combination says that *'Manny'* is marked as a rheme focus by a pitch accent which signals speaker/hearer agreement. The value of the boundary DRS-flag has not yet been determined.

Figure 6.15 shows the further combination of the constituent *'Manny H*'* with the boundary tone LL%. The INF variable I in the active part of the boundary tone sign is unified with the value $\rho{:}+$. However, in the result this value is replaced by ϕ. The boundary feature variable B in the sign for *'Manny H*'* is unified with the constant value s in the active part of the boundary tone sign, and introduced in its appropriate place in the DRS of the former sign. Since the result part of the boundary tone has no BND feature, this feature is absent from the outcome of this combination.

6.7 The Full System

In this section I will recapitulate the main points about information structure in UCCG and illustrate them with examples. In the sub-sections we will have a closer look at more specific phenomena: the analysis of unmarked themes, split themes and rhemes, multiple foci in an intonational phrase, evidence from information structure which explains the need for the syntactic operation of

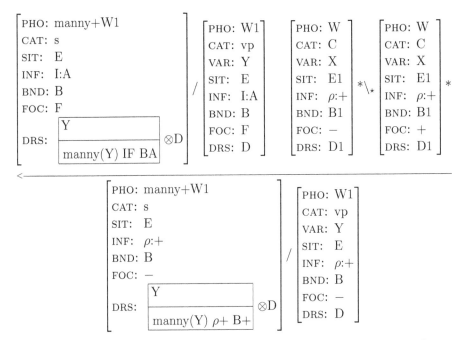

Figure 6.14: Combining the word 'Manny' with the pitch accent H*

type-raising, and issues regarding focus on function words.

Pitch accents are accountable for focus marking $(+, -)$ on word level, and theme/rheme (θ, ρ) and speaker/hearer agreement $(+, -)$ marking on the level of prosodic phrases. When non-prosodic signs are combined with pitch accent signs or other signs whose INF and FOC feature values are already instantiated to constant values, variable unification also introduces the new theme/rheme, $\pm AGREED$ and focus flag values on DRS-conditions. Non-prosodic lexical signs are combined with pitch accent signs before any other combinations take place during the so-called "lexical stage".

Boundary tones signs contribute the dimension of speaker/hearer commitment (s,h) to the semantics. Syntactically, the role of boundary tones is to assign phrase-marking (ϕ) to complete intonational phrases, thereby preventing them from further combinations with any other but similarly phrase-marked signs. The INF feature value ϕ is not allowed as a flag on DRS-conditions. The phrasal marking is blocked from entering into the DRS by giving the INF value

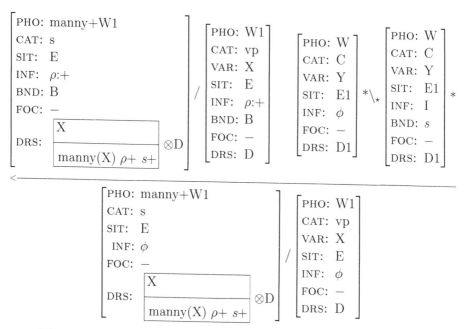

Figure 6.15: Combining 'Manny H*' with the boundary tone LL%

of unmarked signs the form $I{:}A$ (where I is the themeness/rhemeness variable and S is the variable for the $\pm AGREED$ aspect), which cannot directly unify with the single constant value ϕ. The combinations between phrase-marked and non-phrase-marked signs are further prevented by having an extra feature BND in all other signs, save the phrase marked ones. The BND feature is eliminated from other signs when they combine with a boundary tone sign which only contains this feature in its active part, but not in the result part.

In what follows I will give a step by step analysis of the sentence 'Anna L+H* married LH% Manny H* LL%'. Example 6.17 shows the same sentence in an appropriate context. The diagram in Figure 6.16 (to be read bottom-up) sketches the anticipated process of analysis of this sentence. The edges of the graph stand for the combinations performed, and the non-terminal nodes show the value of the INF feature of the result sign after each combination.

(6.17) Q: I know who Mary married, but who did Anna marry?

A: Anna L+H* married LH% Manny H* LL%.

First we perform the lexical stage. This involves looking the input words up in the lexicon and retrieving the corresponding signs. Then the focused words are combined with their respective pitch accent signs. Thus, in the case of the sentence we are analysing, two combinations are performed in the lexical stage: the sign for Anna is combined with the sign for L+H*, and the sign for *Manny* with that for H*.

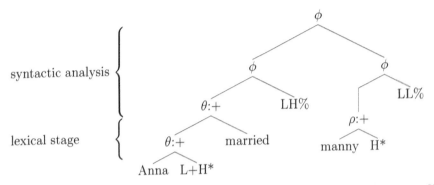

Figure 6.16: Analysis of the sentence *'Anna L+H* married LH% Manny H* LL%'*

Figure 6.17 demonstrates the combination of the sign for *'Anna'* with the sign for L+H*, which is a theme pitch accent and signals that the item carrying it is perceived as uncontentious by the speaker. Note how the FOC variable *F* of the sign for *'Anna'* is unified with the value '+' of the FOC feature in the active part of the pitch accent sign. Via this unification, the variable *F* is replaced by '+' also in the DRS of the noun phrase sign. The positive focus value is only retained in the DRS of the result sign, while the focus feature value of the result sign is '−'. The INF variable *I* of the sign for *'Anna'* gets its new value θ from the pitch accent sign. This unification is recorded both in the INF feature of the resulting sign as well as in the DRS. Similarly, the $\pm AGREED$ variable *A* in the INF feature gets unified with the value '+' in the INF feature of the active part of the pitch accent sign. Again via unification the new value is introduced in the DRS. A similar combination takes place between the sign for *'Manny'* and the rheme pitch accent sign for H*. This combination was illustrated above in Figure 6.14.

The first step in the "post-lexical" syntactic analysis involves combining the theme-marked sign for *'Anna'* with the sign for *'married'* (see Figure 6.18).

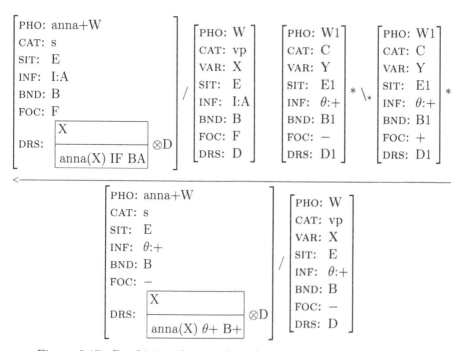

Figure 6.17: Combining the sign for *'Anna'* with the sign for L+H*

The latter is still information-structurally unmarked. During the combination process, the INF values of the two signs are unified, whereby the variable *I* in the INF feature of the sign for *'married'*, as well as on the DRS-condition *marry(E)*, assumes the value θ, and the variable *A* both in the INF feature and in the DRS of *'married'* acquires the constant value '+'. When the FOC features of the signs for *'Anna'* and *'married'* are unified, all four occurrences of the focus variable *F* in the sign for *'married'* are replaced by '−'.

The next step involves combining the now complete theme *'Anna L+H* married'* with the boundary tone LH% (Figure 6.19). During this combination, the INF value θ:+ of the former sign gets replaced by ϕ, which marks it as a complete phrase. This happens, because the boundary tone has different INF values in its active and result part. In the course of this combination, the BND feature finally acquires a constant value. The LH% boundary tone marks the intonational phrases that it completes, as being the hearer's responsibility. The BND feature in the sign for *'Anna L+H* married'* is unified with the value *h* in

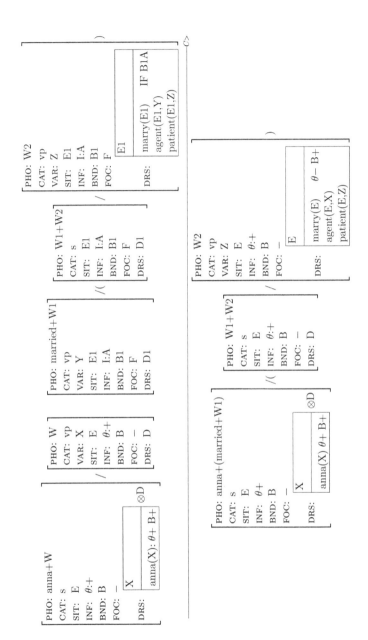

Figure 6.18. Combining the sign for *'Anna L+H*'* with the sign for *'married'*

the active part of the boundary tone sign. Via unification, the new boundary flag value is introduced in the DRS. Since the result part of the boundary tone sign does not contain the BND feature, the feature is absent from the outcome of this combination.

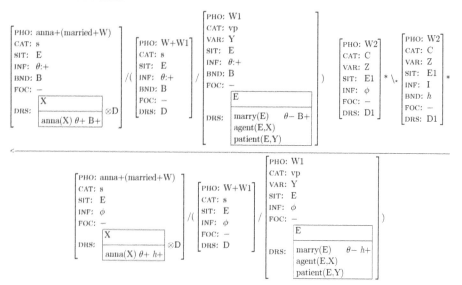

Figure 6.19: Combining *'Anna L+H* married'* with the boundary tone LH%

The theme phrase *'Anna L+H* married LH%'* cannot directly combine with the sign for *'Manny H*'*, since their INF values are different constants and their signs have a different number of features. Therefore, next *'Manny H*'* has to combine with the boundary tone LL%. The INF value of the sign for *'Manny H*'* is replaced by ϕ, the boundary flag s is introduced into the DRS, and the BND feature is removed from the result sign (see Fig. 6.15).

Now that we have two complete intonational phrases with the same number of features, both having the INF value ϕ, we are ready to take the final step in the analysis and combine the two phrases. The constant INF values of the theme phrase *'Anna L+H* married LH%'* and the rheme phrase *'Manny H* LL%'* now unify, and the two signs are combined by forward application (see Fig.6.20). As a result we have successfully parsed the sentence *'Anna L+H* married LH% Manny H* LL%'*.

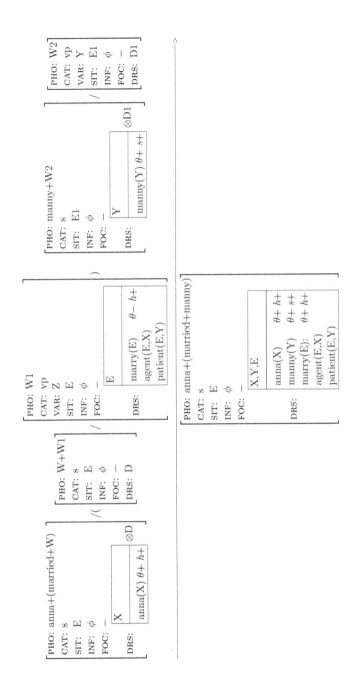

Figure 6.20. Combining two complete intonational phrases: *'Anna L+H* married LH%'* and *'Manny H* LL%'*

6.7.1 Unmarked Themes

In Section 3.3.3, Chapter 3, I already briefly addressed the issue of unmarked themes. I decided not to introduce a special DRS flag for unmarked themes, but rather treat them as being underspecified as far as information structure is concerned, and flag them with a variable. In this section I will argue why this is an appealing and natural solution when seen from the syntactic perspective.

First, a comment is in place regarding unmarked theme boundaries. Unmarked themes, unless sentence final, tend not to be separated from the rest of the utterance by an audible boundary. UCCG formalism, however, assumes that each information-structural phrase is delimited by a boundary: otherwise the unmarked theme gets analysed as a part of the neighbouring information-structural constituent. If a sentence consists of an unmarked theme and a rheme, without the presence of a boundary after the theme, it would be analysed as an all-rheme utterance. I assume the presence of another module that, based on contextual information, takes care of disambiguating the unmarked themes, and enters the delimiters in appropriate locations in an utterance, before it is passed on to the UCCG parser.

The INF value of all UCCG non-prosodic lexical signs is of the form $I{:}A$, where I is a themeness/rhemeness variable, whilst the variable A stands for the $\pm AGREED$ value. Also the FOC value of such signs is a variable. In short: all these values are initially underspecified, and only assume constant values via combinations with prosodic signs. The constant values for the variables I and A can only be contributed by pitch accent signs directly or indirectly, the negative focus value can also be obtained from the boundary tone signs. Hence, it is all very straightforward: if there is no pitch accent in a prosodic phrase, the INF value of the constituents of the phrase remains underspecified until the complete unmarked theme is combined with a boundary tone, when the previous INF value is replaced by ϕ. Since the value is replaced, and not unified, the themeness/rhemeness and $\pm AGREED$ DRS flags never get a constant value and thus remain variables. Due to the absence of pitch accents (which mark words for focus) in an unmarked theme, the focus value remains a variable until the complete unmarked theme is combined with a boundary tone. Then the FOC variable is unified with the constant value '−' of the corresponding feature in the active part of the boundary tone sign. Once an unmarked theme has combined with a boundary tone, it is ready to combine with other complete intonational phrases.

Figure 6.21 shows the combination of the unmarked theme *'Anna married'* with the boundary tone LL%. Example 6.18 shows the unmarked theme used in appropriate context.

(6.18) Q: Who did Anna marry?

A: Anna married LL% Manny H* LL%

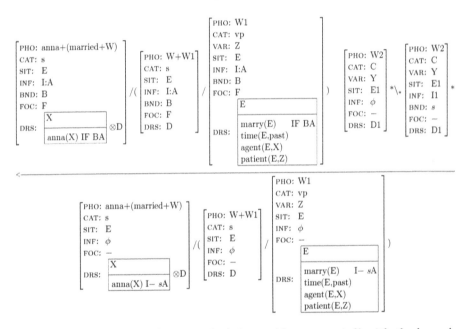

Figure 6.21: Combining the unmarked theme *'Anna married'* with the boundary tone LL%

6.7.2 Need for Type-Raising: Evidence from Information Structure

When we discussed coordination in Section 5.2, chapter 5, we recognised the need for type-raising in order to be able to successfully complete the analysis of well-formed sentences which contain certain kinds of coordination. This was because coordination constrained us to perform the combinations between the signs in a particular order. Thus, we had more combinatory freedom when analysing the sentence *'Mary drove to London'* than when analysing a similar one with coordination *'Mary drove and John flew to London'.* The same is true about information structure: to an extent it prescribes us which path of derivation we have to take.

For example, we are unable to analyse the sentence 6.19a if we only have the category vp for the verb *'drove'* with no access to type-raising. At the same time we would not have any problems analysing the very similar sentence *'Mary drove to London H* LL%'.* The reason why 6.19a poses problems is that we do not have access to the derivation where the post-modification of the verb can directly apply to the verb. The information structure of the sentence prescribes us that we first have to combine all the constituents in each intonational phrase, and only once both phrases are complete can we combine the two together. Ignoring the exact prosodic marking for the time being, the derivation path that intonation structure confines us to would be the one seen in Example 6.20. However, a complete sentence cannot combine with a modifier with the category vp\vp. In order to circumvent the problem we have exactly the same options as were pointed out in connection with the discussion of coordination (see Section 5.2.2, Chapter 5). Introducing a new lexical category vp/(vp\vp) for the verb *'drove'* would help us to provide an analysis for the sentence 6.19a. However, this solution would not be generalizable to the sentence 6.19b: we would again need to add a new lexical category for the verb.

(6.19)

    a)Mary L+H* drove LH% to London H* LL%.

    b)Mary drove from Edinburgh L+H* LH% to London H* LL%.

(6.20) Mary drove | to London

Mary	drove		to	London
s/vp	vp		$vp\backslash vp/(s/vp)$	s/vp

The best and most flexible option still seems to be to use type-raising, which can be applied whenever and if the need arises. Example 6.21 sketches the analysis of the sentence 6.19a if we type-raise the vp before it is combined via forward composition with the noun phrase that precedes it. Type-raising is an attractive solution, because it is generalizable to more complicated examples, and in contrast to the static character of the lexical categories, type-raising allows to create signs with a new category from the signs which are themselves already a result of combinations. For instance, in Example 6.22 first the signs for *'drove'*, *'from'* and *'Edinburgh'* are combined to form a vp, and then this vp is type-raised in order to allow for accommodating another vp modification at a later stage of analysis.

(6.21)

Mary	drove		to	London
s/vp	vp		$vp\backslash vp/(s/vp)$	s/vp

$$\frac{\qquad}{T/(T\backslash vp)} \text{>T}$$
$$\frac{\qquad}{s/(vp\backslash vp)} \text{>B}$$

$$\frac{vp\backslash vp}{\qquad} \text{>}$$

$$\frac{\qquad\qquad\qquad\qquad}{s} \text{>}$$

(6.22)

Mary	drove	from	Edinburgh		to	London
s/vp	vp	$vp\backslash vp/(s/vp)$	s/vp		$vp\backslash vp/(s/vp)$	s/vp

$$\frac{vp\backslash vp}{\qquad} \text{>} \qquad\qquad \frac{vp\backslash vp}{\qquad} \text{>}$$

$$\frac{vp}{\qquad} \text{<}$$

$$\frac{\qquad}{T/(T\backslash vp)} \text{>T}$$

$$\frac{\qquad}{s/(vp\backslash vp)} \text{>B}$$

$$\frac{\qquad\qquad\qquad\qquad}{s} \text{>}$$

6.7.3 Split Themes

Split themes occur when the theme of a sentence is divided into two by an intervening rheme. There is no need to provide any special mechanism in UCCG to handle such themes. In the case of a split theme each part of the theme is an independent intonational phrase. As far as UCCG is concerned this means that a path of derivation needs to be taken where the constituents inside each intonational phrase are combined first, and once the prosodic phrases are complete, the phrases can be combined together.

The sentence *'Mary L+H* drove LH% from Edinburgh H* LL% to London LL%'* contains a split theme (see also Example 6.23). The first part of the theme, *'Mary L+H* drove LH%'*, is marked by a theme pitch accent, the second part, *'to London LL%'*, is unmarked. The two parts of the theme are analysed as independent theme phrases. Due to the way syntax and information structure constrain each other (see the discussion about type-raising in Section 6.7.2), we first need to combine the full theme prosodic phrase *'to London LL%'* with the full rheme phrase *'from Edinburgh H* LL%'*, and only then can we combine the phrase *'from Edinburgh H* LL% to London LL%'* and the sentence initial theme phrase *'Mary L+H* drove LH%'*.

(6.23) Q: Anna drove from Cambridge to London, but where did Mary drive from?

A: Mary L+H* drove LH% from Edinburgh H* LL% to London LL%.

Figure 6.22 shows the combination of the sign for *'from Edinburgh H* LL%'* with that for *'to London LL%'*. Figure 6.23 demonstrates the final step of the analysis of the sentence, where *'Mary L+H* drove LH%'* and *'from Edinburgh H* LL% to London LL%'* are combined. For the last combination to be successful we need to have type-raised the vp *'drove'* before combining it with *'Mary'*. We can observe three different theme/rheme flag values in the final DRS: the conditions $mary(X)$ and $drive(E)$ are marked as a theme (θ), the conditions $edinburgh(Y)$ and $from(E,Y)$ are marked as a rheme (ρ), and the conditions $london(Z)$ and $to(E,Z)$ are flagged with a variable: hence they correspond to an unmarked theme. Two of the conditions are marked as foci $(mary(X), edinburgh(Y))$. The conditions corresponding to the sentence initial theme are marked for hearer commitment by the boundary tone LH% while the rest are marked for speaker commitment by the LL% boundaries. The majority of conditions are marked as uncontentious, while in the case of the two conditions corresponding to the unmarked theme, the $\pm AGREED$ value is undetermined: if a phrase contains no pitch accents the value of the $\pm AGREED$ aspect cannot, strictly speaking, be determined. However, since an unmarked theme is all background, we can assume that it is agreed. Hence, whenever we have a variable flag in the final DRS in the position of the $\pm AGREED$ aspect, we can interpret it as $+AGREED$.

6.7.4   Multiple foci

Multiple words can be accented in an intonational phrase. There is a constraint that the pitch accents occurring in the same minimal prosodic phrase

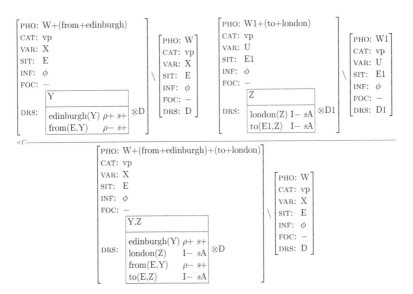

Figure 6.22: Combination of the rheme phrase *'from Edinburgh H* LL%'* with the unmarked theme phrase *'to London LL%'*

(i.e. in the scope of the same boundary tone) have to conform in the features which are projected to the whole intonational phrase: they need to have the same themeness/rhemeness and $\pm AGREED$ value. The prosodic phrase *'from Edinburgh H* to London H* LL%'* (see Example 6.24) complies with this constraint. However, it is not possible to provide an analysis for similar phrases *'from Edinburgh L+H* to London H* LL%'* and *'from Edinburgh H* to London L* LL%'*, since the pitch accents contained in them have clashing themeness/rhemeness or $\pm AGREED$ values.[10] The latter two are not well-formed intonational phrases: their constituents have different constant INF feature values wherefore their information structure features cannot unify.

(6.24) Q: Where did Mary drive from and where did she drive to?

A: Mary drove LL% from Edinburgh H* to London H* LL%.

Figure 6.24 shows the combination of the two rheme-marked prepositional phrases present in the intonational phrase *'from Edinburgh H* to London H* LL%'*. The example illustrates the stage of the derivation where the noun

---

[10]In order to accept these phrases, we require a boundary between the pitch accents with different themeness/rhemeness or $\pm AGREED$ property.

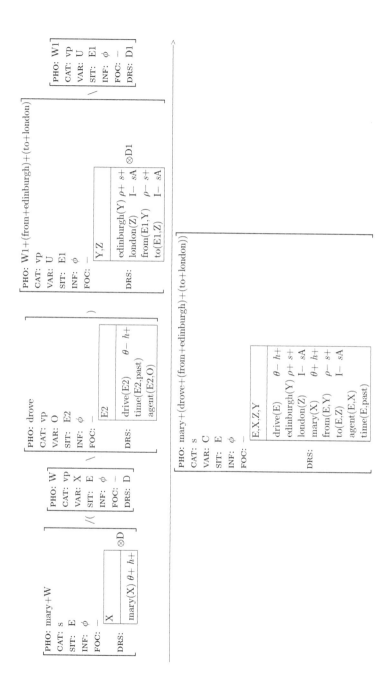

Figure 6.23. Combining the theme phrase 'Mary L+H* drove LH%' with the rheme+theme phrase 'from Edinburgh H* LL% to London LL%'

phrase and the pitch accent sign have already been combined. The signs of
both PPs have the same constant INF value ρ:+. Hence, their INF feature values
unify. No information-structural flags are changed in the DRSs, except the
boundary variables which acquire a new unified value.

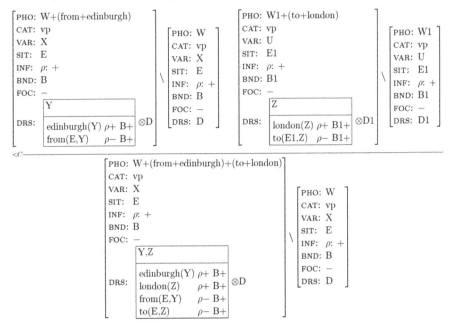

Figure 6.24: Combining two rheme-marked signs: *'from Edinburgh H*'* and *'to
London H*'*

6.7.5   Focus on Function Words

Hitherto, I have demonstrated what happens if the focus occurs on content
words. Even though most pitch accents do fall on content words, counter-
examples are not hard to find. When focus falls on a function word there is
usually some kind of contrast involved.

For instance, in Example 6.25 the contrast is between the prepositions specifying the exact location of the box. As a matter of fact, we already have
all the means present in UCCG which are necessary for handling focus on a
preposition. Remember that prepositions do appear as conditions in the DRS.
Similarly to other signs, the preposition signs include information structure
features, the values of which are introduced in their semantics as DRS flags.

Figure 6.25 shows the combination of the preposition 'on' with the pitch accent H*. As a result of this combination the DRS flags on the condition corresponding to the preposition assume the values that mark it as a rheme focus (ρ+) and +*AGREED*. The sign that corresponds to the whole noun phrase 'the box on H* the table' can be seen in Example 6.26. The DRS shows that the condition introduced by the preposition ($on(X, Y)$) is the focus of this rheme, and while the rhemeness has been projected to other two conditions in the DRS ($box(X)$, $table(Y)$), neither of them is marked as focus.

(6.25) A: I cannot find the box under the table.

B: The box on H* the table LL% is what I need LL%.

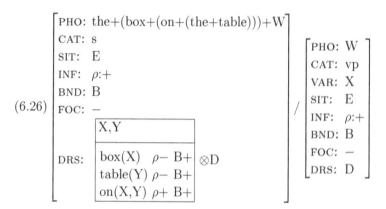

The issue of focus-marking becomes more complicated when we attempt to account for pitch accents on polarity items: negation ('no' and 'not') and *position* (a focused auxiliary). The sentence 6.27a negates the proposition that Anna loves Manny, while the sentence 6.27b negates the proposition that Anna does not love Manny. I will use double negation ($\neg\neg$) to represent position.

(6.27) a) Anna does not H* love Manny LL%.

b) Anna does H* love Manny LL%.

Both the determiner 'no' and the negation particle 'not' wrap a DRS around the DRS of their argument, which they embed as a negated condition in the new DRS. Since any DRS-condition that has a verbal exponent participates in shaping the information structure, the negated DRS can also have information-structural flags attached to it. Hence, accounting for a pitch accent on negation is not that different as compared to content words.

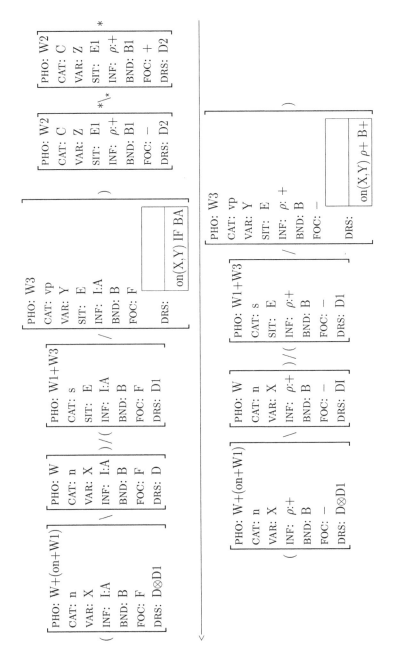

Figure 6.25. Combining the sign for the preposition 'on' with the sign for the pitch accent H*

Figure 6.26 shows the combination of the negation particle *'not'* with the rheme pitch accent H*. The negated sub-DRS in the result part of the negation particle sign has information-structural flags attached to it. During the combination with the pitch accent, three of these flags acquire a constant value via variable unification. Figure 6.27 shows the sign for *'not H*'* being combined with the vp *'love Manny'*. The DRS variable in the active part of the negation sign unifies with the DRS in the vp sign, and thereby the negated sub-DRS in the result part of the negation sign also assumes a constant value. The flags on the DRS-conditions corresponding to the vp inherit the values ρ, +*AGREED* and −*focus* from the negation sign. In the result sign of this combination all the applicable DRS-conditions are marked as rheme and as being uncontentious. Yet, only the negated DRS which corresponds to the negative polarity is marked as focus.

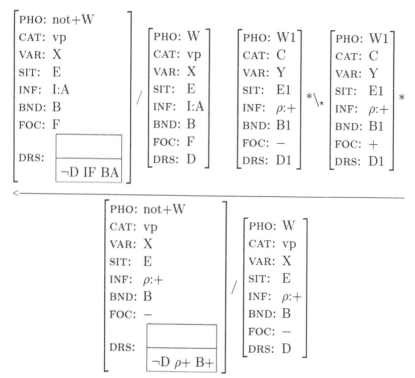

Figure 6.26: Combining the sign for the negation *'not'* with the pitch accent H*

It can also be the positive polarity that is focused (see Example 6.27b). Focus

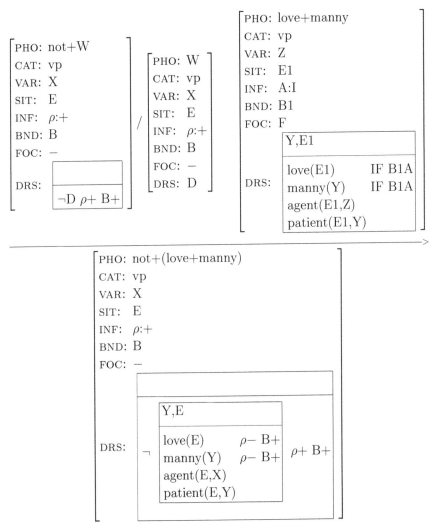

Figure 6.27: Combining the sign for *'not H*'* with the sign for the verb phrase *'love Manny'*

on positive polarity is a more complicated matter than that of focus on the negative polarity. The first problem is that we do not normally express auxiliary verbs in semantics. The sign for auxiliary verbs, as introduced in Section 4.5.1, Chapter 4 and Section 5.1.1, Chapter 5, simply copies the semantics of its argument, possibly adding the tense, and changes the agreement feature from non-finite to finite. If there is no DRS-condition present that corresponds to the auxiliary, there is nothing to attach the information-structural flags to. The analysis does still work with the simple auxiliary signs, however focus information, in that case, is not reflected in the resulting DRS.

Consequently, it seems that we need to change the sign of auxiliary verbs to allow the auxiliaries make a semantic contribution of some kind. However, intuitively, it also seems that the contribution of auxiliary verbs to semantics is far greater if they carry a pitch accent, while when unfocused they seem to be a mere syntactic requirement (see the use of *'does'* in sentences 6.27a and 6.27b). Hence, we need two different categories for auxiliary verbs: one for the case when it carries a pitch accent and one for the case when is does not. Nevertheless, at the same time I do not want to alter my approach to pitch accent signs being independent lexical entries that are combined with their exponent signs during the lexical stage of analysis. This implies that we would need to provide two types of signs for auxiliaries: one that can only be used in connection with a pitch accent, and another that is unable to combine with a pitch accent.

When not focused, the sign for auxiliary verbs is very similar to the original version from Chapters 4 and 5. The only alteration I will make is that I give them a negative focus value already in the lexicon. This focus value cannot unify with the positive focus value in the active part of a pitch accent sign, which guarantees us that this sign is only chosen if there is no pitch accent on the auxiliary. This would be the sign to use in the analysis of the sentence 6.27a. Figure 6.28 shows the combination of the auxiliary verb sign with the sign for the vp *'not H* love Manny'*. Note the FOC value '−' in the auxiliary sign. In this figure I chose to retain the focus features, since this is where the syntactic effect of combining with the auxiliary verb can be seen. The auxiliary verb takes a vp in a base form as its argument, and outputs a finite vp. Also the number and person features acquire constant values (3rd person singular) during the combination. If the auxiliary were combined with a verb phrase which has a variable as the value of its focus feature, then the FOC feature of the vp would get the value '−' from the auxiliary.

Providing a sign for auxiliaries that would only allow them to be used in tandem with pitch accents, is more problematic. Giving them a positive focus

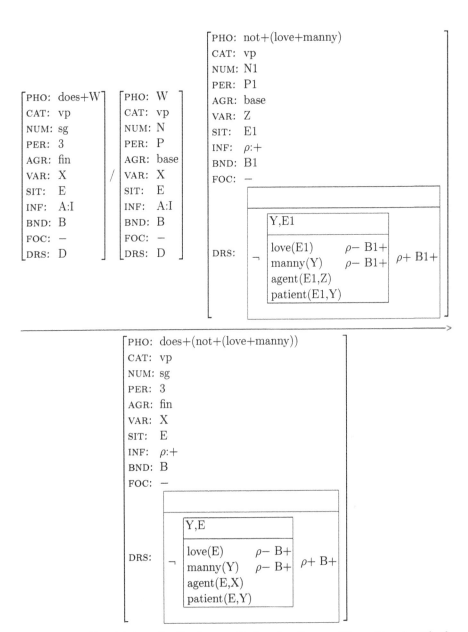

Figure 6.28: Combining the "unfocused" sign for the auxiliary *'does'* with the vp *'not H* love Manny'*

value in the lexicon would not help, since in the case they did not combine with a pitch accent they would project this focus value to other focally unmarked signs that they combined with. The unlicensed use of this version of the auxiliary sign would cause the analysis to halt sooner or later when a sign with a negative focus value would be encountered. However, by that time a lot of time and effort may already have been invested in spurious combinations.

Another option would be to provide focused auxiliaries with a sign which takes a pitch accent sign as an argument. This is the approach I take. Thus, our UCCG sign for a focused auxiliary has the category $(vp/vp)/_\star(C\backslash C)$. The use of the "application-only" modal slash in the category makes it impossible for the sign to compose into the signs that follow it. The focus value of this sign is also determined in the lexicon: the first three sub-signs have the FOC feature value '−', whilst the final sub-sign has the focus value '+'. Setting the focus values to constants is a further precaution to make sure that this auxiliary sign cannot apply to anything else but a pitch accent sign: pitch accent signs are the only signs in our system which have different constant focus feature values in their active and result part. On the other hand, a pitch accent sign is unable to backward apply to the auxiliary sign, since the FOC feature value of the active part of the pitch accent sign is '+', but that of the three first sub-signs of the auxiliary sign is '−', which means that these values cannot unify.

Finally, we discuss the contribution a focused auxiliary makes to semantics. The effect is similar to that of negation: the argument verb's DRS is introduced as a sub-DRS in the result head of the auxiliary sign. This sub-DRS is under the scope of a special position operator. We will use a double negation sign '¬¬' to represent it: a negation of a negation. This sub-DRS is itself a DRS-condition, and has information-structural flags attached to it. The focus DRS-flag is set to '+' already in the lexicon.

Figure 6.29 shows the combination of the position auxiliary sign with the pitch accent 'H^*' via forward application. Only the themeness/rhemeness and $\pm AGREED$ features and flags in the auxiliary sign acquire new values. Figure 6.30 demonstrates the sign for '*does H^**' being combined with the vp '*love Manny*'. The DRS-flags on the conditions *love(E)* and *manny(Y)* get new constant values via the unification of the INF and FOC features of the two signs. The DRS of the vp is introduced as a sub-DRS in the result of the auxiliary sign. Examining the flags on the DRS of the outcome of this combination, we see that the positive polarity is the focus of the utterance.

Lastly, Figure 6.31 shows the signs that correspond to the whole sentences 6.27a and 6.27b. The signs are identical in all other respects except the operator used in the DRS: 6.31a includes a negation operator and 6.31b includes a position operator. In both signs the focus in the DRS is on the polarity.

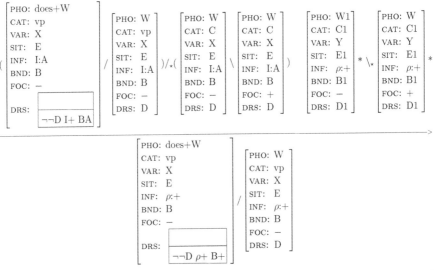

Figure 6.29: The combination of the 'position' auxiliary sign with the pitch accent 'H*'

Determiners. I already explained my approach to representing the information-structural status of the determiner *'no'* above when discussing negation. As far as information structure is concerned, I treat the determiner *'every'* in a very similar manner to the negative determiner: we attach the information-structural flags to the implication condition. The sign for a sentence where the universal quantifier carries a pitch accent, *'Every H* man walks LL%'*, is shown in Example 6.28. The implication condition is followed by the DRS-flags which indicate that the universal quantifier is focused and carries a rheme pitch accent marked as +*AGREED*, and that it is the speaker who is committed to the utterance.

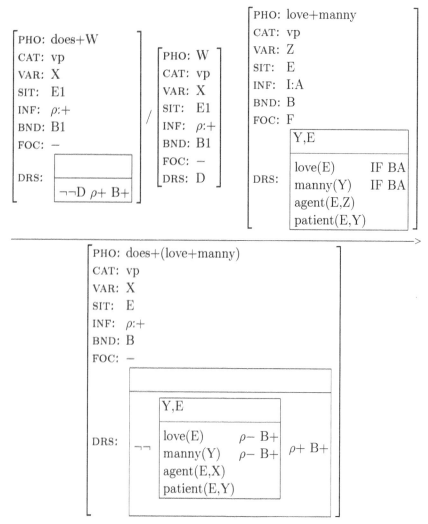

Figure 6.30: The combination of the sign for *'does H*'* with the vp *'love Manny'*

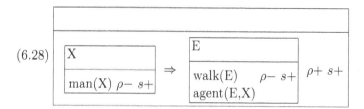

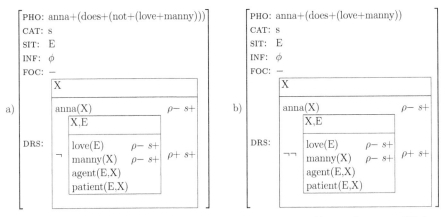

Figure 6.31: The signs corresponding to the sentences *'Anna does not H* love Manny LL%'* and *'Anna does H* love Manny LL%'*

In the case of the negative and the universal determiners, the introduction of information structure in their DRSs was relatively straightforward. But what to do with the definite and indefinite articles, which in the form presented in 5.1.1 only introduce a discourse referent in the domain of the DRS and no DRS-conditions at all? Contrastive focusing of these determiners is definitely possible in certain contexts (see Example 6.29).

(6.29) A: I saw Mary with a guy yesterday.

B: It was not A guy, it was THE guy.

I decided to overlook the complicated and disputed details of the precise semantics of these determiners, and opted for a simple solution which involves letting these determiners introduce a dummy condition *def(X)* or *indef(X)* in their DRSs. The argument of the condition is the discourse referent introduced by the determiner. Now we can proceed in the usual manner and introduce DRS-flags on the condition which describe the information-structural status of the determiner. Example 6.30 shows the DRS corresponding to the sentence *'A H* man walks LL%'*, where the indefinite article carries the rheme pitch accent H*.

$$(6.30) \quad \boxed{\begin{array}{l} \text{X,E} \\ \hline \begin{array}{ll} \text{man(X)} & \rho-\ s+ \\ \text{indef(X)} & \rho+\ s+ \\ \text{walk(X)} & \rho-\ s+ \\ \text{agent(E,X)} \end{array} \end{array}}$$

6.8 Conclusion

The present chapter is the key chapter of the book. It described my approach of extending UCCG with an account of information structure. I broadly followed the prosodic approach of (Steedman, 2000b).

After a brief review of how information structure is included in CCG, I explained the implications of adding information structure for UCCG. In contrast to CCG, both pitch accents and boundary tones are treated as independent signs in UCCG.

My first concern was to include themeness, rhemeness and focus marking in the system. To that end we introduced two new features into UCCG signs: one for themeness/rhemeness and another for focus. By using the same variables as feature values and as DRS-flags, we ensured that the value gets replaced simultaneously in both locations. We proceeded with incorporating boundary tone semantics, which led us to the inclusion of yet another feature in the signs. Again its value was connected to the corresponding flag in the DRS feature. Finally, we implemented the $\pm AGREED$ aspect. Since this aspect, too, is contributed by pitch accents, we included the value of this dimension in the same feature as themeness/rhemenes, rather than introducing a new feature.

In order to allow for a straightforward implementation of my ideas, I aimed at maximum precision about how the effects of information structure are achieved in UCCG. This raised some problems that were not previously mentioned in connection with CCG. Under certain circumstances, the combination of signs only via ordinary unification did not seem a practical or even a practicable choice. Therefore, I introduced the operation of recursive unification. Section 6.7 summarised my approach to information structure in UCCG, and addressed some specific topics: unmarked themes, split themes, the need for type-raising induced by information structure, multiple foci in a prosodic phrase, and focus marking on function words.

Chapter 7

Assessment and Review of the Theses

This chapter presents an assessment of the UCCG formalism and the theses presented in Chapter 1 at the beginning of this book.

In Section 7.1 I will test the UCCG formalism by implementing a parser and parsing a small corpus of intonationally annotated English text. Then I will use the parser in reverse order to make predictions about the soundness of the UCCG formalism.

In 7.2 we will re-examine the theses presented at the beginning of this book. First, we will review Theses 1–3: about the suitability of a first order DRS for representing information structure in semantics, the aptness of a formalism based on CCG to provide a path between intonationally annotated strings and the semantic representation proposed in this book, and the appropriateness of the use of unification as a means of communication between syntactic, semantic and information-structural level of linguistic representation. We will also discuss the implications of the results of the corpus analysis and the generating experiment for the theses. Finally, Section 7.2.4 discusses some ways how the IS-DRS promoted in this book as well as the whole UCCG framework can be extended, thereby providing support for Thesis 4.

7.1 Assessment of the UCCG Formalism

The ultimate objective of the UCCG formalism is to enable generation of intonationally annotated text from information-structurally marked DRSs. Therefore, in order to best assess the formalism, we would need an intonationally annotated corpus. However, that is where the trouble starts: no suitable pre-existing intonationally annotated corpora are available that could be used for evaluation purposes. Assessing the formalism is further complicated by the inadequate definitions of information structure.

A grammar formalism can be tested either via parsing or via generation. Parsing a set of sentences allows one to identify the sentences that a grammar based on the given formalism is able to parse, and the sentences that it cannot handle. Thus, parsing informs us about the linguistic phenomena that the given formal framework can account for. However, there are some problems with this approach:

- There needs to be an appropriate corpus available. This is not the case for intonationally annotated data. The only publicly available corpora use ToBI annotation scheme which is unreliable as pointed out by Steedman (2003, page 13).

- Specific grammars are generally developed based on a set of development data, and therefore a parser is bound to perform well on data similar to that seen in the development set. However, in the case of a rule-based grammar formalism, phenomena that were not included in the development set are likely not to receive a parse at all. Usually, the unparsed phenomena can easily be accommodated by making a minor addition to the parser (e.g. add a missing lexical entry), and therefore it is incorrect to say that the formalism is unable to handle these phenomena. In that case, it would be more appropriate to say that we are evaluating the parser rather than the formalism itself.

- Test sets tend to contain only grammatically correct sentences. Therefore, parsing them only informs us about the performance of the parser on grammatically correct sentences, but it makes no predictions about whether or not ungrammatical sentences would also get accepted.

The alternative approach entails making the formalism generate sentences. This method would reveal whether the formalism allows generating multiple output sentences from a single input, as well as allow one to check whether all the outputs are equally acceptable.

The best solution would be to combine the two approaches, and test the formalism in both directions: via parsing and generation. In a way, I am going to do precisely that. In this book, I will not implement an actual generator – this will be left for future work. However, I will employ the parser to make predictions about the formalism in the generation direction. Some pointers about using CCG for generation and the ensuing problems are in place here: White 2004a,b; White and Baldridge 2003; Hoffman 1995.

7.1.1 Parsing

In order to test the formalism presented in this book, I implemented a UCCG parser. It is a rule-based bottom-up chart parser implemented in SICStus Prolog. I chose the Prolog programming language, because in Prolog unification comes for free: it is already conveniently included as an integral part of the programming language. The main components and features of the parser are described in Appendix A.

Test Data

As mentioned above one of the big challenges of evaluating the UCCG formalism by parsing was caused by the lack of appropriate intonationally annotated corpora. Thus, I needed to create my own test suite. I created it using the examples presented in the papers of Kruijff-Korbayová (2004) and Steedman (2000b, 2003). Steedman's examples were already intonationally annotated (see Ex. 7.1), while Kruijff-Korbayová's had only theme and rheme boundaries marked, and the location of the main rheme accent and theme accent, if present. The theme/rheme boundaries in Kruijff-Korbayová's examples were either visually marked (see Ex. 7.2), or indicated by the question test (see Ex. 7.3).

(7.1) *Anna   married   Manny.*
    L+H*   LH% H* LL%

(7.2) The GERMAN actor writes **POETRY**,
           theme   *rheme*

(7.3) I know the British author writes history books. But what does he read? The British author reads **COMIC** books.

I used Steedman's (2000b; 2003) theory of information structure (summarised in Section 2.2.1, Chapter 2) to provide Kruijff-Korbayová's examples with intonational annotation within the bounds determined by their information structure. For theme focus I used the L+H* accent and for rheme focus the H* accent. I used the most common pitch accent and boundary tone combinations: for sentence final intonational phrases I always used the LL% boundary, in other cases at the end of the theme intonational phrase containing the L+H* pitch accent I used the LH% boundary tone, and at the end of the rheme intonational phrase containing the H* pitch accent I used the LL% boundary tone. I also used the LL% boundary tone to delimit sentence internal unmarked themes. This method led to the addition of the sentences in Example 7.4 to my test suite. Example 7.5 shows the same examples in the linearised form.

(7.4) *The   German   actor   writes   poetry.*
       L+H*   LH%   H* LL%
    The British   author   reads   comic   books.
                    L+H*LH%   H*   LL%

(7.5) The German L+H* actor LH% writes poetry H* LL%.
    The British author reads L+H* LH% comic H* books LL%.

The full test suite contains one hundred and forty-five sentences. The examples are relatively short and syntactically simple, reflecting the nature of the examples presented in papers about information structure.

Nevertheless, there is some variety in the syntactic phenomena they cover. In addition to the simplest sentences, there are sentences containing coordination, sentences with relative clauses, topicalised sentences, passive sentences, clefts, pseudo-clefts and reverse pseudo-clefts. As far as information structure is concerned, the corpus contains all-rheme and all-theme utterances, sentences containing a theme and a rheme in either order and sentences with a split theme. Both marked and unmarked themes are represented. Some of the theme/rheme intonational phrases contain multiple foci. The full corpus can be seen in Appendix B.

Analysis of Results

One hundred and thirty-nine sentences of the total of one hundred and forty-five in the whole corpus were accepted by the UCCG parser. The six sentences which did not receive a parse were rejected correctly: their information structure was incompatible with their syntactic structure. Here, the main aim is to evaluate the coverage of the formalism of different intonation contours, rather than its syntactic coverage. In what follows we will first view several information-structural phenomena that were present in the test suite, and that the parser handled successfully. Then I will give a very brief sketch of syntactic phenomena present in the test suite that the parser dealt with effectively. Finally, we will turn our attention to the six sentences in the test suite that were rejected, and explain the reasons behind their rejection.

The simplest case as far as information structure is concerned, are all-rheme and all-theme utterances. All-rheme utterances are very common, especially at the beginning of a discourse or as an answer to a question of the kind *'what happened?'*. An all-rheme utterance can be seen in Example 7.6. From the parsing point of view, since an all-rheme utterance has no utterance-internal information-structural bracketing, its analysis proceeds much like that of a sentence with no prosodic annotation. However, the output IS-DRSs of an all-rheme utterance and a similar sentence with no prosodic annotation differ in that in the former case the flags of the DRS-conditions acquire constant values, whilst in the latter case they remain variables. The IS-DRS 7.6a corresponds to the all-rheme sentence in Example 7.6. The applicable DRS-conditions in it are marked as rheme (ρ), focus ($+$) or background ($-$), and $+AGREED$. This marking is due to the pitch accent H*. In addition, they are marked for speaker commitment (s) by the boundary tone LL%. The conditions of the IS-DRS 7.6b have none of this marking: all the DRS flags are variables.

(7.6) John writes novels H* LL%.

a)
X,Y,E	
write(E)	$\rho- \ s+$
novels(Y)	$\rho+ \ s+$
john(X)	$\rho- \ s+$
patient(E,Y)	
agent(E,X)	

b)
X,Y,E	
write(E)	IF BA
novels(Y)	IF BA
john(X)	IF BA
patient(E,Y)	
agent(E,X)	

All-theme utterances are less common than all-rheme utterances. There were four such sentences in the test suite. Example 7.7 shows one of them together with its corresponding IS-DRS. This sentence contains the less common L*+H theme pitch accent that marks the theme as contentious ($-AGREED$).

(7.7) I am a millionaire L*+H LH%.

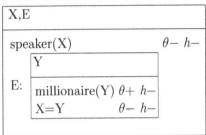

Theme and rheme can appear in a sentence in either order. This poses no obstacles to the UCCG parser. Example 7.8a illustrates the case where the theme is followed by the rheme, while 7.8b exemplifies the opposite case where the rheme precedes the theme. In 7.8a we have a marked theme where a word bears an L+H* pitch accent on it, while in 7.8b the theme is unmarked. Notice the difference in the flags on the DRS-conditions of the two DRSs in 7.8: ignoring the semantic roles, in DRS a° the theme (θ) includes the condition *john(X)* and the rheme the conditions *write(E)* and *novels(Y)*, while in DRS b° the condition *john(X)* constitutes the rheme, and the theme partition comprises *write(E)* and *novels(Y)*. As I said, the theme in the second sentence is unmarked: no word in it carries a pitch accent. Pitch accents are what gives an intonational phrase its themeness or rhemeness character. Since unmarked themes do not contain any pitch accents, their themeness/rhemeness value remains a variable. The same applies to the $\pm AGREED$ aspect: if a phrase contains no pitch accent, this flag also remains undetermined. In the first DRS two conditions are flagged as focus by '+': the theme and the rheme focus respectively. In the second DRS only the rheme focus (*john(X)*) bears a focus flag. In sentence 7.8a (DRS a°) two different boundary tones are present: LH% marks the theme for hearer commitment (*h*), while the rheme is marked for speaker commitment (*s*) by LL%. In 7.8b (DRS b°), both phrases end with the low boundary LL%, and hence, all the DRS conditions are marked with '*s*'.

(7.8) a) John L+H* LH% writes novels H* LL%.

     b) John H* LL% writes novels LL%.

X,Y,E	
john(X)	$\theta+\ h+$
novels(Y)	$\rho+\ s+$
write(E)	$\rho-\ s+$
agent(E,X)	
patient(E,Y)	

a°)

X,Y,E	
john(X)	$\rho+\ s+$
novels(Y)	$I-\ sA$
write(E)	$I-\ sA$
agent(E,X)	
patient(E,Y)	

b°)

Each information-structural phrase can contain multiple foci. The parser successfully parses a phrase with multiple foci, as long as the accents in an intonational phrase are compatible with each other in that they all belong either to the set of theme pitch accents or they all belong to the rheme pitch accents. All the accents in the same phrase must also have the same $\pm AGREED$ value. Example 7.9 illustrates this point. Notice how among the discourse conditions two, namely *london(Y)* and *paris(Z)*, are flagged as rheme focus ($\rho+$).

(7.9) John L+H* flew LH% from London H* to Paris H* LL%.

X,Y,Z,E	
fly(E)	$\theta-\ h+$
john(X)	$\theta+\ h+$
london(Y)	$\rho+\ s+$
paris(Z)	$\rho+\ s+$
from(E,Y)	$\rho-\ s+$
to(E,Z)	$\rho-\ s+$
agent(E,X)	
time(E,past)	

The theme of the sentence can be split by an intervening rheme. This poses no difficulty for the parser. As long as all the theme fragments are delimited by a boundary tone, they all represent separate intonational phrases. Thus, the parser needs no additional capabilities in order to analyse split themes as compared to unsplit themes. An example of the analysis of an utterance with a split theme can be seen in Example 7.10: the rheme 'to London' divides the theme of the sentence into two parts. The first theme phrase contains a pitch accent, and therefore receives the analysis of a marked theme. The second theme phrase is unmarked, and the corresponding DRS-conditions are flagged with variables for themeness/rhemeness and $\pm AGREED$.

(7.10) John L+H* flew LH% from London H* LL% to Paris LL%.

E,X,Z,Y	
fly(E)	$\theta-$ $h+$
john(X)	$\theta+$ $h+$
london(Y)	$\rho+$ $s+$
paris(Z)	I− sA
from(E,Y)	$\rho-$ $s+$
to(E,Z)	I− sA
agent(E,X)	
time(E,past)	

Now we will very briefly turn our attention to some syntactic phenomena that the parser handled successfully, whilst parsing the test suite. All the syntactic phenomena are viewed in the context of a specific information structure.

First, there were some examples of coordination in the test suite. UCCG's approach to coordination was explained in Section 5.2.2, Chapter 5. Information structure adds a layer of complexity to coordination: the two conjuncts need to also have the same themeness/rhemeness (theme, rheme or phrase) and $\pm AGREED$ marking. Example 7.11 illustrates the result of parsing a sentence containing coordination. In 7.11 the two conjuncts are part of the same rheme.

(7.11) Bill cooked H* and Fred ate H* L the beans L+H* LH%.

X,Y,Z,E,E1		
beans(Y)	$\theta+$ $h+$	
bill(X)	$\rho-$ $s+$	
cook(E)	$\rho+$ $s+$	
eat(E1)	$\rho+$ $s+$	
fred(Z)	$\rho-$ $s+$	
agent(E1,Z)		agent(E,X)
patient(E1,Y)		patient(E,Y)
time(E1,past)		time(E,past)

Example 7.12 shows the result IS-DRS of the analysis of a sentence with a relative clause. Due to the syntactic category of the relative pronoun *who*, (n\n)/vp in the subject relative clause or (n\n)/(s/(s/vp)) in the object relative clause, the relative clause cannot have further information-structural bracketing in itself, unless there is a boundary between the relative clause and the head

noun and the combination takes place at the phrasal level. The relative clause either belongs to the same intonational phrase as the noun it modifies (like in Example 7.12), or there is a boundary between the noun and the relative clause and they belong to two separate intonational phrases. These two cases correspond to the restrictive and non-restrictive relative clause respectively. A restrictive relative clause is not separated from its head noun by an audible break, while a non-restrictive clause is (hence a comma in writing). This way the syntactic category of the relative pronoun makes some important assumptions about the information structure of relative clauses: only non-restrictive relative clauses can have an independent information structure of their own, restrictive relative clauses have to be part of the same information-structural unit as the noun they are modifying. These assumptions need further empirical study.

(7.12) People who like bombazine L+H* LH% like corduroy H* LL%.

X,Y,Z,E,E1	
bombazine(Y) $\theta+$ $h+$	
corduroy(Z) $\rho+$ $s+$	
like(E) $\theta-$ $h+$	
like(E1) $\rho-$ $s+$	
people(X) $\theta-$ $h+$	
agent(E,X)	agent(E1,X)
patient(E,Y)	patient(E1,Z)

The result of the analysis of a sentence containing a complement clause can be seen in Example 7.13. Basically, in the approach proposed in this book, complement clauses are viewed as introducing a new event or situation or possible world, and the complement taking verbs as relations between the event expressed by themselves and by the one represented by the complement clause. The phrase *'am sure'* makes a contribution to semantics that is very similar to that of a propositional attitude verb like *'believe'*. However, we treat *'am'* and *'sure'* as two separate lexical entries rather than taking the easier road of viewing it as a single unit *'am_sure'*. *'Sure'* is treated as a complement taking adjective, and the copula funtions as a predicator (see Chapter 5 about the signs for adjectives and the copula). It is the copula that introduces the event variable and the sub-DRS which describes the event. The adjective specifies the event variable as "the state of X being sure about T". The content of T is described in a sub-DRS. In contrast to relativisers, the syntax of the complementiser places no constraints on the information-structural bracketing inside the complement clause. In the case of 7.13 we have a sentence initial rheme *'I am sure'*, while the rest of the utterance forms an unmarked theme.

(7.13) I am sure H* LL% that Mary likes corduroy LL%.

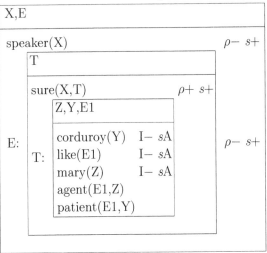

Intuitively, in the case of topicalised sentences it might seem more natural that the topicalised material represents the theme, and the rheme focus is somewhere else in the sentence. If this were the case, it would be possible to encode this information already in the signs of UCCG, independently of the prosodic features. However, it turns out that the topicalised material can also be the rheme of the sentence. There were both kinds of topicalised sentences in the corpus. Example 7.14 illustrates such sentences accompanied by their respective DRSs. In the theme-first case (7.14a,a°) the DRS condition *comics(X)* is marked by a theme-focus flag, the condition *john(Y)* with a rheme-focus flag, and *hate(E)* with a rheme-background flag. In the rheme-first case (7.14b,b°) the condition *comics(X)* carries a rheme-focus flag, and the rest of the sentence is an unmarked theme.

(7.14) a) Comics L+H* LH% John hates H* LL%.

b) Comics H* LL% John hates LL%.

	X,Y,E			X,E,Y	
	comics(X)	$\theta+$ $h+$		comics(X)	$\rho+$ $s+$
a°)	hate(E)	$\rho+$ $s+$	b°)	hate(E)	I— sA
	john(Y)	$\rho-$ $s+$		john(Y)	I— sA
	agent(E,Y)			agent(E,Y)	
	patient(E,X)			patient(E,X)	

Passive constructions were represented in the corpus by the Hallidayan example *'Dogs must be carried'*. Strictly speaking, the □-operator (*necessarily*) is not part of the first order logic language. However, modal operators can easily be translated into first order logic. The IS-DRS corresponding to the above sentence can be seen in Example 7.15.

(7.15) Dogs L+H* LH% must be carried H* LL%.

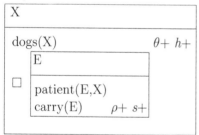

There was another group of interesting syntactic constructions represented in the data: clefts, pseudo-clefts and reverse pseudo-clefts. These constructions are often thought of as syntactically determining the focus position. However, as argued by Delin (1990) and Hedberg (1990), this is a misconception. Hedberg uses the topic-comment approach to information structure, but for the current purposes we can equate these with theme and rheme. One of the topic-clause cleft examples used by Hedberg (1990) is as follows:

'Just so. And of course, we've only got his version of the niece and the nurse – and he obviously had what the Scotch call ta'en a scunner at the nurse. We mustn't lose sight of her, by the way. She was the last person to be with the old lady before her death, and **it was she who administered that injection**.'

'Yes, yes – but the injection had nothing to do with it. If anything's clear, that is.' [Sayers, 1987, unnatural Death, p.17]

While *'she'* in the quote above bears the accent of a contrastive theme, the main rheme accent falls on *'injection'*. Thus, tempting though it is, we cannot key information structure in the signs that are specific to clefts. The theme/rheme division is still made by the pitch accents.

Cleft sentences also provided a syntactic puzzle due to their extraordinary structure. There are two basic views concerning the structure of cleft sentences: the expletive and the extrapositional approaches. According to the expletive approach both the cleft pronoun and the copula are dummies, they are present only for syntactic purposes. However, the extrapositional approach views the cleft pronoun as referential and the copula as a regular copula. In previous categorial grammar approaches to cleft sentences (Carpenter, 1998; Hockenmaier, 2003) the expletive view had been followed, but I found the extrapositional account more credible. Pseudo-cleft sentences exhibit especially close structural similarity to "normal" copular sentences (see Example 7.16), and hence the special treatment of copulas in cleft constructions does not seem justified. My UCCG analysis of clefts is described at length in Appendix C.

(7.16) These books   are comics.
        What John likes   are comics.
        $\underbrace{\text{The things that John likes}}_{NP}$ $\underbrace{\text{are comics,}}_{VP}$

After an ardent argument for the importance of understanding that the partitioning of information structure is not determined by the syntax of cleft constructions, I have to admit that the corpus used here only contained the "canonical" type of clefts, pseudo-clefts and reverse pseudo-clefts, where the clefted element indeed does carry the main rheme focus. The analysis of the cleft and pseudo-cleft in Example 7.17 resuts in the same DRS, thus they are viewed as being semantically equivalent. The cleft pronoun introduces a discourse referent *(Y)* into the universe of the main DRS. The same discourse referent appears in the discourse condition *patient(E1, Y)*. However, in order to find out about the identity of this discourse referent, we need to look inside the equality event *(E)* introduced by the copula, where we learn that *Y* is the same as *Z*, which means it refers to comics. The equality relation and the DRS-condition *comics(Z)* represent the rheme of this cleft and pseudo-cleft, and are therefore marked by ρ and $+/-$ according to their focus or background status.

The relative clause forms the theme of the given cleft/pseudo-cleft and therefore the corresponding DRS-conditions are marked by θ. The DRS-condition *hate(E1)* is marked by '+' since it carries the theme focus. Thus, the sentences in 7.17 contain a contrastive theme.

(7.17) It is comics H* L John hates L+H* LL%.
       What John hates L+H* LL% is comics H* LL%.

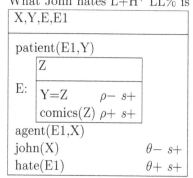

(7.18) Comics H* are L what John hates L+H* LL%.

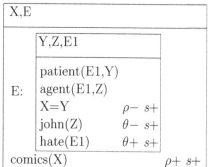

In the case of the reverse pseudo-cleft expressing the same (read "similar") meaning to the cleft and pseudo-cleft in example 7.17, the DRS has a slightly different appearance (see Example 7.18). This is caused by the different order in which the discourse referents are introduced in the cleft/pseudo-cleft and in the reverse pseudo-cleft, and their position in relation to the copula. In the former the discourse referents introduced by the pronouns come first, while in the latter the referent to come first is the one introduced by *'Comics'*. Therefore, most of the information we had in the main DRS in the former case is now placed in the sub-DRS, while the conditions found previously in the sub-DRS now move

to the main DRS. It would be interesting to know whether the order in which
the discourse referents are introduced has an effect on cognitive processing, in
which case the difference in the appearance of the DRS for cleft/pseudo-cleft
and reverse pseudo-cleft would not be purely representational, but would have
a deeper significance.

In what follows, we will examine the six sentences that the parser rejected.
The sentences can be seen in Example 7.19.

(7.19) a) Bill cooked and Fred H* L ate the beans L+H* LH%

b) My older L+H* LH% sister ate the green beans H* LL%

c) The beans that Fred H* L ate were delicious L+H* LH%

d) The beans that Fred L+H* LH% ate were delicious H* LL%

e) What Bill L+H* LH% writes is poetry H* LL%

f) The British H* L author reads history books LL%

Examples 7.19a and 7.19b were presented by Steedman (2000b) as sentences
that should not be processed due to the incongruence between syntax and
information structure. Here syntax puts constraints on the order in which
syntactic signs should be combined, the information structure, however, blocks
the required syntactic combinations. Coordination in 7.19a requires that the
coordinated constituents be of the same syntactic category, thus *'Bill cooked'*
and *'Fred ate'*. However, there is a prosodic boundary between *'Fred'* and *'ate'*.
Material in different prosodic phrases cannot be combined, unless the phrases
are complete. Therefore, the coordinated constituents cannot be combined.

7.19b illustrates a phenomenon called the *NP island constraint*. Here the
noun phrase is split into two with part of it belonging to one prosodic phrase
and the other part to another prosodic phrase. The syntactic combination is
blocked in the second prosodic phrase: the syntactic category of a noun does
not provide it with the ability to combine with a verb phrase that follows it,
only a full noun phrase is capable of that.

As a matter of fact, 7.19c–f bear witness to the same phenomenon as 7.19b.
The structure of 7.19f is completely parallel to that of 7.19b, except the order
of the theme and the rheme, which is not relevant at this point. 7.19c and
7.19d have the same intonational partitioning as each other. An intonational
boundary is inserted in the relative clause which post-modifies the noun phrase.
Here syntactic combinations cannot be successfully completed in either of the

prosodic phrases. In the first prosodic phrase *'that'* needs a vp after it, and cannot directly combine with a noun phrase on its right. In the second prosodic phrase the verb *'ate'* cannot take a vp as its argument, and therefore cannot combine with the material following it.

As we saw in Example 7.16, the left-hand side of the copula in pseudo-clefts can be viewed as a noun phrase. Therefore, also in 7.19e we have a violation of the NP island constraint. The reason why syntactic processes cannot conclude in the second prosodic phrase in 7.19e is the same as in 7.19c and d: the syntactic category of the verb *'writes'* does not provide for a vp argument after it.

From the previous discussion it seems that NP island constraints play a crucial role in deciding which kind of information-structural partitionings are permitted for sentences. Now the question arises whether the NP island constraint can never be violated by information structure. At a closer look at the sentences that the parser accepted, it occurs that among them is at least one sentence where information structure seems to violate the NP island constraint (see Example 7.20). This means that our grammar predicts that NP island violations are allowed at certain points of division: if the head noun, possibly with post-modification, forms a separate prosodic phrase, which means that the combination of the prenominal material with the head noun can take place at the phrasal level, then the division of the noun phrase is permitted. Whether this is indeed the case and makes sense from the information structure point of view, needs further empirical study. In case the empirical study showed that NP island constraint can never be violated, we would need to introduce multi-modal slashes (as seen previously in the prosodic signs) in the syntactic category of prenominal adjectives (n/n) and as the last slash in the syntactic category of determiners ((s/vp)/n), that would limit the combinatory capabilities of these slashes to application only. This way we would constrain the prenominal adjectives and determiners to first combine with their head noun, and only then could the full noun phrase combine with the linguistic material preceding the noun phrase.

(7.20) FRED L+H* ate the green LH% BEANS H* LL%

7.1.2   Parser as a Generator

In this section I will make some predictions about the strings that the UCCG formalism would generate. The tool I will use for this is my UCCG parser. However, I will use it in a particular way. The basic idea is to first create a large body of different configurations of input and then parse it. Whenever the parse of different sentences results in the same DRS we can conclude that this particular DRS would generate all the sentences concerned. However, I have to limit the task, since for practical reasons it is not feasible to create all the possible configurations of word orders of all existing words with all different intonational configurations. Therefore, I will use fixed strings of words, and only vary the prosody on them. Consequently, the predictions made will concern only information-structural/prosodic configurations that a grammar set in the UCCG formal framework would generate, rather than offering a comment on the overall grammaticality of the linguistic expressions that the formalism allows. The principal questions of interest here are:

- Does our framework generate prosodically unacceptable sequences?
- Does a single input DRS allow for generating multiple output sentences that differ in their prosody?

I will answer the first question by reasoning. In order to provide an answer for the second question I will pursue the methodology sketched above, which can be summed up into the following three steps:

- First we generate all the legal prosodic configurations of a sentence consisting of a particular string of words.
- Then we parse all the configurations from the previous step.
- Finally we compare the output DRSs. If the parse of different prosodic configurations produces the same DRS, we can conclude that this particular DRS would generate all these prosodic configurations.

Does the UCCG framework generate prosodically unacceptable sequences?

First, I need to explain what it means for a prosodic sequence to be unacceptable. The most blatantly unacceptable prosodic sequences are the ones that contain an utterance or phrase initial pitch accent or boundary tone before the occurrence of any words (remember that our representation uses a linear layout). Prosodic configurations with multiple pitch accents or boundary tones following each other without any intervening lexical material are equally nonsensical. Another class of unacceptable intonational configurations comprises sequences where incompatible pitch accents appear in the same prosodic phrase, or where the utterance-final boundary tone is missing. Finally, the sequences can be unacceptable due to the way they are aligned with syntactic constituents. In order to illustrate the final point, Example 7.21 presents a sentence from Steedman 2000b, where the syntactic and prosodic structure are incongruent with each other.

(7.21) *Three mathematicians L+H* LH% in ten derive a lemma H* LL%

However, as far as CCG is concerned, all categories, either lexical or derived as a result of the combinatorial process, are valid prosodic constituents. Whenever there is a clash between the syntactic and prosodic structure (see also Example 7.19 above) the utterance is not accepted by the grammar. That is true of Example 7.21: the string *'in ten derive a lemma'* in the second intonational phrase cannot be combined into a single syntactic category, and therefore the analysis of this sentence fails. Hence, when attempting to define syntactically acceptable prosodic constituents in CCG terms, we end up with a circular definition: whenever a prosodic constituent is accepted by a CCG grammar, it is correct, because the grammar says so. In this sense, it simply never happens that a CCG grammar accepts sentences where intonation and syntax do not agree. However, we could look around for a different definition of acceptable intonational constituents. We cannot rely on any notion which requires the intonational constituents to conform to the "traditional" syntactic constituents: on the one hand, this does not reflect the reality; on the other hand, CCG's flexible constituents are its main *droit de vivre*. Finally, there is Selkirk's *Sense Unit Condition* (1984, page 286), which says that the immediate constituents of an intonational phrase must together form a sense unit. This is a very credible condition. However, it is rather philosophical in its nature rather than being formally precise, and, as such, open to different interpretations. We finish our discussion about syntactic/semantic constraints on the validity of intonational constituents, and delegate the issue to future empirical studies.

Hereby we return to the more straightforward issues concerning the acceptability conditions on intonational sequences. Phrase initial pitch accents are not allowed by the UCCG formalism, because on the one hand the pitch accent signs contain an "application-only" multimodal slash, that does not allow for composition into them, on the other hand, no sign can backward apply to a pitch accent sign as a whole, because the accent sign has the FOC value '+' in its active part and the value '−' in its result part, and there are no signs permitting different FOC values in their active part. Phrase initial boundary tones are also disallowed. Similarly to pitch accents, they contain a multimodal slash which prohibits composition into the boundary tone sign. Furthermore, the boundary tone signs have a different number of features in their active part and passive part. Since there are no signs whose active part could unify with the whole boundary tone sign, no sign can combine with the boundary tone in the phrase initial position.

It is easy to show that our formalism does not allow for multiple pitch accents on a single word. On the one hand, pitch accent signs cannot combine with each other, because they have different constant FOC values in their result and active parts, and all prosodic signs make use of a multi-modal slash that allows them to only combine via backward application. On the other hand, whenever a pitch accent sign combines with a lexical sign, the FOC feature of the result becomes '−'. A pitch accent sign has the FOC value '+' in its active part and therefore cannot combine with a sign that has a negative focus feature value. For example, if we combine the signs for *'John'* and H*, the resulting sign for *'John_H*'* has the FOC value '−'. Combining *'John_H*'* with another H* would not succeed, since the pitch accent sign expects a FOC value in its argument sign that is capable of unifying with the FOC value '+'.

Also the sequence of two or more adjacent boundary tones is disallowed. Boundary tones cannot combine with each other, firstly, due to their multi-modal slash, and secondly, due to the different number of features in their result and active parts. Whenever a boundary tone sign combines with a lexical sign, the INF feature value of the result becomes *phrase* (ϕ), and the BND feature is removed from the sign. A second boundary tone cannot be applied, because the boundary tone sign expects an argument where the BND feature is still present. Therefore, after *'John'* has combined with LL%, it is not possible to combine the sign for '*John_LL%*' with another LL%.

Since neither multiple adjacent pitch accents nor boundary tones are allowed, the maximum number of prosodic markings between any two words in a sentence is two: one pitch accent and one boundary tone. These two have a restriction on their ordering: the pitch accent always has to precede the boundary tone. If the boundary tone were to precede the pitch accent, it would first be combined with the lexical sign to its left. The INF feature value of the result would be ϕ. The INF value of the argument of the pitch accent sign has to unify with either *theme* (θ) or *rheme* (ρ). A unit like '*John_LL%*' cannot be further combined with H*, since the two different constant INF values of the signs (ϕ and ρ) do not unify. Furthermore, such combinations are prevented by the different number of features in a phrase-marked sign and in the active part of a pitch accent sign.

A single prosodic phrase can only include pitch accents which have the same themeness/rhemeness and the same $\pm AGREED$ value. Example 7.22 contains hypothetical utterances where this is not the case. For example, in the second prosodic phrase of 7.22b, two pitch accents are present: H* and L+H*. The former is a rheme pitch accent and the latter is a theme pitch accent. They project their respective information-structural marking to other signs in the phrase. However, signs with different constant themeness/rhemeness values cannot be combined, since their INF features fail to unify. The two pitch accents in the first prosodic phrase in 7.22d are both rheme accents, but they differ in their $\pm AGREED$ value. Again signs with a different constant $\pm AGREED$ value cannot be combined.

(7.22) a) john H* walks L+H* LH%

      b) john L*+H LH% loves H* mary L+H* LH%

      c) john L+H* LL% flew L*+H to london H* LH%

      d) john L* flew to H* LL% london L*+H LL%

We can also conceive of cases where the utterance final prosodic phrase is incomplete: a boundary tone is missing. Such hypothetical cases are illustrated by Example 7.23. For example, the intonational phrases in 7.23a cannot combine, because due to the missing boundary tone at the end of the phrase '*walks L**', the sign for this phrase cannot acquire the INF value ϕ, and rid itself of the BND feature, which would allow it to combine with the complete intonational phrase *'John L+H* LH%'*.

(7.23) a) John L+H* LH% walks L*
 b) John L*+H LH% loves H* LL% Mary L+H*
 c) John H* LL% flew L+H* to LH% London L*+H

Generating the Data

Our first task is to define legal prosodic configurations. Again, to set boundaries
for the task, we will only use the four pitch accents: H*, L+H*, L* and L*+H,
and the two boundary tones: LH% and LL%, familiar from earlier in this book.
We conceded in the previous section that the maximum number of prosodic
markings between any two words in an utterance is two: one pitch accent
and one boundary tone, whereas the pitch accent always has to precede the
boundary tone. This leaves us with the following options of prosodic marking
between any two words in a sentence:

- insert nothing
- insert a single pitch accent or a boundary tone: H*, L+H*, L*, L*+H,
  LL% or LH%.
- insert a pitch accent and a boundary tone: H* LL%, H* LH%, L+H* LL%,
  L+H* LH%, L* LL%, L* LH%, L*+H LL% or L*+H LH%

We also need to bear in mind that only the same kind of pitch accents can
occur in the same prosodic phrase (e.g. H* and L+H* cannot appear in the
same intonational phrase, since one of them signals theme, while the other
signals rheme). The finite state automaton in Figure 7.1 graphically describes
how we generate from strings of words intonationally annotated strings which
follow the criteria specified above.

I implemented the prosody assignment finite state automaton in Sicstus Prolog, and generated all the configurations permitted by the automaton for the
following five sentences: *'John walks'*, *'John loves Mary'*, *'John flew to London'*, *'The man that wins smiles'* and *'John flew from Paris to London'*. Table
7.1 shows how the number of prosodic configurations per sentence grows as sentences become longer: by adding a word to the sentence, the number of possible
prosodic configurations grows 12.52 times (except when going from length 1 to
length 2, where the growth is 12.6 times). I was going to use the automaton

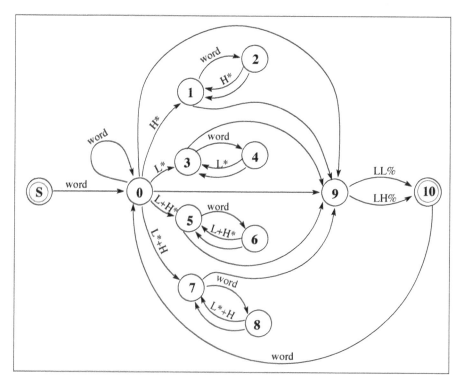

Figure 7.1: Automaton for generating all legal prosodic configurations

to generate even longer sentences, but it turned out that already parsing all the prosodic configurations of a sentence that was six words long and classifying the corresponding DRSs exceeded the capacity of Sicstus Prolog's dynamic memory (the data exhausted the atom table). In order to be able to examine longer and syntactically more complex sentences in spite of the limitations of the computational memory, I generated the prosodic configurations for longer sentences with a reduced set of prosodic marking. The test sentences in this category were *'John flew from Paris to London'*, *'Anna believes that John does love Mary'* and *'Mary admires the woman who directed the musical'*. When generating the configurations for our test sentences of length six and seven, I used only the two most common pitch accents, H* and L+H*, and a single boundary tone, LL%. For the sentence of length eight, I had to constrain the set of prosodic marking even further, using only the pitch accent H* and the boundary tone LL%.

I make no claims about the naturalness of the prosody of the configurations generated by the automaton on Figure 7.1. It is true that many of the configurations would sound rather strange if pronounced with the given prosody. For example, it is definitely undesirable to accent each word in the sentence or to have a boundary after each single word. It would also be a difficult exercise to come up with an appropriate context for each configuration. However, it is not the task of the grammar to determine the exact placement of accents, but to provide a range of alternatives, and to define the relationship between intonation, syntax and semantics. It is up to the language user to find their way in this dynamic system and to make sensible and purposeful choices about which prosody to use. Should the grammar developers prefer, it is possible to impose some constraints on UCCG signs which determine whether the words corresponding to these signs or their arguments are capable of bearing a pitch accent. This can be done straightforwardly by adjusting the FOC feature values in the lexicon accordingly. We will briefly discuss this approach in Section 7.1.2 below.

Table 7.1: The tip of the iceberg: the number of different intonation contours as determined by the sentence length when using four pitch accents and two boundary tones

Number of words	Prosodic configurations
1	10
2	126
3	1578
4	19758
5	247386
6	3097470

Analysis of Results

This section will supply an answer to the question postulated above about whether a single input DRS allows for generating multiple sentences that differ in their prosody. The answer is found by parsing all the prosodic configurations for a selection of test sentences of varied length (see the previous section) and comparing the output DRSs. Whenever the parse of different sentences results in the same DRS, we conclude that the given DRS would generate all the sentences concerned. In the final part of this section we will take a brief look at the intonational configurations which were rejected by the parser.

Before continuing, we need to establish what it means for DRSs to be different. With the relatively simple examples that I use, I do not expect any major differences as far as the semantic roles of verbs or variable bindings are concerned. The differences we are after lie in the information-structural flags attached to the DRS-conditions. The four DRSs in Figure 7.2 illustrate this point. Two DRSs are considered identical only in the case where the value of each DRS-flag in one DRS coincides with the value of the same flag in the other DRS. Hence, all the four DRSs in Figure 7.2 are different.

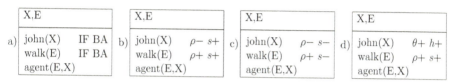

Figure 7.2: DRSs differing in the values of the DRS-flags

Table 7.2 summarises the results of the comparison of DRSs obtained by parsing all the prosodic configurations generated for the test sentences. Each column of the table contains the results for a different test sentence. The column titles refer to sentence length. The DRS were divided into classes according to the number of sentences that correspond to them. Each row expresses the number of the DRSs in the given class. The three bottom rows of the table contain information about how many prosodic configurations were originally created, how many different DRSs where produced by parsing them, and how many configurations were rejected by the parser.

For example, altogether 126 prosodic configurations were generated for the sentence '*John walks*'. All of them were accepted by the parser, and their parse produced 116 distinct DRSs. In the case of 106 configurations there was a one-to-one correspondence between a sentence and a DRS, while in the case of 10 DRSs, 2 sentences corresponded to each of them (details will follow). For the sentence '*John flew to London*' 19758 prosodic configurations were created. All of them received a parse. In total the parser produced 15376 different DRSs. Now there was a one-to-one correspondence between 11866 DRS and sentence pairs, while in the case of 3030 DRSs, 2 sentences corresponded to each of them, in the case of 160 DRSs, 3 sentences corresponded to each, 294 DRSs "generated" 4 sentences, 16 DRSs generated 6 sentences, while the remaining 10 DRSs each generated 8 sentences. Inspection of the sets of parsed and not parsed sentences confirmed that these sets corresponded to the results expected.

Table 7.2: DRS comparison results for the sentences 'John walks', 'John loves Mary', 'John flew to London', 'The man that wins smiles', 'John flew from Paris to London', 'Anna believes that John does love Mary' and 'Mary admires the woman who directed the musical'

	2 words	3 words	4 words	5 words	6 words[a]	7 words[a]	8 words[b]
Sentences per DRS	No. of DRSs						
1 sentence	106	1122	11866	8000	1174	34	51
2 sentences	10	196	3030	992	1068	114	117
3 sentences	–	8	160	800	226	111	65
4 sentences	–	10	294	96	344	143	120
5 sentences	–	–	–	80	86	20	31
6 sentences	–	–	16	8	78	186	105
7 sentences	–	–	–	8	42	58	5
8 sentences	–	–	10	–	38	53	121
9 sentences	–	–	–	–	14	76	11
10 sentences	–	–	–	–	20	10	38
11-14 sentences	–	–	–	9980	24	261	116
15-19 sentences	–	–	–	80	4	219	85
20-24 sentences	–	–	–	–	3	182	62
25-29 sentences	–	–	–	–	–	104	14
30-34 sentences	–	–	–	–	–	89	24
35-39 sentences	–	–	–	–	–	134	8
40-44 sentences	–	–	–	–	–	59	9
45-49 sentences	–	–	–	–	–	62	8
50-69 sentences	–	–	–	–	–	153	8
70-110 sentences	–	–	–	–	–	92	2
Total No. of sentences	126	1578	19758	247386	12064	63168	32768
Total No. of DRSs	116	1336	15376	11984	3121	2160	1000
No. of unparsed sentences	–	–	–	22528	4464	15744	22528

[a]Data generated using only two pitch accents (H*, L+H*) and a single boundary tone (LL%)
[b]Data generated using only one pitch accent (H*) and a single boundary tone (LL%)

As we see from Table 7.2, in a large number of cases there is a one-to-one correspondence between a sentence and a DRSs. That means that in such cases the semantics fully determines the shape of the intonational contour of the output. However, there are other cases where a single DRS corresponds to multiple sentences. As the sentence length grows, the ambiguity grows too.

When I examined the sets of sentences "generated" by a single DRS, I found that the ambiguity was largely caused by boundary tones (see Examples 7.24,

7.25 and 7.26). Boundary tones do have their own semantics and they do make their unique contribution to semantics. However, in certain cases it is not possible to tell from the semantics whether we have one long intonational phrase ending with the given boundary tone, or several short ones, all ending with the same boundary tone. Note that for such ambiguity to arise, all the phrases need to contain either only theme pitch accents, only rheme pitch accents or no pitch accents at all. For example, the eight sentences which correspond to the DRS in Example 7.25 all differ in their phrasing. The first sentence consists of four separate intonational phrases: *'John L+H* LH%'*, *'flew L+H* LH%'*, *'to L+H* LH%'* and *'London L+H* LH%'*. The second sentence contains three phrases: *'John L+H* LH%'*, *'flew L+H* LH%'* and *'to L+H* London L+H* LH%'*. So does the third sentence, but the phrasing is different from the second sentence: *'John L+H* LH%'*, *'flew L+H* to L+H* LH%'* and *'London L+H* LH%'*. The eighth sentence is one long intonational phrase with a single boundary at the end of the sentence: *'John L+H* flew L+H* to L+H* London L+H* LH%'*. The presence of multiple boundaries versus just one is not reflected in the DRT semantics. Notice that regardless of how many phrases there are in this particular sentence all of them are theme phrases. In the case of the DRS in Example 7.26 the corresponding utterance contains (minimally) a theme phrase and a split rheme phrase, but the variation in phrasing only applies to the theme part.

(7.24)

X,E
agent(E,X) walk(E) $\rho+$ $s+$
john(X) $\rho+$ $s+$

john H* LL% walks H* LL%
john H* walks H* LL%

(7.25)

X,Y,E
time(E,past)
agent(E,X)
to(E,Y) $\theta+$ $s+$
london(Y) $\theta+$ $s+$
john(X) $\theta+$ $s+$
fly(E) $\theta+$ $s+$

john L+H* LH% flew L+H* LH% to L+H* LH% london L+H* LH%
john L+H* LH% flew L+H* LH% to L+H* london L+H* LH%
john L+H* LH% flew L+H* to L+H* LH% london L+H* LH%
john L+H* LH% flew L+H* to L+H* london L+H* LH%
john L+H* flew L+H* LH% to L+H* LH% london L+H* LH%
john L+H* flew L+H* LH% to L+H* london L+H* LH%
john L+H* flew L+H* to L+H* LH% london L+H* LH%
john L+H* flew L+H* to L+H* london L+H* LH%

(7.26)
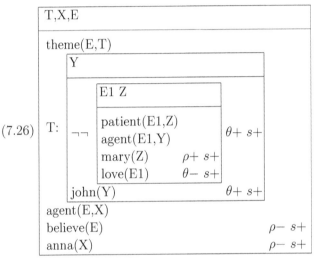

anna believes that H* LL% john L+H* LL% does L+H* LL% love LL% mary H* LL%
anna believes that H* LL% john L+H* LL% does L+H* love LL% mary H* LL%
anna believes that H* LL% john L+H* does L+H* love LL% mary H* LL%

However, also a different kind of ambiguity can be found among the results. This is caused by relativisers and complementisers. The problem is that these words do not manifest themselves in semantics, which means that, in principle, one could put any prosody on them and the semantics would still be the same. This causes an explosion of ambiguity. If the relativiser/complementiser forms a separate prosodic phrase (i.e. it is separated from the preceding and the following words by boundaries), then we have a choice of putting no pitch accent on it or using any of the four pitch accents in our set in combination with any boundary tone with no change in the semantics. If the relativiser/complementiser does not form a separate intonational phrase, our choices are more constrained due to the rule which says that the pitch accents in the same prosodic phrase need to have the same themeness/rhemeness and $\pm AGREED$ features, however, in most of the cases we still have a choice between using a pitch accent and using no pitch accent.

This kind of ambiguity can be observed in Example 7.27 where eleven sentences correspond to the same DRS. 7.27a and 7.27b are different from each other, because in the former the relativiser is followed by the boundary tone LH%, while in the latter it is followed by the boundary LL%. 7.27a, 7.27c, 7.27e, 7.27g and 7.27i differ from each other by the pitch accent on the complementiser (L*+H, L+H*, L*, H* and no pitch accent). 7.27i, 7.27j and 7.27k differ from each other by the kind of boundary tone after the complementiser: LH%, LL% and no boundary.

$$(7.27)$$

X,E,E1	
agent(E,X)	
agent(E1,X)	
win(E1)	I− hA
def(X)	I− sA
smile(E)	$\theta+\ h-$
man(X)	$\rho+\ s+$

a) the LL% man H* LL% who L*+H LH% wins LH% smiles L*+H LH%
b) the LL% man H* LL% who L*+H LL% wins LH% smiles L*+H LH%
c) the LL% man H* LL% who L+H* LH% wins LH% smiles L*+H LH%
d) the LL% man H* LL% who L+H* LL% wins LH% smiles L*+H LH%
e) the LL% man H* LL% who L* LH% wins LH% smiles L*+H LH%
f) the LL% man H* LL% who L* LL% wins LH% smiles L*+H LH%
g) the LL% man H* LL% who H* LH% wins LH% smiles L*+H LH%
h) the LL% man H* LL% who H* LL% wins LH% smiles L*+H LH%
i) the LL% man H* LL% who LH% wins LH% smiles L*+H LH%
j) the LL% man H* LL% who LL% wins LH% smiles L*+H LH%
k) the LL% man H* LL% who wins LH% smiles L*+H LH%

When the two kinds of ambiguity co-occur, the number of sentences created by a single DRS can shoot to the sky. This happens in the case of the test sentences which contain relativisers or complementisers. Among the data, I encountered the biggest ambiguity in connection with the sentence *'Anna believes that John does love Mary'* where the most ambiguous IS-DRSs "generate" 108 sentences (see Example 7.28). As a matter of fact, it is possible to constrain the ambiguity caused by function words which do not manifest themselves in semantics. We will discuss how this can be done in the next section.

(7.28)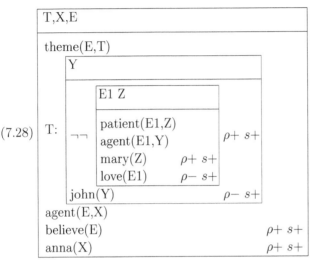

anna H* LL% believes H* LL% that L+H* LL% john H* LL% does H* LL% love LL% mary H* LL%
anna H* LL% believes H* LL% that L+H* LL% john H* LL% does H* LL% love mary H* LL%
anna H* LL% believes H* LL% that L+H* LL% john H* LL% does H* love LL% mary H* LL%
anna H* LL% believes H* LL% that L+H* LL% john H* LL% does H* love mary H* LL%
anna H* LL% believes H* LL% that L+H* LL% john H* does H* love LL% mary H* LL%
anna H* LL% believes H* LL% that L+H* LL% john H* does H* love mary H* LL%
anna H* LL% believes H* LL% that H* LL% john H* LL% does H* LL% love LL% mary H* LL%
anna H* LL% believes H* LL% that H* LL% john H* LL% does H* LL% love mary H* LL%
anna H* LL% believes H* LL% that H* LL% john H* LL% does H* love LL% mary H* LL%
anna H* LL% believes H* LL% that H* LL% john H* LL% does H* love mary H* LL%
anna H* LL% believes H* LL% that H* LL% john H* does H* love LL% mary H* LL%
anna H* LL% believes H* LL% that H* LL% john H* does H* love mary H* LL%
anna H* LL% believes H* LL% that H* john H* LL% does H* LL% love LL% mary H* LL%
anna H* LL% believes H* LL% that H* john H* LL% does H* LL% love mary H* LL%
anna H* LL% believes H* LL% that H* john H* LL% does H* love LL% mary H* LL%
anna H* LL% believes H* LL% that H* john H* LL% does H* love mary H* LL%
anna H* LL% believes H* LL% that H* john H* does H* love LL% mary H* LL%
anna H* LL% believes H* LL% that H* john H* does H* love mary H* LL%
anna H* LL% believes H* LL% that LL% john H* LL% does H* LL% love LL% mary H* LL%
anna H* LL% believes H* LL% that LL% john H* LL% does H* LL% love mary H* LL%
anna H* LL% believes H* LL% that LL% john H* LL% does H* love LL% mary H* LL%
anna H* LL% believes H* LL% that LL% john H* LL% does H* love mary H* LL%
anna H* LL% believes H* LL% that LL% john H* does H* love LL% mary H* LL%
anna H* LL% believes H* LL% that LL% john H* does H* love mary H* LL%
anna H* LL% believes H* LL% that john H* LL% does H* LL% love LL% mary H* LL%
anna H* LL% believes H* LL% that john H* LL% does H* LL% love mary H* LL%
anna H* LL% believes H* LL% that john H* LL% does H* love LL% mary H* LL%
anna H* LL% believes H* LL% that john H* LL% does H* love mary H* LL%
anna H* LL% believes H* LL% that john H* does H* love LL% mary H* LL%

anna H* LL% believes H* LL% that john H* does H* love mary H* LL%
anna H* LL% believes H* that H* LL% john H* LL% does H* LL% love LL% mary H* LL%
anna H* LL% believes H* that H* LL% john H* LL% does H* LL% love mary H* LL%
anna H* LL% believes H* that H* LL% john H* LL% does H* love LL% mary H* LL%
anna H* LL% believes H* that H* LL% john H* LL% does H* love mary H* LL%
anna H* LL% believes H* that H* LL% john H* does H* love LL% mary H* LL%
anna H* LL% believes H* that H* LL% john H* does H* love mary H* LL%
...

Leaving the ambiguity caused by relativisers and complementisers aside, the general tendency is that the longer the sentence to be generated, the more prosodic configurations can be generated from a single DRS, because there are more insertion points for boundary tones. However, as the sentence length grows, more syntactic factors come into play in determining the possible prosodic constituents, and thereby restrict the number of outputs generated from a specific DRS. Syntactic factors were one of the two reasons why numerous prosodic configurations of the longer test sentences were not accepted (see Table 7.2).

Example 7.29 shows two prosodic configurations that received no parse. In 7.29a the problem is that the relative clause would need to combine with its head noun, but this is not possible, because the head noun is in a different prosodic phrase. The noun is forced to first combine with its determiner to form a complete noun phrase. However, the relative clause cannot combine with a complete noun phrase. In 7.29b the main problem lies in the final prosodic phrase: *'wins smiles H* LL'*. This phrase cannot be combined into a single syntactic category.

(7.29) a) The man H* LL% that LL% wins H* LL% smiles L* LL%

     b) The man L+H* that LL% wins smiles H* LL%

Discussion

As we saw above there are two reasons why there is no strict one-to-one correspondence between IS-DRSs and sentences that they generate. The reason was that in the case of certain prosodic configurations, it is not possible to tell from the IS-DRS whether we have a single long theme or rheme phrase, or multiple short ones following each other. Thus, the first case of ambiguity was caused by boundary tones. The second kind of ambiguity was caused by function words which do not manifest themselves in semantics (such as relativisers and complementisers). Since they do not leave a trace in semantics, more often than not, we cannot tell whether such words carry a pitch accent or not, and if they do, we are likely not to be able to determine the type of the accent. In the following we will briefly discuss what can be done to rectify these two kinds of ambiguity.

We will start with function words. There is an easy way to fix the problem: we can stipulate that words with no semantic content (i.e. function words that do not manifest themselves in semantics) can never bear a pitch accent. We do not need to formulate a separate rule expressing this condition: it is enough to adjust the lexical signs accordingly. If we introduce the negative FOC value in the corresponding signs already in the lexicon, we can make sure that such signs will never combine with pitch accent signs, as the latter require that their arguments' FOC value be able to unify with the focus value '+'.

I chose not to introduce this restriction in the lexical signs of function words in the present implementation, since it is not entirely correct that these words can never bear a pitch accent. In a dynamic system like a natural language there are not many restrictions that cannot be broken under any circumstances. For example, we can come up with a context where a language learner uses a wrong word instead of the relativiser *'that'*. In that case a person correcting her is likely to put a contrastive focus on the relativiser. However, one can argue that this is a different use of a pitch accent, the so-called "quotative" use, as opposed to the new information or contrastive use in their more traditional sense, and as such it is out of the scope of the present study. Alternatively, one can say that the occurrences of focused function words, such as relativisers and complementisers, are so rare that we can take the freedom to ignore them. However, I leave these decisions to the implementers of specific systems, on the grounds that at present we do not have enough empirical evidence to completely ban accents on focus words.

There is also a rather simple recipe for avoiding the generation of multiple outputs from a single IS-DRS due to different prosodic phrasing. We can formulate a *Principle of Efficiency* which says that during generation as few boundaries should be used as possible. It is very questionable anyway, whether multiple adjacent themes and rhemes can be found at all. Empirical study into this question would be needed. The Principle of Efficiency can be worded as follows: do not insert a boundary tone unless it is not possible to proceed otherwise. In the parsing direction we need no such rule: it is actually positive that the parser is robust enough to allow reasonable variation in its input.

A different approach to controlling the proliferation of different prosodical phrasings could be taken if we had the knowledge about possible syntactic constraints on where boundary tones can or cannot occur. However, this is another point where empirical study would need to precede the implementation decisions. For example, we can hypothesize that boundary tones are undesirable between a determiner and a noun phrase, i.e. that there is a noun phrase island constraint requiring the whole noun phrase to be in the same intonational phrase. In that case, we could introduce a new feature, the value of which would determine whether the given sign can or cannot be combined with a boundary tone. We could call this feature HEAD, and allow it to have two constant values: '+' and '−'. Once this is done, we can stipulate that boundary tones cannot combine with signs which have the negative HEAD feature value (Steedman, PC).

7.2 Review of the Theses

In this section we will review the four theses that were presented at the beginning of the book, and recapitulate the evidence that was provided in the previous chapters and sections of the book to back them up.

7.2.1 IS-DRS

The first thesis said: "First order DRS is suitable for representing information structure in semantics." When I first presented the thesis, I pointed out that I had practical goals in mind (which foremost concerned the determination of appropriate intonation from IS marking in the DRS), and were not going to specify semantic computations with information structure. Throughout the book, I have shown the suitability of first order DRSs for representing different aspects of information structure relevant for inferring prosody.

In Section 3.3 of Chapter 3 I presented a way of including information-structural flags on DRS-conditions. These reflected the information-structural status of DRS-conditions, whether they were part of the context already (theme: θ), or they represented information that was new to the discourse (rheme:ρ). The focus flag $(+/-)$ adjacent to the themeness/rhemeness flag showed whether the lexical item corresponding to the given DRS-condition in the surface representation bore a phrasal stress. Besides the aforementioned two flags there was another polar $(+/-)$ flag expressing the agreement between the speaker and the hearer, and a flag representing boundary tone semantics.

In Section 7.1.1 of the present chapter I provided a first order DRS representation for all the 137 sentences in the corpus which contained no discrepancy between syntax and information structure. The syntax and information structure of these sentences varied. Our first order IS-DRS proved adequate for accounting for the semantics of these non-trivial sentences.

It is true that first order DRSs exhibit the usual problems of FOL representation, and are not able to convey all the richness of meaning of a natural language. For example, it has been pointed out that generalised quantifiers like *most* cannot be expressed in first order logic. This means that some kind of approximation has to be made, for example $\forall$ to represent *most*. I agree, that this way some of the precision is lost, but as said at the very beginning of this book I chose the particular logic language to make my representations compatible with first order model checkers/builders and theorem provers. I believe that the best way to convey the meaning of a natural language, is the natural language itself, which, however, is not too well suited for computational purposes.

Since our focus in this book is on representing information-structural phenomena, we need to consider the expressiveness of IS-DRSs in terms of how well they succeed in representing information structure. As shown throughout the book IS-DRSs are very clear about whether a certain DRS-condition (the ones that have an overt expression in the surface structure) belongs to a theme or a rheme, and whether it represents focused or backgrounded information. For example, in Example 7.30 the condition *john(X)* is unambiguously marked as a theme focus $(\theta+)$, the condition *novels(Y)* is equally unambiguously marked as a rheme focus $(\rho+)$ and the condition *write(E)* is marked as a rheme background $(\rho-)$. The semantic role conditions do not have information-structural flags, since no constituent corresponds to them in the surface representation, and as such these conditions do neither clearly belong to theme nor to rheme.

(7.30) John L+H* LH% writes novels H* LL%.

X,Y,E	
patient(E,Y)	
agent(E,X)	
write(E)	$\rho-$ $s+$
novels(Y)	$\rho+$ $s+$
john(X)	$\theta+$ $h+$

However, on certain occasions focus does not get reflected in IS-DRSs. This is the case when the focus is on a function word that does not manifest itself in DRS semantics. However, this problem is not specifically intrinsic to a first order representation, but to any semantic representation which involves a degree of simplification and does not literally mirror the surface representation.

In Section 7.1.2, I showed that a certain ambiguity existed between the mapping of DRSs and surface prosodic representation: sometimes utterances with slightly different prosodic phrasing map to the same DRS. However, the difference between these phrasings is only minor, since the ambiguity can only arise between utterances which either have a single longer phrase of a certain type of information structure or several shorter adjacent ones of the same type. The reason for this ambiguity is the boundary tone semantics used: the boundaries mark the whole phrase as speaker's or hearer's, and leave no trace at the particular position where they actually occurred.

Everything added together, my general conclusion is that first order DRSs are well suited for representing information structure. Particular support for the conclusion is offered by the fact that I was able to represent accurately the 137 sentences in my corpus where syntactic and information-structural constituents did not clash. The special cases of focus on function words, that IS-DRS cannot currently handle, is an issue for future research.

7.2.2 CCG as a starting point

The second thesis claimed that Combinatory Categorial Grammar provided a suitable starting point for developing a formalism to supply a path between a first order DRS annotated with information structure and an intonationally marked text.

CCG is especially suited for handling information structure, due to its flexible syntactic constituents. I showed above in Section 2.1 (Chapter 2) that information-structural constituents do not necessarily correspond to standard syntactic constituents.

I have provided support for the second thesis by having developed a formalism based on CCG that computes semantics with information structure from a prosodically annotated text. Most importantly, in Chapter 5 I described the process of integrating information structure in the UCCG framework, and in Section 7.1.1 of the present chapter I showed how the formalism allowed computing a corresponding IS-DRS for each of the sentences in the test suite which contained no discrepancy between syntax and information structure.

7.2.3   Unification

The third thesis stated that unification was a suitable means for facilitating the collaboration between the different levels of linguistic representation: syntax, semantics, and information structure.

Throughout the book I have demonstrated the use and usefulness of unification to achieve a tight connection between syntax, semantics and information structure. In Chapter 4, I showed how unification allows us to simultaneously construct semantics based on lambda calculus for a linguistic expression, while syntactically combining the signs that correspond to the sub-parts of the expression. The use of the same variables inside the feature structures and the semantic representation allowed us to replace the values in both locations at the same time. When we replaced lambda calculus with DRT semantics in Chapter 5 the close relationship between syntax and semantics was retained. Later, in Chapter 6 we introduced information structure in the framework. When introducing information structure, we added three new features, INF, FOC and BND, to the syntactic signs. However, the variables that were used as the values of these syntactic features were recycled as information-structural flags on the DRS-conditions in semantics. This approach ensured that whenever a variable in the INF, FOC or BND feature acquired a new value, the corresponding information-structural flag was replaced by the same value.

A practical proof of the usefulness of unification as a tool for achieving collaboration between different levels of linguistic representation is provided by the UCCG parser, which I implemented in Sicstus Prolog. With this parser, replacement of variable values is achieved via unification, as described in the theoretical part of the present book. A short description of the UCCG parser can be found in Appendix A.

7.2.4   Extensions of IS-DRS and UCCG

The fourth thesis asserted that both IS-DRS and the UCCG formalism were easily extendable. In this section I will briefly discuss some ways to extend them.

It is definitely possible to develop both IS-DRS and the UCCG formalism further in several directions. Probably the first thing one could think of would be to write UCCG grammars for languages other than English. This would enable exploring how or whether the word order variation caused by information structure can be accounted for in the UCCG framework. It is possible that for other languages additional or a different set of information-structural DRS-flags might prove useful. It would not be difficult to substitute the DRS-flags with different ones or add new flags to the existing ones.

As far as introducing new features in signs goes, UCCG is infinitely extendable. The number of features required depends on the demands that a specific application makes for precision and detail.

IS-DRS and UCCG do not necessarily have to be used together. Either of them can be combined with a different formalism: IS-DRS can be used as the semantics for a different grammar formalism, and UCCG can be combined with a different semantic framework.

Semantic computations can be specified for IS-DRSs to account for special phenomena like focus sensitive particles, and IS can be taken into account when choosing an accommodation site in a DRS (global vs. local accommodation) to ensure the correct accessibility constraints.

In this book we only made very little use of the capabilities that Multi-Modal CCG has to offer. Adding more insights from Multi-Modal CCG to

UCCG would be another way to improve the present formalism, and to make it more precise and more efficient.

Once more empirical, prosodically annotated data becomes available, it would be interesting to study whether there are some function words that never occur with a pitch accent. Similarly, it is conceivable that certain lexical items can only occur at a certain location in a sentence if they are focused. If the former were the case, this would allow us to specify the corresponding signs with a negative focus value already in the lexicon. If the latter is true, we would need to play around with the combination of specific syntactic categories with specific focus and possibly also other information-structural values in the lexicon. Hence, both multimodal slashes and the lexically specified information-structural properties are ways to shape the combinatorial space.

Another obvious way to extend the UCCG formalism would be to introduce the remaining CCG combination rules that were not made use of in the current implementation: forward and backward substitution, and forward and backward crossed substitution rules, in order to extend the formalism's coverage to more complex syntactic constructions (e.g. "parasitic gap" constructions).

Finally, a very attractive avenue would be to generalise the framework as to allow for use in combination with tree-bank size wide-coverage grammars. It would take relatively little effort to use UCCG jointly with a stochastic CCG parser in order to produce wide-coverage semantic representations. There is no particular reason, why a stochastic UCCG parser should not be possible, but a)implementing it from scratch would require more work, and b) there are already efficient stochastic CCG parsers available off-the-shelf. Moreover, it is more efficient to only compute the semantics for the most probable parse, once all the syntactic ambiguities have been resolved.

Using UCCG in tandem with a stochastic CCG parser would be very similar to what is described in Bos et al. 2004 and Bos 2005. After specifying the corresponding UCCG signs for the categories in CCG-bank, we would reduce the four steps of the algorithm in Bos et al. 2004 (Section 4.2) into just its first step: "assigning semantic representation to the lexical items". This done, we would trace the parse tree output by the stochastic CCG parser starting from its leaves and use UCCG's combinatory rules according to the information in the nodes of the CCG parse tree. By combining the UCCG signs (the DRSs in the semantics feature of the UCCG signs would be combined, too), the final semantic representation would be built up simultaneously.

However, it would still be problematic to fully benefit from the information-structural capacities of UCCG. The most serious problem is that there is no training data which includes prosodic categories: these are not included in the present CCG-bank. We would need a new ToBI[1] annotated treebank. The second, related problem is that at present there are no appropriate large corpora of intonationally annotated text available that we might want to parse.

7.3 Conclusion

This chapter presented a preliminary assessment of the UCCG formalism. In order to judge its coverage of syntactic and information-structural phenomena, I compiled a small corpus of intonationally annotated data and parsed it with my UCCG parser (see Appendix A). I found that the formalism allowed to adequately account for information-structural phenomena: all-rheme utterances, sentences containing a theme and a rheme in either order and sentences with a split theme, marked and unmarked themes, and theme/rheme intonational phrases with single focus or multiple foci. As far as syntactic phenomena are concerned, the parser successfully handled simple sentences, sentences containing coordination or sub-ordination, topicalised sentences, passive sentences, clefts, pseudo-clefts and reverse pseudo-clefts.

By using the parser in a reverse order, I made predictions about UCCG's suitability for generation: first, all possible intonational permutations of the selected example sentences were created, then all the permutations were parsed, and the result DRSs compared. I found that there was no absolute one-to-one correspondence between DRSs and corresponding surface intonational annotation.

This ambiguity had two sources: boundary tones and function words. I observed that in certain cases it is not possible to tell from the semantics whether we have to do with one long intonational phrase ending with the given boundary tone, or several short ones, all ending with the same boundary tone. However, the issue of whether multiple theme or rheme intonational phrases

---

[1]See the footnote on page 24 about problems with ToBI annotation.

following each other are empirically possible needs further study. The problem with function words is due to the fact that usually they are not reflected in semantics, which means that there is no record about the prosodic marking on them.

Subsequently, I re-examined the four theses which were presented at the beginning of the book, concluding that sufficient proof had been provided for all of them. It was possible to provide a first order DRS representation with information-structural flags for all the sentences in the corpus which contained no disagreement between syntax and information structure. The proof for the suitability of CCG as a starting point for a formalism providing a path between prosodically annotated text and information-structurally marked DRSs was provided by developing Unification-based Combinatory Categorial Grammar, implementing a UCCG parser, and parsing a corpus of intonationally annotated sentences providing an IS-DRS for each "correct" (the information structure and the syntax of which are compatible) sentence in the corpus. The above also provided sufficient support for the usefulness of unification as a means of achieving collaboration between different levels of linguistic representation. Finally, I discussed some ways to extend IS-DRS and UCCG.

Chapter 8

Conclusion

This book presented an approach for integrating Discourse Representation Theory (DRT), information structure (IS) and Combinatory Categorial Grammar (CCG) into a single framework. DRT, IS and CCG have existed a long time and their usefulness in automatic natural language processing has been proved by considerable bodies of research. However, until now they have remained largely independent, and no detailed proposal has existed to show how they could be combined. In this book I have used the three as building blocks for a unification-based realisation of CCG, which I have entitled Unification-based Combinatory Categorial Grammar (UCCG).

The UCCG formalism was developed step by step throughout the book. As the first step, information structure was introduced in DRT. This resulted in a new kind of Discourse Representation Structure (DRS): IS-DRS. An IS-DRS is a DRS annotated for information structure. The next step involved expanding CCG categories into feature structures called signs, and bringing in feature structure unification. Here the core of UCCG was worked out. Subsequently, the provisional predicate-calculus-based semantic representation in UCCG signs was replaced by the traditional DRT representation. The final step in the process involved replacing the DRSs with IS-DRSs, and modifying the UCCG signs to accommodate information-structural features.

I introduced information structure in DRT by assigning information-structural flags to DRS-conditions. In this book I used these flags to determine the appropriate intonation for utterances, but in the future they could also be used to specify semantic computations with information structure. There are four kinds of flags. First, there is a flag for themeness/rhemeness, which can have two constant values θ (theme) or ρ (rheme). This flag is followed by the focus flag. The two constant values that the focus flag can assume are '+' and '−'. The third flag that I use stands for speaker or hearer "commitment", indicating whether the speaker presents the information in an utterance as if s/he or the hearer was committed to it. This commitment flag can have the constant value s (speaker) or h (hearer). Finally, there is a flag marking "agreement": whether the speaker presents the information in an utterance as if it was contentious or uncontentious. This flag, too, has two polar constant values: '+' and '−'. Besides the constant values, the value of any of the information-structural flags can be a variable, standing for an unspecified value. The general scheme of the four different aspects of the semantics of information structure is due to Steedman (2003). In his approach these values are tightly connected with prosody: the themeness/rhemeness, focus and agreement aspects are contributed by pitch accents, while the commitment aspect is contributed by boundary tones. These IS-DRSs, which are relatively uncomplicated first order structures, allow us to accurately describe the semantics of a non-trivial fragment of English (Thesis 1).

I used CCG to provide a path from an intonationally annotated text to the IS-DRS representation, and vice versa. Information-structural constituents frequently do not coincide with the traditional syntactic constituents. As such, CCG is especially well suited for handling information structure, because of its flexible notion of constituency (Thesis 2). I enriched the CCG categories with a variety of linguistic information, and due to their attractive transparency and compactness, I used feature structures to present these information bundles. In the case of UCCG, the usual categorial unification of CCG applies to the whole feature structures called signs. These developments relate UCCG to Unification Categorial Grammar (UCG). However, differently from UCG there is no recursive sign embedding in UCCG. Moreover, UCCG uses CCG's rich system of combinatory rules. In the first version of UCCG I employ predicate calculus to represent semantics. After a brief introduction to the main signs and combinatory rules, illustrated with ample examples, where among other things I demonstrated the usefulness of unification for passing values between different levels of linguistic representation (Thesis 3), I replaced the provisional semantic representation with DRT semantics.

Finally, I introduced information structure into UCCG. This involved replacing the DRT semantic representation by IS-DRSs, and introducing information-structural features into signs. Even more significantly I brought in new, prosodic signs, which correspond to pitch accents and boundary tones. It is the pitch accent and boundary tone signs which ultimately determine the information-structural flags on the IS-DRSs of the outcome of the analysis of an intonationally annotated utterance. This is achieved in the following way:

- The information-structural feature values of lexical (non-prosodic) signs start as variables.

- When lexical signs are combined with prosodic signs the latter replace the information-structural variables in the corresponding features of lexical signs with constant values for themeness/rhemeness, focus, etc.

- Since I use the same variables as information-structural feature values and the values of the corresponding IS-DRS flags, whenever the feature acquires a new value, the same value is introduced into the IS-DRS via unification (Thesis 3).

The final part of the book presented a preliminary assessment of the UCCG formalism. In this assessment I used a parser based on the UCCG formalism, which I implemented in Sicstus Prolog. The parser successfully handled a non-trivial fragment of English producing an IS-DRS for each of the legitimate[1] input sentences of my test suite. However, I observed a certain ambiguity between intonationally annotated sentences and IS-DRSs: sometimes a single IS-DRS corresponded to multiple slightly different intonation contours. This ambiguity is not inherent to the way information structure, DRT and CCG are combined in UCCG, but rather it is already native to UCCG's building blocks themselves. The reason for why we cannot precisely infer the information-structural properties of certain function words from an IS-DRS lies in the fact that these function words are not explicitly reflected in DRT semantics. Similarly, the ambiguity caused by boundary tones is already native to the prosodic approach to information structure first proposed inside the CCG framework.

It is possible to further develop both the IS-DRSs and the UCCG formalism in several directions (Thesis 4). These are issues to be addressed in future work.

---

[1] I mean the sentences which contain no disagreement between syntax and information structure.

One of the most obvious developments would involve writing UCCG grammars for languages other than English. A natural consequence would be having to confront the question about how or whether the word order variation caused by information structure can be accounted for in the UCCG framework. It is also probable that additional or a different set of information-structural DRS-flags might prove useful. There is certainly no obstacle to substituting the DRS-flags with different ones or adding new flags to the existing ones. Similarly, UCCG signs can in principle be indefinitely extended with new features, depending on the precision and detail needed for a specific application. Moreover, IS-DRSs and UCCG do not necessarily have to be used in tandem. Either of them can be combined with a different formalism: IS-DRSs can be used as the semantics for a different grammar formalism, and UCCG can be combined with a different semantic framework.

Currently, I have only made very little use of the capabilities that Multi-Modal CCG has to offer. Adding more insights from Multi-Modal CCG to UCCG would be another way to make the existing formalism better, more precise and more efficient. Once more empirical data becomes available, it would be interesting to study whether there are some function words that on no occasion bear a pitch accent. Similarly, it is conceivable that certain lexical items can only occur at a certain location in a sentence if they are focused. In the former case this would mean that we can specify the corresponding signs with a negative focus value already in the lexicon. In the latter case we would need to experiment with the combination of specific syntactic categories with specific focus and possibly also other information-structural values in the lexicon. Hence, both multimodal slashes and the lexically specified information-structural properties are ways to shape the combinatorial space.

Finally, a very attractive avenue would be to generalise the framework as to allow for use in combination with tree-bank sized wide-coverage grammars. However, in the case of this application, having access to appropriate intonationally annotated corpora is crucial.

Appendix A

UCCG Parser

This appendix briefly describes the main predicates of a UCCG chart parser which is implemented in Sicstus Prolog. The parser is a bottom-up chart parser.

First we have a look at the lexicon. I implemented the UCCG basic signs as Prolog lists. The complex signs are represented by complex terms made up of lists and slash operators.[1] I use the lists of the same length for all signs. However, I only specify constant values for the features relevant to the particular category, as described in Chapters 4, 5 and 6 of this book. The constant length of lists allows us to keep the program simple[2] and compact. Each list contains eleven[3] elements: pho:W, cat:C, num:N, per:P, agr:A, var:V, sit:E, info:I:D, bnd:B, foc:F and drs:D. The lexical entries are presented by the predicate *sign/2*. The two arguments of this predicate are the actual lexical item and the corresponding sign. The lexical entry for the basic sign for *'child'* looks like follows:

sign([child],

    [phon:child, cat:n, num:sg, per:3, agr:_, var:X,

    sit:_, info:I:A, bnd:B, foc:F, drs:drs([ ],[child(X):I:F:B:A])]).

The verb has the following lexical entry:

---

[1] The slash operators are defined as follows (the second declaration concerns the "application-only" modal slashes):

    :- op(400,yfx, [/,\]).
    :- op(400,yfx, [/^,\^]).

[2] This regards, for example, the easy implementation of the unification during the combination of prosodic signs with lexical signs, as well as allowing direct access to the values of specific features based on their position in the list.

[3] Exceptionally the lists corresponding to the result part of the boundary tones consists of ten elements, since they do not include the boundary feature any more (see Chapter 6).

sign([loves],

    [phon:loves+W1, cat:vp, num:sg, per:3, agr:fin, var:X,

    sit:E, info:I:A, bnd:B, foc:F, drs:B1] /

    ([phon:W1+W2, cat:s, num:N, per:P, agr:sent, var:_,

    sit:E, info:I:A, bnd:B, foc:F, drs:B1] /

    [phon:W2, cat:vp, num:N, per:P, agr:_, var:Y, sit:E, info:I:A,

    bnd:B, foc:F, drs:drs([E],[love(E):I:F:B:A, agent(E,X), patient(E,Y)])])])).

The entry for the prosodic sign H* is expressed as follows:

sign(['H*'],

    [phon:W, cat:C, num:N, per:P, agr:L, var:X,

    sit:E, info:rheme:pos, bnd:B, foc:nil, drs:D] \^

    [phon:W, cat:C, num:N, per:P, agr:L, var:X, sit:E,

    info:rheme:pos, bnd:B, foc:foc, drs:D]).

The principal parsing predicate has three main tasks to perform: it has to initialise the chart, drive the combination of edges, and finally, print the resulting IS-DRSs. The predicate looks like follows:

parse(I):-

    retractall(edge(_,_,_,_)),

    retractall(max(_)),

    initialise_chart(I,0),

    chartParse,!,

    printResult.

The first two calls to the predicate *retractall/1* serve to clear Prolog's dynamic memory. Then the predicate *initialise_chart/2* initialises the chart. It has two arguments: the first of them is the input, and the second stands for the leftmost position in the chart: position 0. Chart initialisation introduces a separate edge for each input word and prosodic boundary. Pitch accents form an exception: no individual edges are introduced for them. Pitch accents are already combined during chart initialisation with the word that carries them. This is done, because, in order to achieve the correct focus marking, pitch accents need to be combined with their exponent words before any other combinations take place (see Chapter 6). The predicate *chartParse/0* performs the actual combining of edges, and printResult/0 prints the resulting IS-DRSs.

The predicate *chartParse/0* combines the edges stored in the dynamic memory of Prolog. When this predicate is first called the only edges present are the ones that were introduced by chart initialisation. After each successful combination, a new edge is introduced in the chart.

First, *chartParse/0* picks out two edges which satisfy the condition that the end position of the first edge corresponds to the start position of the second edge. Then it tries to combine them by means of any of the combinatory rules. If the combination succeeds, then the edge is compared against the already existing edges, and if it turns out to be a novel edge (note that when comparing the edges, we ignore the fourth argument: here we do not care about the exact derivation that produced the edge) it is stored in Prolog's dynamic memory. If everything is successful up to this point, the predicate *chartParse/0* is called recursively and the combination of edges continues. If at any point the program encounters a problem, Prolog's in-built back-tracking mechanism is used to seek for alternative solutions. If no more combinations are possible, then Prolog back-tracks up to the point when *chartParse/0* was first called. Then the second, non-recursive, clause of *chartParse/0* is resorted to, which succeeds in any case.

```
chartParse:-
    edge(S1,A,B,_),[4]
    edge(S2,B,C,_),
    combine(S1,S2,S3,D),
    \+ edge(S3,A,C,_),
    addEdge(S3,A,C,D),
    chartParse.

chartParse.

addEdge(S,Start,End,D):-
```

[4] The *edge/4* predicate has the following arguments: the UCCG sign which spans the edge, start position of the edge, end position of the edge, the derivation by means of which the UCCG sign was formed. For edges originating from chart initialisation, the value of the fourth argument of *edge/4* is '*init*'

```
asserta(edge(S,Start,End,D))).
```

The *combine/4* predicate chooses the appropriate combinatory rule, and combines the two signs S1 and S2. The result of the combination (S3) and information about the derivation are stored in the new edge of the chart.

I have implemented the following combinatory rules in the parser: forward application (*fa/3*), backward application (*ba/3*), generalised forward composition (*fc/3*) and generalised backward composition (*bc/3*). Besides these I implemented the unary rules of type-raising and NP-conversion. For practical (tractability) reasons I only implemented type-raising for a limited set of UCCG signs. The NP-conversion rules were needed to turn the signs of plural nouns into indefinite noun phrases according to necessity.

For forward application the rules are very straightforward. Two rules were needed to provide for the multi-modal slash as well.

```
fa(A/B,B,A).
fa(A/^B,C,D):- fa(A/B,C,D).
```

For backward application, I had to implement the recursive application (needed for prosodic signs) besides the traditional one. Here I present two rules for recursive backward application (omitting the ones providing for multi-modal slashes inside the argument signs). For recursive backward application we first check that the functor sign is a prosodic sign (here we slightly diverge from what was explained in Chapter 6, where we explicitly marked the recursive signs with a star (*)). We identify the prosodic signs by checking that the category of the sub-sign on each side of the backslash is a variable. Next we make a copy of the functor sign. Then we (recursively) unify the active part of the original functor with the left-hand side of the argument, and record the outcome of the unification in the left-hand side of the result sign. Subsequently, we (recursively) unify the active part of the copy of the functor with the right-hand side of the argument, and record the outcome of the unification in the right-hand side of the result.

```
ba(A,B\A,B).

ba(A/B,B1\A1,C/D):-
    B1=[phon:_, cat:Cat|_],
```

A1=[phon:__, cat:Cat|__],
var(Cat),
copy_term(B1\A1,NewB1\NewA1),
ba(A,B1\A1,C),
ba(B,NewB1\NewA1,D),!.

ba(A\B,B1\A1,C\D):-
    B1=[phon:__, cat:Cat|__],
    A1=[phon:__, cat:Cat|__],
    var(Cat),
    copy_term(B1\A1,NewB1\NewA1),
    ba(A,B1\A1,C),
    ba(B,NewB1\NewA1,D),!.

ba(A,B\^C,D):- ba(A,B\C,D).

I implemented three clauses for both generalised forward and generalised backward composition, limiting the depth of embedding to three.

fc(A/B,B/C,A/C):-!.
fc(A/B,(B/C)/D,(A/C)/D):-!.
fc(A/B,((B/C)/D)/E,((A/C)/D)/E).

bc(B\C,A\B,A\C):-!.
bc((B\C)\D,A\B,(A\C)\D):-!.
bc(((B\C)\D)\E,A\B,((A\C)\D)\E).

Whenever it is possible (i.e. the DRS-variables have acquired a constant value of an actual DRS), the IS-DRSs in the result head are merged after each combination. This operation is performed by the *merge/2* predicate. The first argument of this predicate is a list of DRSs, and the second argument is the result of the merge. The list of DRSs is sorted such that the instantiated DRSs come before the DRS-variables.

The first clause of *merge/2* corresponds to the base case where the list of DRSs contains a single element. This means that no merging needs to be done: we simply extract the DRS from the list.

The second clause represents the recursive case. We pick out the two first elements in the DRS-list, and check that neither of them is a variable. If this condition is fulfilled, then we can merge the two DRSs together. The predicate *reduceDrs/2* checks whether among the DRS-conditions of the given DRS any sub-DRSs need to be merged, and if this is the case, merges them (by redirecting them to *merge/2*). Once the sub-DRSs have been sorted out, we can continue with the merging of the main DRSs. However, we still also need to check for duplicate variables in the two DRSs, and if present, rename the variables of one of the DRSs. That is what the predicate *convertVar/3*[5] does. Subsequently, using *append/3* from the lists package of the Prolog library, we join the lists of the discourse referents of the two DRSs together. The same is done with the DRS-conditions. After that, we call *merge/2* again, and see if we can merge another DRS with the one we just formed.

Finally, the third clause of *merge/2* is used if after merging some DRSs by means of the second clause DRS-variables are encountered, i.e. there are still uninstantiated variables in the merge list.

```
merge([Merged],Merged):-!.

merge([B1,B2|Tail],Merged):-
    \+ var(B1),
    \+ var(B2),!,
    reduceDrs(B1,drs(D1,C1)),
    reduceDrs(B2,drs(D,C)),
    convertVar(drs(D1,C1),drs(D,C),drs(D2,C2)),
    append(D1,D2,D3),
    append(C1,C2,C3),
    sort(D3,D4),
    sort(C3,C4),
    merge([drs(D4,C4)|Tail],Merged).

merge(Merged,merge(Merged)).
```

---

[5]This predicate is taken from Blackburn and Bos 2006.

Appendix B

Test Suite

B.1 The Complete Test Suite

Dogs must be CARRIED H* LL%
DOGS L+H* LH% must be CARRIED H* LL%
DOGS H* LL% must be carried LL%
DOGS H* LL% must be CARRIED L+H* LH%
John writes NOVELS H* LL%
JOHN L+H* LH% writes NOVELS H* LL%
JOHN H* LL% writes novels LL%
JOHN H* LL% writes NOVELS L+H* LH%
John flew from London to PARIS H* LL%
John flew from LONDON L+H* LH% to PARIS H* LL%
JOHN L+H* flew from London LH% to PARIS H* LL%
JOHN L+H* flew LH% from London to PARIS H* LL%
John flew L+H* LH% from London to PARIS H* LL%
JOHN L+H* LH% flew from London to PARIS H* LL%
JOHN L+H* flew from LH% LONDON H* LL% to PARIS L+H* LH%
JOHN L+H* flew from LH% LONDON H* LL% to Paris LL%
John flew from LONDON H* LL% to Paris LL%
John flew to PARIS L+H* from LH% LONDON H* LL%
JOHN L+H* flew to PARIS L+H* from LH% LONDON H* LL%
John flew to Paris from LONDON H* LL%
JOHN H* LL% flew from LONDON L+H* to Paris LH%
JOHN H* LL% flew from London to PARIS L+H* LH%
JOHN H* LL% flew from London to Paris LL%
JOHN L+H* LH% FLEW H* LL% from LONDON L+H* to PARIS L+H* LH%
JOHN L+H* LH% FLEW H* LL% from London to PARIS L+H* LH%
JOHN L+H* LH% FLEW H* LL% from London to Paris LL%
John FLEW H* LL% from London to Paris LL%
John FLEW H* LL% from London to PARIS L+H* LH%
John FLEW H* LL% from LONDON L+H* to PARIS L+H* LH%

233

The British author reads COMIC H* books LL%
The BRITISH H* ACTOR H* LL% reads comic books LL%
The BRITISH ACTOR H* LL% reads comic books LL%
The British author READS L+H* LH% COMIC H* books LL%
The British author READS L+H* LH% history PAPERS H* LL%
The British author READS L+H* LH% DETECTIVE H* STORIES H* LL%
The American ACTOR H* LL% reads history books LL%
The BRITISH H* LL% author reads history books LL%
The BRITISH H* ACTOR H* LL% reads history books LL%
The BRITISH L+H* author reads LH% COMICS H* LL%
The American ACTOR L+H* reads LH% COMICS H* LL%
COMICS L+H* LH% John HATES H* LL%
COMICS H* LL% John hates LL%
It is JOHN H* LL% who hates comics LL%
It is JOHN H* LL% who hates COMICS L+H* LH%
It is COMICS H* LL% John hates LL%
It is COMICS H* LL% JOHN L+H* hates LH%
It is COMICS H* LL% John HATES L+H* LH%
What John HATES L+H* LH% are COMICS H* LL%
What JOHN L+H* hates LH% are COMICS H* LL%
What John HATES L+H* are LH% COMICS H* LL%
COMICS H* are LL% what John HATES L+H* LH%
COMICS H* are LL% what John hates LH%
COMICS H* LL% are what John HATES L+H* LH%
COMICS H* LL% are what JOHN L+H* hates LH%
John gave Mary a BOOK H* LL%
John gave MARY L+H* LH% a BOOK H* LL%
John gave a book to MARY H* LL%
John gave a BOOK L+H* LH% to MARY H* LL%
John gave a BOOK L+H* to LH% MARY H* LL%
COMICS L+H* are hated LH% by JOHN H* LL%
Comics are hated by JOHN H* LL%
COMICS L+H* are hated by LH% JOHN H* LL%
BILL L+H* writes LH% POETRY H* LL%
POETRY H* LL% is written by BILL L+H* LH%
POETRY H* LL% is written by Bill LL%
It is POETRY H* LL% BILL L+H* writes LH%
What BILL L+H* LH% writes is POETRY H* LL%
POETRY H* LL% BILL L+H* writes LL%
BILL L+H* LH% writes POETRY H* LL%
Bill writes POETRY H* LL%
BILL L+H* writes LH% POETRY H* LL%

BILL H* LL% writes POETRY L+H* LH%
BILL H* LL% writes poetry LL%
BILL L+H* LH% WRITES H* LL% POETRY L+H* LH%
BILL L+H* LH% WRITES H* LL% poetry LL%
Bill WRITES H* LL% poetry LL%
The GERMAN L+H* actor LH% writes POETRY H* LL%
The German ACTOR L+H* LH% writes POETRY H* LL%
The GERMAN H* actor LL% writes POETRY L+H* LH%
The GERMAN H* actor LL% writes poetry LL%
The German ACTOR H* LL% writes POETRY L+H* LH%
The German ACTOR H* LL% writes poetry LL%
On the Shetlands one speaks ENGLISH H* LL%
On the SHETLANDS L+H* one speaks LH% ENGLISH H* LL%
On the Shetlands one SPEAKS L+H* LH% ENGLISH H* LL%
One speaks ENGLISH L+H* LH% on the SHETLANDS H* LL%
OFFICERS L+H* always escorted LH% BALLERINAS H* LL%
Officers always ESCORTED L+H* LH% BALLERINAS H* LL%
Officers always escorted BALLERINAS H* LL%
OFFICERS L+H* always LH% escorted BALLERINAS H* LL%
OFFICERS H* LL% always escorted BALLERINAS L+H* LH%
OFFICERS H* LL% always ESCORTED L+H* ballerinas LH%
OFFICERS H* LL% always escorted ballerinas LL%
Mary ADMIRES L+H* LH% the woman who DIRECTED H* the musical LL%
ANNA H* LL% married MANNY L+H* LH%
ANNA L+H* LH% married MANNY H* LL%
Mary likes BOMBAZINE H* LL%
Mary likes BOMBAZINE L+H* LH%
Well, she likes BOMBAZINE L+H* LH%
And people who like BOMBAZINE L+H* LH% like CORDUROY H* LL%
So I am SURE H* LL% that Mary likes corduroy LL%
Mary is ALWAYS H* on time LL%
Mary is USUALLY L+H* on time LH%
Anna married MANNY H* LL%
Mary WANTS L+H* LH% IPSWICH H* LL% to WIN L+H* LH%
Harry doesn't READ H* LL% BOOKS L+H* LH%
Harry doesn't READ H* books LL%
Harry doesn't READ H* LL% books LL%
FRED L+H* LH% ate the BEANS H* LL%
FRED H* LL% ate the BEANS L+H* LH%
FRED H* LL% ate the beans LL%
FRED H* ate the beans LL%
MARY L+H* says he ate LH% BEANS H* LL%

FRED L+H* LH% ate the GREEN H* beans LL%
FRED L+H* LH% ate the GREEN H* BEANS H* LL%
Mary wrote a book about BATS H* LL%
NIXON H* died LL%
NIXON H* LL% died LL%
FRED L+H* LH% ATE H* the beans LL%
FRED L+H* LH% ATE H* LL% the beans LL%
FRED H* LL% ATE L+H* the beans LH%
Fred ATE L+H* LH% the BEANS H* LL%
Fred ATE H* LL% the BEANS L+H* LH%
Fred LL% ATE H* LL% the BEANS L+H* LH%
FRED L+H* LH% ate the BEANS H* LL%
FRED H* ate LL% the BEANS L+H* LH%
Bill COOKED H* and Fred ATE H* LL% the BEANS L+H* LH%
It was the BEANS H* LL% that FRED ATE L+H* LH%
It was the BEANS H* LL% that Fred ATE L+H* LH%
It was the beans that FRED H* ate LL%
It was the beans that Fred ATE H* LL%
The beans that FRED H* LL% ate were DELICIOUS L+H* LH%
The beans that FRED L+H* LH% ate were DELICIOUS H* LL%
I am a MILLIONAIRE H* LL%
I am a MILLIONAIRE L* LL%
I am a MILLIONAIRE H* LH%
I am a MILLIONAIRE L* LH%
I am a MILLIONAIRE L+H* LL%
I am a MILLIONAIRE L*+H LL%
I am a MILLIONAIRE L+H* LH%
I am a MILLIONAIRE L*+H LH%

Not to be processed due to the incompatibility of syntactic and information-structural constituents:

Bill cooked and FRED H* LL% ate the BEANS L+H* LH%
My OLDER L+H* LH% sister ate the green BEANS H* LL%
FRED L+H* ate the green LH% BEANS H* LL%

B.2   Syntactic Phenomena Covered

In this section the sentences (the positive examples) in the test suite are classified according to syntactic phenomena present in them. Each sentence has been included only in a single class, even though in the case of several sentences they could, in principle, fit under the title of more than one class.

Intransitive verbs

NIXON H* died LL%
NIXON H* LL% died LL%

Copula

I am a MILLIONAIRE H* LL%
I am a MILLIONAIRE L* LL%
I am a MILLIONAIRE H* LH%
I am a MILLIONAIRE L* LH%
I am a MILLIONAIRE L+H* LL%
I am a MILLIONAIRE L*+H LL%
I am a MILLIONAIRE L+H* LH%
I am a MILLIONAIRE L*+H LH%

Transitive verbs

John writes NOVELS H* LL%
JOHN L+H* LH% writes NOVELS H* LL%
JOHN H* LL% writes novels LL%
JOHN H* LL% writes NOVELS L+H* LH%
BILL L+H* writes LH% POETRY H* LL%
BILL L+H* LH% writes POETRY H* LL%
Bill writes POETRY H* LL%
BILL L+H* writes LH% POETRY H* LL%
BILL H* LL% writes POETRY L+H* LH%
BILL H* LL% writes poetry LL%
BILL L+H* LH% WRITES H* LL% POETRY L+H* LH%
BILL L+H* LH% WRITES H* LL% poetry LL%
Bill WRITES H* LL% poetry LL%
ANNA H* LL% married MANNY L+H* LH%
ANNA L+H* LH% married MANNY H* LL%
Mary likes BOMBAZINE H* LL%
Mary likes BOMBAZINE L+H* LH%
Anna married MANNY H* LL%
FRED L+H* LH% ate the BEANS H* LL%
FRED H* LL% ate the BEANS L+H* LH%
FRED H* LL% ate the beans LL%
FRED H* ate the beans LL%

FRED L+H* LH% ATE H* the beans LL%
FRED L+H* LH% ATE H* LL% the beans LL%
FRED H* LL% ATE L+H* the beans LH%
Fred ATE L+H* LH% the BEANS H* LL%
Fred ATE H* LL% the BEANS L+H* LH%
Fred LL% ATE H* LL% the BEANS L+H* LH%
FRED L+H* LH% ate the BEANS H* LL%
FRED H* ate LL% the BEANS L+H* LH%

Ditransitive verbs

John gave Mary a BOOK H* LL%
John gave MARY L+H* LH% a BOOK H* LL%
John gave a book to MARY H* LL%
John gave a BOOK L+H* LH% to MARY H* LL%
John gave a BOOK L+H* to LH% MARY H* LL%

Verbal post-modification

John flew from London to PARIS H* LL%
John flew from LONDON L+H* LH% to PARIS H* LL%
JOHN L+H* flew from London LH% to PARIS H* LL%
JOHN L+H* flew LH% from London to PARIS H* LL%
John flew L+H* LH% from London to PARIS H* LL%
JOHN L+H* LH% flew from London to PARIS H* LL%
JOHN L+H* flew from LH% LONDON H* LL% to PARIS L+H* LH%
JOHN L+H* flew from LH% LONDON H* LL% to Paris LL%
John flew from LONDON H* LL% to Paris LL%
John flew to PARIS L+H* from LH% LONDON H* LL%
JOHN L+H* flew to PARIS L+H* from LH% LONDON H* LL%
John flew to Paris from LONDON H* LL%
JOHN H* LL% flew from LONDON L+H* to Paris LH%
JOHN H* LL% flew from London to PARIS L+H* LH%
JOHN H* LL% flew from London to Paris LL%
JOHN L+H* LH% FLEW H* LL% from LONDON L+H* to PARIS L+H* LH%
JOHN L+H* LH% FLEW H* LL% from London to PARIS L+H* LH%
JOHN L+H* LH% FLEW H* LL% from London to Paris LL%
John FLEW H* LL% from London to Paris LL%
John FLEW H* LL% from London to PARIS L+H* LH%
John FLEW H* LL% from LONDON L+H* to PARIS L+H* LH%
One speaks ENGLISH L+H* LH% on the SHETLANDS H* LL%

Frequency adverbs: verbal pre-modification

OFFICERS L+H* always escorted LH% BALLERINAS H* LL%
Officers always ESCORTED L+H* LH% BALLERINAS H* LL%
Officers always escorted BALLERINAS H* LL%
OFFICERS L+H* always LH% escorted BALLERINAS H* LL%
OFFICERS H* LL% always escorted BALLERINAS L+H* LH%
OFFICERS H* LL% always ESCORTED L+H* ballerinas LH%
OFFICERS H* LL% always escorted ballerinas LL%
Mary is ALWAYS H* on time LL%
Mary is USUALLY L+H* on time LH%

Adjectives: nominal pre-modification

The British author reads COMIC H* books LL%
The BRITISH H* ACTOR H* LL% reads comic books LL%
The BRITISH ACTOR H* LL% reads comic books LL%
The British author READS L+H* LH% COMIC H* books LL%
The British author READS L+H* LH% history PAPERS H* LL%
The British author READS L+H* LH% DETECTIVE H* STORIES H* LL%
The American ACTOR H* LL% reads history books LL%
The BRITISH H* LL% author reads history books LL%
The BRITISH H* ACTOR H* LL% reads history books LL%
The BRITISH L+H* author reads LH% COMICS H* LL%
The American ACTOR L+H* reads LH% COMICS H* LL%
The GERMAN L+H* actor LH% writes POETRY H* LL%
The German ACTOR L+H* LL% writes POETRY H* LL%
The GERMAN H* actor LL% writes POETRY L+H* LH%
The GERMAN H* actor LL% writes poetry LL%
The German ACTOR H* LL% writes POETRY L+H* LH%
The German ACTOR H* LL% writes poetry LL%
FRED L+H* LH% ate the GREEN H* beans LL%
FRED L+H* LH% ate the GREEN H* BEANS H* LL%

Nominal post-modification

Mary wrote a book about BATS H* LL%

Sentential modification

On the Shetlands one speaks ENGLISH H* LL%
On the SHETLANDS L+H* one speaks LH% ENGLISH H* LL%

On the Shetlands one SPEAKS L+H* LH% ENGLISH H* LL%
Well, she likes BOMBAZINE L+H* LH%

Topicalised sentences

COMICS L+H* LH% John HATES H* LL%
COMICS H* LL% John hates LL%
POETRY H* LL% BILL L+H* writes LL%

Passive sentences

Dogs must be CARRIED H* LL%
DOGS L+H* LH% must be CARRIED H* LL%
DOGS H* LL% must be carried LL%
DOGS H* LL% must be CARRIED L+H* LH%
COMICS L+H* are hated LH% by JOHN H* LL%
Comics are hated by JOHN H* LL%
COMICS L+H* are hated by LH% JOHN H* LL%
POETRY H* LL% is written by BILL L+H* LH%
POETRY H* LL% is written by Bill LL%

Co-ordination

Bill COOKED H* and Fred ATE H* LL% the BEANS L+H* LH%

Relative clauses

Mary ADMIRES L+H* LH% the woman who DIRECTED H* the musical LL%
And people who like BOMBAZINE L+H* LH% like CORDUROY H* LL%
The beans that FRED H* LL% ate were DELICIOUS L+H* LH%
The beans that FRED L+H* LH% ate were DELICIOUS H* LL%

Complement clauses

So I am SURE H* LL% that Mary likes corduroy LL%
Mary WANTS L+H* LH% IPSWICH H* LL% to WIN L+H* LH%
MARY L+H* says he ate LH% BEANS H* LL%

Clefts

It is JOHN H* LL% who hates comics LL%
It is JOHN H* LL% who hates COMICS L+H* LH%

It is COMICS H* LL% John hates LL%
It is COMICS H* LL% JOHN L+H* hates LH%
It is COMICS H* LL% John HATES L+H* LH%
It is POETRY H* LL% BILL L+H* writes LH%
It was the BEANS H* LL% that FRED ATE L+H* LH%
It was the BEANS H* LL% that Fred ATE L+H* LH%
It was the beans that FRED H* ate LL%
It was the beans that Fred ATE H* LL%

Pseudo-clefts

What John HATES L+H* LH% are COMICS H* LL%
What JOHN L+H* hates LH% are COMICS H* LL%
What John HATES L+H* are LH% COMICS H* LL%
What BILL L+H* LH% writes is POETRY H* LL%

Reverse pseudo-clefts

COMICS H* are LL% what John HATES L+H* LH%
COMICS H* are LL% what JOHN L+H* hates LH%
COMICS H* LL% are what John HATES L+H* LH%
COMICS H* LL% are what JOHN L+H* hates LH%

Negation

Harry doesn't READ H* LL% BOOKS L+H* LH%
Harry doesn't READ H* books LL%
Harry doesn't READ H* LL% books LL%

B.3 Information-Structural Phenomena Covered

In this section the sentences (the positive examples) of the test suite are classified according to their information structure. Again each example is only included in one class, even though often it would fit under several class descriptions (e.g. "unmarked themes" and "rheme followed by theme").

All-rheme utterances

Dogs must be CARRIED H* LL%
John writes NOVELS H* LL%

John flew from London to PARIS H* LL%
John flew to Paris from LONDON H* LL%
The British author reads COMIC H* books LL%
John gave Mary a BOOK H* LL%
John gave a book to MARY H* LL%
Comics are hated by JOHN H* LL%
Bill writes POETRY H* LL%
On the Shetlands one speaks ENGLISH H* LL%
Officers always escorted BALLERINAS H* LL%
Mary likes BOMBAZINE H* LL%
Mary is ALWAYS H* on time LL%
Anna married MANNY H* LL%
Harry doesn't READ H* books LL%
FRED H* ate the beans LL%
Mary wrote a book about BATS H* LL%
NIXON H* died LL%
It was the beans that FRED H* ate LL%
It was the beans that Fred ATE H* LL%
I am a MILLIONAIRE H* LL%
I am a MILLIONAIRE L* LL%
I am a MILLIONAIRE H* LH%
I am a MILLIONAIRE L* LH%

All-theme utterances

Mary likes BOMBAZINE L+H* LH%
Well, she likes BOMBAZINE L+H* LH%
Mary is USUALLY L+H* on time LH%
I am a MILLIONAIRE L+H* LL%
I am a MILLIONAIRE L*+H LL%
I am a MILLIONAIRE L+H* LH%
I am a MILLIONAIRE L*+H LH%

Unmarked theme

DOGS H* LL% must be carried LL%
JOHN H* LL% writes novels LL%
JOHN H* LL% flew from London to Paris LL%
The BRITISH ACTOR H* LL% reads comic books LL%
The American ACTOR H* LL% reads history books LL%
The BRITISH H* LL% author reads history books LL%
It is JOHN H* LL% who hates comics LL%

It is COMICS H* LL% John hates LL%
POETRY H* LL% is written by Bill LL%
BILL H* LL% writes poetry LL%
Bill WRITES H* LL% poetry LL%
So I am SURE H* LL% that Mary likes corduroy LL%
Harry doesn't READ H* LL% books LL%
FRED H* LL% ate the beans LL%
NIXON H* LL% died LL%

Theme followed by rheme

DOGS L+H* LH% must be CARRIED H* LL%
JOHN L+H* LH% writes NOVELS H* LL%
John flew from LONDON L+H* LH% to PARIS H* LL%
JOHN L+H* flew from London LH% to PARIS H* LL%
JOHN L+H* flew LH% from London to PARIS H* LL%
John flew L+H* LH% from London to PARIS H* LL%
JOHN L+H* LH% flew from London to PARIS H* LL%
John flew to PARIS L+H* from LH% LONDON H* LL%
The British author READS L+H* LH% COMIC H* books LL%
The British author READS L+H* LH% history PAPERS H* LL%
The British author READS L+H* LH% DETECTIVE H* STORIES H* LL%
The BRITISH L+H* author reads LH% COMICS H* LL%
The American ACTOR L+H* reads LH% COMICS H* LL%
COMICS L+H* LH% John HATES H* LL%
What John HATES L+H* LH% are COMICS H* LL%
What JOHN L+H* hates LH% are COMICS H* LL%
What John HATES L+H* are LH% COMICS H* LL%
John gave MARY L+H* LH% a BOOK H* LL%
John gave a BOOK L+H* LH% to MARY H* LL%
John gave a BOOK L+H* to LH% MARY H* LL%
COMICS L+H* are hated LH% by JOHN H* LL%
COMICS L+H* are hated by LH% JOHN H* LL%
BILL L+H* writes LH% POETRY H* LL%
What BILL L+H* LH% writes is POETRY H* LL%
BILL L+H* LH% writes POETRY H* LL%
BILL L+H* writes LH% POETRY H* LL%
The GERMAN L+H* actor LH% writes POETRY H* LL%
The German ACTOR L+H* LH% writes POETRY H* LL%
On the SHETLANDS L+H* one speaks LH% ENGLISH H* LL%
On the Shetlands one SPEAKS L+H* LH% ENGLISH H* LL%
One speaks ENGLISH L+H* LH% on the SHETLANDS H* LL%

OFFICERS L+H* always escorted LH% BALLERINAS H* LL%
Officers always ESCORTED L+H* LH% BALLERINAS H* LL%
OFFICERS L+H* always LH% escorted BALLERINAS H* LL%
Mary ADMIRES L+H* LH% the woman who DIRECTED H* the musical LL%
ANNA L+H* LH% married MANNY H* LL%
And people who like BOMBAZINE L+H* LH% like CORDUROY H* LL%
FRED L+H* LH% ate the BEANS H* LL%
MARY L+H* says he ate LH% BEANS H* LL%
FRED L+H* LH% ate the GREEN H* beans LL%
FRED L+H* LH% ATE H* the beans LL%
Fred ATE L+H* LH% the BEANS H* LL%
FRED L+H* LH% ate the BEANS H* LL%
The beans that FRED L+H* LH% ate were DELICIOUS H* LL%

Rheme followed by theme

DOGS H* LL% must be CARRIED L+H* LH%
JOHN H* LL% writes NOVELS L+H* LH%
John flew from LONDON H* LL% to Paris LL%
JOHN H* LL% flew from LONDON L+H* to Paris LH%
JOHN H* LL% flew from London to PARIS L+H* LH%
COMICS H* LL% John hates LL%
It is JOHN H* LL% who hates COMICS L+H* LH%
It is COMICS H* LL% JOHN L+H* hates LH%
It is COMICS H* LL% John HATES L+H* LH%
COMICS H* are LL% what John HATES L+H* LH%
COMICS H* are LL% what JOHN L+H* hates LH%
COMICS H* LL% are what John HATES L+H* LH%
COMICS H* LL% are what JOHN L+H* hates LH%
POETRY H* LL% is written by BILL L+H* LH%
It is POETRY H* LL% BILL L+H* writes LH%
POETRY H* LL% BILL L+H* writes LL%
BILL H* LL% writes POETRY L+H* LH%
The GERMAN H* actor LL% writes POETRY L+H* LH%
The GERMAN H* actor LL% writes poetry LL%
The German ACTOR H* LL% writes POETRY L+H* LH%
The German ACTOR H* LL% writes poetry LL%
OFFICERS H* LL% always escorted BALLERINAS L+H* LH%
OFFICERS H* LL% always ESCORTED L+H* ballerinas LH%
OFFICERS H* LL% always escorted ballerinas LL%
ANNA H* LL% married MANNY L+H* LH%
Harry doesn't READ H* LL% BOOKS L+H* LH%

FRED H* LL% ate the BEANS L+H* LH%
FRED H* LL% ATE L+H* the beans LH%
Fred ATE H* LL% the BEANS L+H* LH%
FRED H* ate LL% the BEANS L+H* LH%
It was the BEANS H* LL% that FRED ATE L+H* LH%
It was the BEANS H* LL% that Fred ATE L+H* LH%
The beans that FRED H* LL% ate were DELICIOUS L+H* LH%

Split theme

JOHN L+H* flew from LH% LONDON H* LL% to PARIS L+H* LH%
JOHN L+H* flew from LH% LONDON H* LL% to Paris LL%
JOHN L+H* LH% FLEW H* LL% from LONDON L+H* to PARIS L+H* LH%
JOHN L+H* LH% FLEW H* LL% from London to PARIS L+H* LH%
JOHN L+H* LH% FLEW H* LL% from London to Paris LL%
BILL L+H* LH% WRITES H* LL% POETRY L+H* LH%
BILL L+H* LH% WRITES H* LL% poetry LL%
Mary WANTS L+H* LH% IPSWICH H* LL% to WIN L+H* LH%
FRED L+H* LH% ATE H* LL% the beans LL%
Fred LL% ATE H* LL% the BEANS L+H* LH%

Multiple foci in theme

JOHN L+H* flew to PARIS L+H* from LH% LONDON H* LL%

Multiple foci in rheme

The BRITISH H* ACTOR H* LL% reads comic books LL%
The BRITISH H* ACTOR H* LL% reads history books LL%
FRED L+H* LH% ate the GREEN H* BEANS H* LL%
Bill COOKED H* and Fred ATE H* LL% the BEANS L+H* LH%

Appendix C

Extrapositional Account of Cleft Sentences in UCCG

This paper provides an account of cleft sentences in English in the framework of Unification-based Combinatory Categorial Grammar (UCCG) (Traat and Bos, 2004) in the lines of the extrapositional approach to clefts (Hedberg, 1990). There are no previous accounts to cleft sentences in UCCG. However, cleft sentences have received some treatment in Combinatory Categorial Grammar (CCG) framework (Steedman, 2000b) and related CG formalisms, but always following the expletive tradition (Hockenmaier, 2003; Carpenter, 1998).

C.1 Introduction

Cleft sentences have puzzled linguists for a long time. As the name given to the group of syntactic constructions implies there is something non-standard about them. But their special status makes them all the more appealing. Both the syntax and the semantics of the cleft family are out of the ordinary, to the extent that there is still no complete consensus neither about what the syntactic building blocks of cleft sentences are, nor the exact details of the semantics. The two major approaches to clefts are discussed in Section C.2 of the present paper.

The main purpose of the present paper is providing an extrapositional account to cleft sentences in the Combinatory Categorial Grammar tradition (Steedman, 2000b) – more precisely in the Unification-based Combinatory Categorial Grammar framework (Traat and Bos, 2004). To date the few attempts on clefts in frameworks related to CCG have always followed the expletive tradition. Section C.3 briefly touches upon the expletive cleft analysis in CCG.

Section C.4 discusses some issues related to the semantics of clefts, while Section C.5 contains the main contribution of the present paper: the extrapositional cleft analysis in UCCG.

C.2 The Two Approaches to Clefts

Following (Hedberg, 1990) the structural components of cleft sentences are as follows:

(C.1)
$$\underbrace{\text{It}}_{\substack{\text{cleft} \\ \text{pronoun}}} + \underbrace{\text{is}}_{\text{copula}} + \underbrace{\text{beans}}_{\substack{\text{clefted} \\ \text{constituent}}} + \underbrace{\text{that I like}}_{\substack{\text{cleft} \\ \text{clause}}}$$

There are two main approaches to the structure of clefts. The first one of them is known as the extraposition approach. This approach views clefts as copular sentences (see Example C.2). The cleft pronoun is viewed as a normal pronoun, i.e. it is referential and, therefore, has semantic content. The clefted constituent functions as the predicate complement, and the cleft clause is a relative clause. Again following Hedberg: on the level of pragmatic interpretation, the cleft pronoun and the cleft clause function as a discontinuous constituent, while syntactically the clefted constituent and the cleft clause form a constituent.

(C.2) PRONOUN + COPULA + PREDICATE COMPLEMENT +
RELATIVE CLAUSE

An alternative to the above would be to take the stand of the expletive approach (see Example C.3) according to which the clefted constituent is the actual subject of the sentence, and the cleft clause is the predicate. The rest is just a mere structural eccentricity. Thus, the cleft pronoun is viewed as a dummy subject and the copula as a dummy verb, neither of them making a contribution to the meaning of the sentence.

(C.3) DUMMY SUBJECT + DUMMY VERB + SUBJECT + PREDICATE

According to the expletive approach the sentences a) and b) in Example C.4 are semantically identical.

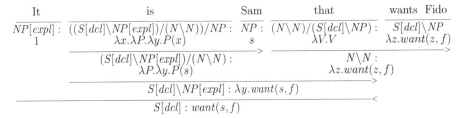

Figure C.1: A CCG derivation of *It is Sam that wants Fido*.

(C.4) a) Sam wants Fido.

b) It is Sam that wants Fido.

However, languages generally do not like redundancy. If the cleft pronoun and the copula are as devoid of meaning as the expletive approach states then the question arises: why has the English language not done away with the cleft constructions?

I subscribe to the position of the extrapositional approach. In my view, while C.4a and C.4b have the same truth conditions, they have distinct semantics.[1]

C.3 Cleft Analysis in CCG and Related CG Frameworks

As mentioned above the analyses of clefts in CCG have followed the expletive tradition. Hockenmaier (2003) provides a purely syntactic analysis of clefts in CCG. Carpenter's (1998) approach in what he calls Applicative Categorial Grammar, is similar to Hockenmaier's, but he also provides semantics. Figure C.1 illustrates the expletive analysis of clefts in CCG. We use Hockenmaier's syntactic categories, since her Combinatory Categorial Grammar (CCG) notation is closer to that of UCCG than Carpenter's, coupled with the semantics similar to that provided by the latter.

As seen in Fig. C.1 the final result of the analysis of the cleft *It is Sam that wants Fido* presents us with exactly the same semantics as the corresponding

---

[1]Outside the context of clefts, Atlas and Levinson (1981) have shown that sentences with the same truth conditions can have different semantics, e.g.:

It's done.   p

It's done, and if it's done it's done.   p & (p → p)

non-cleft sentence *Sam wants Fido* would have done. However, we want these two to be semantically distinct. Some of the reasons for that are outlined in the next section.

C.4   Cleft Semantics

Clefts differ from their corresponding non-cleft counterparts in some important respects. One of them is the fact that clefts are presupposition-inducing syntactic structures (Delin, 1990).

(C.5) a) Sam wants Fido.

  Sam does not want Fido.

  b) It is Sam that wants Fido.

  It is not Sam that wants Fido.

  c) Somebody wants Fido.

While the sentences in C.5a and C.5b have the same truth conditions, only the cleft preserves inference to C.5c under negation and questioning. Therefore, quoting Atlas and Levinson (1981):

> Sentences that give rise to presuppositions should on this analysis differ from their corresponding presuppositionless sentences at least in logical form if not also in truth conditions.

The above leads us to the following semantic representations:

(C.6) a) Sam wants Fido. $wants(s,f)$

  b) It is Fido that Sam wants. $\lambda x(wants(s,x))(f)$

  c) It is Sam who wants Fido. $\lambda x(wants(x,f))(s)$

  d) What Sam wants is Fido. $\lambda x(wants(s,x))(f)$

Even though logically equivalent, the logical forms of C.6a, C.6b and C.6c are distinct. While C.6a is a simple two-place predicate expressing a relation between Sam and Fido, C.6b and C.6c are complex one-place predicates, where the portion immediately following the lambda-expression is the presupposition induced by the cleft, and the final part of the logical form is the assertion that supplies the value for the variable in the presupposition. The cleft in C.6b and the pseudo-cleft in C.6d share the same presupposition and, therefore, have the same semantics.

Another important way clefts differ from their non-cleft counterparts is the fact that the instantiation of the variable in the presupposition of clefts is governed by the uniqueness or maximality condition. C.6b "conventionally implicates" (Halvorsen, 1978) *Fido is the only thing Sam wants*, while C.6b has no such restriction – Fido could be just one among any number of things desired by Sam. Atlas and Levinson (1981) have worked out a nice semantic representation to express this property of clefts in the Radical Pragmatics framework:

(C.7) a) It is Fido that Sam wants.

   b) $\lambda x(x{=}Fido)(\gamma x.want(Sam,x))^a$

   c) Meaning of b: A group of individuals wanted by Sam is identical to Fido.

---

   [a]γA produces a collective term $\gamma x A(x)$, i.e. a term which denotes a group

In this paper, although we are generally going to adopt the approach of Atlas and Levinson to cleft semantics, we simplify it by omitting the group operator.

C.5   Cleft Analysis in UCCG

C.5.1   Syntax

In extrapositional approach the copula in clefts is considered just a regular copula, playing its usual linking role. Therefore, we cannot directly use the CG syntactic categories used in the expletive account, as these give the copula a particular status in cleft constructions. The motivation for viewing clefts as similar to other copular structures is transparent in the case of pseudo-clefts, which are syntactically somewhat more straightforward structures:

(C.8) a) What Sam wants is Fido.

   b) This dog's name is Fido.

In Example C.8a the constituent *what Sam wants* seems to be functionally no different from this dog's name in C.8b: they both function as the subject of the sentence. Assuming that they, indeed, would have the same syntactic category in CG, there is no reason whatsoever to give the copula a different category in the two sentence under discussion.

The real clefts can be viewed as not so very different from pseudo-clefts. In fact, there have been proposals that cleft sentences are syntactically derived from pseudo-clefts (Akmajian, 1970; Gundel, 1977). Analyses where clefted constituent is viewed as the predicate complement and the cleft clause as a dislocated relative clause modifying the cleft pronoun are by no means a news (Fowler and Fowler, 1919; Jespersen, 1927).

(C.9) a) It$_i$ is Fido [that Sam wants]$_i$.

   b) *It that Sam wants is Fido.[2]

The sentence in C.9b is not grammatically correct English, but it does succeed in conveying the meaning, and is presented here to illustrate the similarity between clefts if their relative clause were not "dislocated" and pseudo-clefts like in C.8a.

Now that we have established two important facts about clefts and pseudo-clefts, namely that they are structurally related, and that the copula occurring in them is just a regular copula, we are ready to work out the necessary UCCG syntactic categories. At a closer look, the only categories specific to clefts are these of the pronouns *what* and *it*.

Before proceeding just a quick note on some relevant UCCG syntactic categories (Traat and Bos, 2004): they are similar to CCG categories, but differ in some respects. UCCG does not have a category *np* for noun phrases, instead the noun phrases have a functor category s/vp. Therefore, the category for verb phrases is just *vp* rather than s\np. This leads us to the following UCCG syntactic categories in our cleft examples:

(C.10)

Sam, Fido	:=	s/vp
wants	:=	vp/(s/vp)
is	:=	vp/(s/vp)
that	:=	(n\n)/vp
that	:=	(n\n)/(s/(s/vp))

---

[2] In some other languages this construction is perfectly acceptable, e.g in Estonian:
See,   kes   mulle meeldib, on Martin.
This who   I   like   is Martin.

Now we need to fit in the missing pieces in the puzzle, namely the cleft pronouns. We will start with the pseudo-clefts' *what*. In the approach outlined here, the cleft pronoun has the semantics of a regular pronoun, but syntactically it participates in two slots in the sentence:

(C.11)   Sam wants something (= what).   wants(s,x)

   The wanted thing (= what) is Fido.   x=f

Therefore, the syntactic category of *what* has to be specific to pseudo-clefts. The category to do the job in the case the clefted constituent is an object is $(s/vp)/(s/(s/vp))$. An additional justification for this category is that *what* can be paraphrased *the one that* or *the thing that*, which we cannot directly combine into a unit in UCCG, but if we relaxed the constraint on the order that the arguments need to be dealt away with (first combining the category for *that* with the noun on its left), that would be the category that we would get.

(C.12)   the   one   that

        $(s/vp)/n$ n $(n\backslash n)/(s/(s/vp))$

An analysis of the pseudo-cleft *What Sam wants is Fido* is illustrated in Fig. C.2. First we combine *what Sam wants* to form a noun phrase, and *is Fido* to form a verb phrase, and then combine these two to form a sentence.

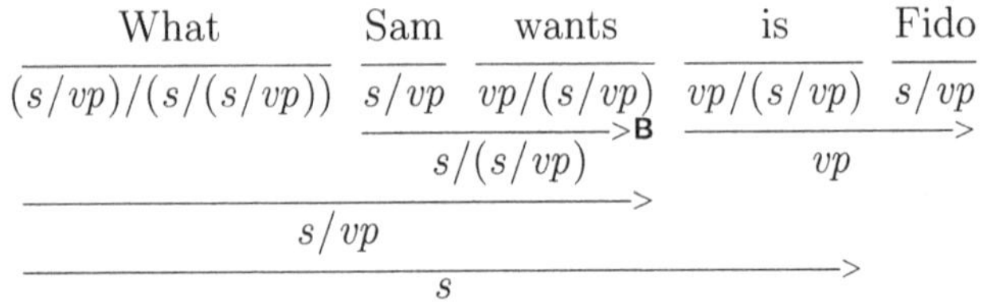

$$
\begin{array}{ccccc}
\text{What} & \text{Sam} & \text{wants} & \text{is} & \text{Fido} \\
\hline
(s/vp)/(s/(s/vp)) & s/vp & vp/(s/vp) & vp/(s/vp) & s/vp \\
& \multicolumn{2}{c}{\underline{}\text{>B}} & \multicolumn{2}{c}{\underline{}\text{>}} \\
& \multicolumn{2}{c}{s/(s/vp)} & \multicolumn{2}{c}{vp} \\
\hline
\multicolumn{3}{c}{s/vp} \text{>} & & \\
\hline
\multicolumn{5}{c}{s} \text{>}
\end{array}
$$

Figure C.2: A CCG derivation of *What Sam wants is Fido*.

For the other type of pseudo-clefts, which seem to be less frequent, where the subject of the sentence is the clefted constituent (see Fig. C.3) the syntactic category for *what* would be $(s/vp)/vp$.

In clefts, similarly to pseudo-clefts, the pronoun fits into two syntactic slots. Consider the sentence *It is Sam that wants Fido*:

(C.13)   Somebody (=it) wants Fido.   wants(x,f)

       This person (=it) is Sam.   x=f

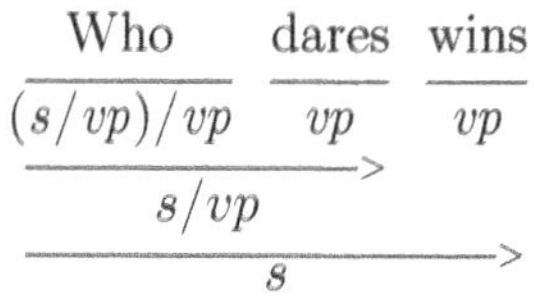

$$
\begin{array}{ccc}
\text{Who} & \text{dares} & \text{wins} \\
\hline
(s/vp)/vp & vp & vp \\
\end{array}
$$

Figure C.3: A CCG derivation of *Who dares, wins*.

As it turns out, we only need a single syntactic category for *it*: $(s/(n\backslash n))/vp$. This category works in both cases – when the constituent is the subject and when it is the object of the sentence, the differences are taken care by the category for the relativiser *that*. Figure C.4 provides the extrapositional syntactic analysis of the cleft that was analysed in expletive tradition in Fig. C.1. First *it is Sam* and *that wants Fido* are combined to form constituents, and then the two syntactic categories are combined resulting in a complete sentence.

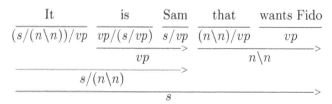

Figure C.4: A CCG derivation of *It is Sam that wants Fido*.

C.5.2 Semantics

In fact, the most significant difference between the expletive and the extrapositional approach to clefts lies in semantics. Thus, in extrapositional approach as opposed to the expletive approach we do need to provide semantics to pronouns.

UCCG uses DRT semantics. The semantics we are going to use for pronouns is actually very simple indeed: all the pronoun does is introducing a discourse referent to the domain. Thus, the semantics for the cleft *it* or *what* would look like follows:

(C.14)
$$
\boxed{\begin{array}{c} X \\ \hline \\ \end{array}}
$$

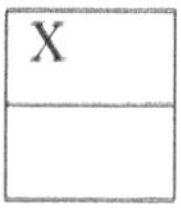

The semantics we provide for the copula is illustrated in Example C.15. Since we use neo-Davidsonian event-semantics, the copula introduces an event variable E in the domain. The discourse condition states that the event is an identity relation between two discourse referents.

(C.15)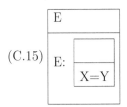

Following the ideas of Atlas and Levinson (1981) as explained above, the final DRS we are aiming for for the sentence in Fig. C.4 is as follows:

(C.16)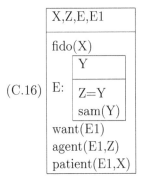

Note that the proper name *Sam* has not been promoted to the main DRS. This is because, for the time being, we use the same approach to all noun phrases. For example, if we analysed the sentence *It is a car that Sam wants*, the sub-DRS would unquestionably be the correct place for the discourse referent for *a car*. The above could be fixed by providing a simple mechanism of promoting proper names to the top-level DRS.

The crucial problem is making the variables in the resulting DRS assume the correct values. In UCCG this is achieved via variable unification (Traat and Bos, 2004). Therefore, we really need to view the semantics in the context of the complete UCCG signs. Thus, the sign for the copula would look as follows:

$$(C.17) \quad \begin{bmatrix} \text{PHO:} & \text{is+W} \\ \text{CAT:} & \text{vp} \\ \text{VAR:} & \text{X} \\ \text{SIT:} & \text{E} \\ \text{DRS:} & \boxed{\begin{array}{c} \text{E} \\ \hline \\ \hline \text{E:D} \end{array}} \end{bmatrix} /(\begin{bmatrix} \text{PHO:} & \text{W+W1} \\ \text{CAT:} & \text{s} \\ \text{SIT:} & \text{E} \\ \text{DRS:} & \text{D} \end{bmatrix} / \begin{bmatrix} \text{PHO:} & \text{W1} \\ \text{CAT:} & \text{vp} \\ \text{VAR:} & \text{Y} \\ \text{SIT:} & \text{E} \\ \text{DRS:} & \boxed{\begin{array}{c} \\ \hline \\ \hline \text{X=Y} \end{array}} \end{bmatrix})$$

The whole sign for the cleft pronoun would be as seen in Example C.18.

$$(C.18) \quad (\begin{bmatrix} \text{PHO:} & \text{it+W+W1} \\ \text{CAT:} & \text{s} \\ \text{SIT:} & \text{E} \\ \text{DRS:} & \boxed{\begin{array}{c} \text{X} \\ \hline \\ \hline \end{array}} ; \text{D1} \end{bmatrix} /(\begin{bmatrix} \text{PHO:} & \text{W2+W1} \\ \text{CAT:} & \text{n} \\ \text{VAR:} & \text{X} \\ \text{DRS:} & \text{D1} \end{bmatrix} \backslash \begin{bmatrix} \text{PHO:} & \text{W2} \\ \text{CAT:} & \text{n} \\ \text{VAR:} & \text{X} \\ \text{DRS:} & \text{D} \end{bmatrix}))/ \begin{bmatrix} \text{PHO:} & \text{W} \\ \text{CAT:} & \text{vp} \\ \text{VAR:} & \text{X} \\ \text{SIT:} & \text{E} \\ \text{DRS:} & \text{D} \end{bmatrix}$$

In what follows we are going to concentrate our attention to it-clefts and provide an extrapositional UCCG analysis of the sentence previously analysed in Figures C.1 and C.4. In essence, UCCG analysis of pseudo-clefts is very similar to that of it-clefts.

The first step of analysis of *It is Sam that wants Fido* is combining the signs for the copula and the word *Sam* (see Fig. C.5). It is done by forward application. Via unification the variable W in the PHO feature of the result sign receives the value *sam*, thus the complete value of the phonology feature of the result is *is+sam*. The CAT feature values of the argument of the copula sign and the noun phrase sign unify successfully. The discourse referent values Y and Z in the VAR feature of the signs unify. At this point another important thing happens: the corresponding discourse referent variable unification also takes place inside the DRSs. Thus, at this point we know that Sam is represented in the model by the referent Y, and we also know that Sam is identical to something, currently unknown, represented by X. The event variables E and E1 of the signs also unify both in the SIT feature as well as in the DRSs. Via unification the DRS variable D1 receives the value C.19a, which is subsequently merged with the DRS C.19b into C.19c. The result of this merged DRS becomes the value of the DRS variable D. This new value of D is then introduced at the corresponding place in the DRS of the result sign. The final DRS informs us about an event E with a participant Y, who is Sam, and of the fact that Sam is equal to something X.

(C.19) a)
$$\boxed{\begin{array}{c} \\ \hline X=Y \end{array}}$$
b)
$$\boxed{\begin{array}{c} Y \\ \hline sam(Y) \end{array}}$$
c)
$$\boxed{\begin{array}{c} Y \\ \hline sam(Y) \\ X=Y \end{array}}$$

The next step, illustrated by Figure C.6 combines the result sign from the previous with the sign of the cleft pronoun *it*. The most important things happening at this stage are the unification of discourse referent variables X and Z both in the VAR feature of the signs and in the DRSs. Now the unknown thing that Sam is known to be identical to is marked by Z in the semantics of the result sign. Also the event variables unify in the SIT feature as well as the DRSs. This step does not give us a single result DRS, since due to the pieces of semantics being scattered around in different parts of the complex result sign, the DRSs cannot be merged.

We are going to skip the following two steps in the analysis, and continue at the point where the signs for the words in the string *that wants Fido* have already been combined into a single sign. Figure C.7 illustrates the combining of the two principal constituents of the cleft sentence – the sign for *it is Sam* which we obtained in step 2 of the analysis, and the sign for *that wants Fido*. This is performed, yet again, via forward application. After the PHO variable W1 unifies with the constant value *(that+(wants+fido))*, the complete constant value of the PHO feature in the result sign becomes *it+(is+sam)+(that+(wants+fido))*. The CAT feature values prove to be no obstacle in the unification process. The discourse referent variables Z and T are unified, and appropriate replacements are made in the semantics. Now the DRS variable D receives the constant value of the DRS describing the identity event. Then the new value of D gets merged with the DRS containing the event of there being somebody wanting Fido. The merged DRS value is subsequently assigned to the DRS variable D1. D1 is also replaced in the result sign. After that the final merging of DRSs in the result sign takes place. When comparing the result DRS with the one in Example C.16 we can report success: the UCCG analysis has produced the DRS we set as our goal.

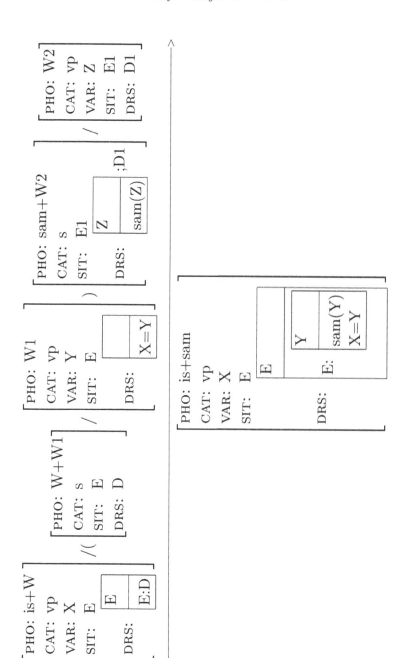

Figure C.5. A UCCG derivation of *is Sam*.

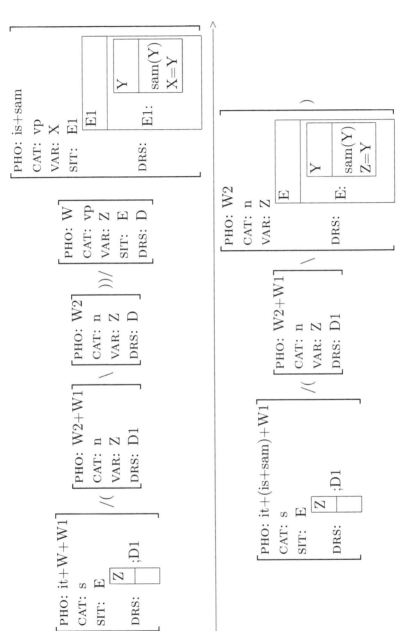

Figure C.6.A CCG derivation of *It is Sam.*

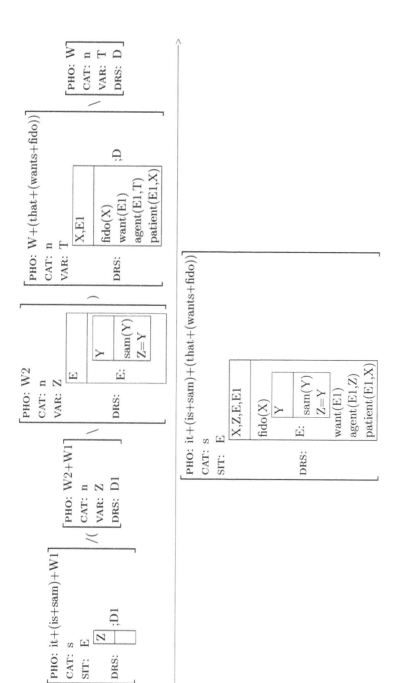

Figure C.7. A CCG derivation of *It is Sam that loves Fido.*

C.6   Conclusion

The present paper discussed several issues connected with the cleft and pseudo-cleft constructions in English. In particular, it provided an extrapositional account of cleft sentence analysis in Unification-based Combinatory Categorial Grammar. Previously, only an expletive analysis had been provided to clefts in the Combinatory Categorial Grammar and related formalisms.

Bibliography

Ajdukiewicz, K. (1935). Die syntaktische Konnexität. *Studia Philosophica*, 1:1–27. Translated as "Syntactic Connection" in Storrs McCall, ed., *Polish Logic 1920-1939*, pages 207-231. Oxford University Press, Oxford.

Akmajian, A. (1970). On deriving cleft sentences from pseudo-cleft sentences. *Linguistic Inquiry*.

Atlas, J. D. and Levinson, S. C. (1981). It-clefts, informativeness, and logical form: Radical pragmatics (revised standard version). In Cole, P., editor, *Radical Pragmatics*, pages 1–62. Academic Publisher, New York.

Baldridge, J. (2002). *Lexically Specified Derivational Control*. PhD thesis, The University of Edinburgh.

Baldridge, J. and Kruijff, G.-J. (2002). Coupling CCG and hybrid logic dependancy semantics. In *Proceedings of 40th Annual Meeting of the Association for Computational Linguistics*, pages 319–326.

Beckman, M. and Hirschberg, J. (1999). The ToBI annotation conventions. URL http://ling.ohio-state.edu/ tobi/ame tobi/annotation conventions.html. Ms. Ohio State University.

Bende-Farkas, A., Genabith, J. V., and Kamp, H. (2003). DRT: An updated survey. course at ESSLLI 2003.

Blackburn, P. and Bos, J. (2003a). Computational semantics. *Theoria: revista de teoria, historia y fundamentos de la ciencia*, 18(46).

Blackburn, P. and Bos, J. (2003b). Computational semantics for natural language. Course Notes for NASSLLI 2003, Indiana University.

Blackburn, P. and Bos, J. (2005). *Representation and Inference for Natural Language. A First Course in Computational Semantics*. CSLI.

Blackburn, P. and Bos, J. (2006). Working with Discourse Representation Theory. an advanced course in computational semantics. Current draft downloadable from www.blackburnbos.org.

Blackburn, P., Bos, J., Kohlhase, M., and de Nivelle, H. (1998). Automated theorem proving for natural language understanding. In Baumgartner, P., Furbach, U., Kohlhase, M., McCune, W., Reif, W., Stickel, M., and Uribe, T., editors, *CADE-15 Workshop "Problem-solving Methodologies with Automated Deduction"*. Paper available at URL: http://www.uni-koblenz.de/~peter/cade-15-ws/.

Bolinger, D. L. (1965). *Forms of English: Accent, Morpheme, Order*. Harvard Universtiy Press, Cambridge, Massachusetts.

Bos, J. (2005). Towards wide-coverage semantic interpretation. In *Proceedings of Sixth International Workshop on Computational Semantics IWCS-6*, pages 42–53.

Bos, J., Clark, S., Steedman, M., Curran, J. R., and Hockenmaier, J. (2004). Wide-coverage semantic representations from a CCG parser. In *Proceedings of the 20th International Conference on Computational Linguistics (COLING '04)*, Geneva, Switzerland.

Buráňová, E., Hajičová, E., and Sgall, P. (2000). Tagging of very large corpora: Topic-focus articulation. In *COLING 2000: 18th International Conference on Computational Linguistics, July 31 - August 4, 2000*, pages 139–144, Universität des Saarlandes, Saarbrücken, Germany.

Büring, D. (1995). *The 59th Street Bridge Accent*. PhD thesis, Univerity of Tübingen.

Calder, J., Klein, E., and Zeevat, H. (1988). Unification Categorial Grammar: A concise, extendable grammar for natural language processing. In *Proceedings of the 12th International Conerence on Computational Linguistics*, Budapest.

Calhoun, S. (2004). Phonetic dimension of intonational categories – the case of l+h* and h*. In *Prosody 2004*, Nara, Japan.

Calhoun, S. (2006). *Information Structure and the Prosodic Structure of English: a Probabilistic Relationship.* PhD thesis, The University of Edinburgh.

Carpenter, B. (1998). *Type-Logical Semantics.* MIT Press.

Chafe, W. L. (1976). Givenness, contrastiveness, definiteness, subjects, topic, and point of view. In Li, C., editor, *Subject and Topic*, pages 25–55. Academic Press, New York.

Cresswell, M. and von Stechow, A. (1982). De re belief generalized. *Linguistics and Philosophy*, 5:503–535.

Davidson, D. (1967). The logical form of action sentences. In Rescher, N., editor, *The Logic of Decision and Action*, pages 81–95. The University Press, Pittsburgh.

Delin, J. L. (1990). A multi-level account of cleft constructions in discourse. In *Coling 90: Proceedings of the 13th International Conference on Computational Linguistics*, Helsinki.

Flickinger, D., Pollard, C., and Wasow, T. (1985). Structure-sharing in lexical representation. In *Proceedings of the 23rd Annual Meeting of the Association of Computational Linguistics, University of Chicago, Chicago, Illinois, July 1985*, pages 262–267.

Fowler, H. W. and Fowler, F. G. (1919). *The King's English.* Clarendon Press, Oxford, second edition.

Frege, G. (1891). Function und Begriff. Translated as "Function and Concept" in Geach & Black, eds., *Translations from the Philosophical Writings of Gottlob Frege'*, pages 21-41. Blackwell, Oxford, 1980.

Frege, G. (1892). Über Sinn und Bedeutung. Translated as "On Sense and Reference" in Geach & Black, eds., *Translations from the Philosophical Writings of Gottlob Frege*, pages 56-78. Blackwell, Oxford, 1980.

Gardent, C. (2000). Deaccenting and higher-order unification. *Journal of Logic, Language and Information*, 9(3):313–338.

Gardent, C. and Kohlhase, M. (1996a). Focus and higher-order unification. In *Proceedings of COLING*, Copenhaguen, Denmark.

Bibliography

Gardent, C. and Kohlhase, M. (1996b). Higher-order coloured unification and natural language semantics. In *Proceedings of the 34th Annual Meeting of the Association for Computational Linguistics*, Santa Cruz, USA.

Geurts, B. (1999). *Presuppositions and Pronouns.* Elsevier Science, Amsterdam.

Geurts, B. and van der Sandt, R. (2004). Interpreting focus. *Theoretical Linguistics*, 30:1–44.

Gundel, J. K. (1977). Where do cleft sentences come from? *Language*, 53(3).

Gussenhoven, C. (1983). *On the Grammar and Semantics of Sentence Accent.* Foris, Dordrecht.

Hajičová, E. (1993). *Issues of Sentence Structure and Discourse Patterns*, volume 2 of *Theoretical and Computational Linguistics.* Charles University Press, Prague, Czech Republic.

Hajičová, E., Partee, B. H., and Sgall, P. (1998). *Topic-Focus Articulation, Tripartite Structures, and Semantic Context.* Studies in Language and Philosophy. Kluwer Academic Publishers, Dordrecht,Boston,London.

Hajičová, E. and Sgall, P. (2004). Degrees of contrast and the topic-focus articulation. In Steube, A., editor, *Information Structure. Theoretical and Empirical Aspects.*, volume 1 of *Language, Context, and Cognition.* de Gruyter, Berlin.

Halliday, M. A. K. (1967). Notes on transitivity and theme in english, part ii. *Journal of Linguistics*, 3:199–244.

Halvorsen, P.-K. (1978). The syntax and semantics of cleft constructions. *Texas Linguistic Forum*, 11. Department of Linguistics, University of Texas, Austin.

Hamblin, C. L. (1973). Questions in Montague English. *Foundations of Language*, pages 41–53.

Hedberg, N. and Sosa, J. M. (2001). The prosodic structure of topic and focus in spontaneous English dialogue. Paper presented at 'Topic and Focus: A Workshop on Intonation and Meaning', Linguistic Society of America. University of California, Santa Barbara.

Hedberg, N. A. (1990). *Discourse Pragmatics and Cleft Sentences in English.* PhD thesis, The University of Minnesota.

Hockenmaier, J. (2003). *Data and Models for Statistical Parsing with Combinatory Categorial Grammar.* PhD thesis, The University of Edinburgh.

Hoffman, B. (1995). *Computational Analysis of the Syntax and Interpretation of "Free" Word-Order in Turkish.* PhD thesis, University of Pennsylvania.

Jackendoff, R. S. (1972). *Semantic Interpretation in Generative Grammar.* MIT Press, Cambridge, MA.

Jespersen, O. (1927). *A Modern English Grammar III.* Allen and Unwin, London.

Kamp, H. (2004). Information structure in a dynamic theory of meaning. In *Proceedings of the Linguistic Society of Korea.*

Kamp, H., Ágnes Bende-Farkas, and Riester, A. (2003). Four formalisms, one example. Ms, IMS Stuttgart.

Kamp, H. and Reyle, U. (1993). *From Discourse to Logic.* Kluwer Academic Publishers, London.

Kay, M. (1979). Functional grammar. In *Proceedings of the fifth annual meeting of the Berkeley Linguistic Society,* pages 142–159.

Kay, M. (1985). Unification in grammar. In Dahl, V. and Saint-Dizier, P., editors, *Natural language understanding and logic programming: proceedings of the First International Workshop on Natural Language Understanding and Logic Programming, Rennes, France, 18-20 September, 1984,* pages 233–241, Amsterdam. Elsevier Science Publishers.

Klein, W. and von Stechow, A. (1982). Intonation und Bedeutung von Fokus. Technical report, SFB, University of Konstanz.

König, E. (1991). *The Meaning of Focus Particles. A Comparative Perspective.* Routledge, London.

Krifka, M. (2005). Focus and/or context: A second look at second occurrence expressions. In Kamp, H. and Partee, B., editors, *Context-Dependence in the Analysis of Linguistic Meaning.* Elsevier Publications.

Krifka, M. (2006). Association with focus phrases. In Molnár, V. and Winkler, S., editors, *Architecture of Focus*. Mouton de Gruyter, Berlin.

Kruijff, G.-J. M. (2001). *A Categorial-Modal Logical Architecture of Informativity*. PhD thesis, Charles University, Prague.

Kruijff-Korbayová, I. (1998). *The Dynamic Potential of Topic and Focus: A Praguian Approach to Discourse Representation Theory*. PhD thesis, Faculty of Mathematics and Physics, Charles University, Prague.

Kruijff-Korbayová, I. (2004). Modeling information structure for discourse and dialog processing. COLING 2004 Tutorial T4, Geneva.

Kruijff-Korbayová, I. and Steedman, M. (2003). Discourse and information structure. *Journal of Logic, Language and Information*, 12:249–259.

Kuschert, S. (1996). Higher order dynamics: relating operational and denotational semantics for λ-DRT. Research Report CLAUS-Report 72, Saarbrücken University, Germany.

Ladd, D. R. (1980). *The Structure of Intonational Meaning*. Indiana University Press, Bloomington.

Ladd, D. R. and Schepman, A. (2003). "Sagging transition" between high pitch accents in english: experimental evidence. *Journal of Phonetics*, 31(1):81–112.

Lambek, J. (1958). The mathematics of sentence structure. *American Mathematical Monthly*, 65:154–170.

Landman, F. (2000). *Events and Plurality. The Jerusalem Lectures*, volume 76 of *Studies in Linguistics and Philosophy*. Kluwer Academic Publishers, Dordrecht.

Parsons, T. (1990). *Events in the Study of English. A Study in Subatomic Semantics*. The MIT Press, Cambridge, Massachusetts.

Peregrin, J. (1996). Topic and focus in a formal framework. In Partee, B. H. and Sgall, P., editors, *Discourse and Meaning: Papers in honour of Eva Hajičová*. Benjamins, Amsterdam.

Pierrehumbert, J. (1980). *The Phonetics and Phonology of English Intonation*. PhD thesis, Massachusetts Institute of Technology, Bloomington, IN. Published 1988 by Indiana University Linguistics Club.

Pierrehumbert, J. and Hirschberg, J. (1990). The meaning of intonational contours in the interpretation of discourse. In Cohen, P., Morgan, J., and Pollack, M., editors, *Intentions in Communication*, pages 271–312. MIT Press, Cambridge, MA.

Poesio, M., Isard, S., Wright, H., Hieronymus, J., Cooper, R., Larsson, S., and Bos, J. (2000). Prosodic cues for information structure. Technical report, TRINDI. Deliverable 4.2.

Pollard, C. (1988). Categorial Grammar and Phrase Structure Grammar: An excursion on the syntax-semantics frontier. In Oehrle, R., Bach, E., and Wheeler, D., editors, *Categorial Grammars and Natural Language Structures*, pages 391–415. Reidel, Dordrecht.

Pollard, C. and Sag, I. (1994). *Head-Driven Phrase Structure Grammar*. University of Chicago Press, Chicago.

Rooth, M. (1985). *Association with Focus*. PhD thesis, University of Massachusetts, Amherst.

Rooth, M. (1992). A theory of focus interpretation. *Natural Language Semantics*, 1(1):75–116.

Schmerling, S. (1981). The proper treatment of the relationship between syntax and phonology. Paper presented at the 55th annual meeting of the Linguistic Society of America.

Selkirk, E. O. (1984). *Phonology and Syntax: The Relation between Sound and Structure*. The MIT Press, Cambridge, Massachusetts.

Sgall, P., Hajičová, E., and Panevová, J. (1986). *The meaning of the sentence in its semantic and pragmatic aspects*. Reidel, Dordrecht, The Netherlands.

Shieber, S. M. (1986). *An Introduction to Unification-Based Approaches to Grammar*. The University of Chicago Press, Chicago, Illinois.

Steedman, M. (1987). Combinatory Grammars and human language process-ing. In Garfield, J., editor, *Modularity in Knowledge Representation and Natural Language Processing*, pages 187–205. MIT Press/Bradford Books, Cambridge, MA.

Steedman, M. (1990). Gapping as constituent coordination. *Linguistics and Philosophy*, 13.

Steedman, M. (1991a). Structure and intonation. *Language*, 67:262–296.

Steedman, M. (1991b). Surface structure, intonation, and focus. In Klein, E. and Veltman, F., editors, *Natural Language and Speech: Proceedings of the Symposium, ESPRIT Conference, Brussels, Nov. 1991*, pages 21–38, Dordrecht. Kluwer.

Steedman, M. (1996). *Surface Structure and Interpretation*. MIT Press. Linguistic Inquiry Monograph No.30.

Steedman, M. (1999). Categorial Grammar. In Wilson, R. and Keil, F., editors, *The MIT Encyclopedia of Cognitive Sciences*. MIT Press, Cambridge, MA.

Steedman, M. (2000a). Information structure and the syntax-phonology inter-face. *Linguistic Inquiry*, 31(4):649–689.

Steedman, M. (2000b). *The Syntactic Process*. The MIT Press, Cambridge, Massachusetts.

Steedman, M. (2003). Information-structural semantics of English intonation. In *LSA Summer Institute Workshop on Topic and Focus*, Santa Barbara, July 2001. Draft 2.2.

Traat, M. and Bos, J. (2004). Unificational Combinatory Categorial Grammar: A formalism for parsing and generating prosodically annotated text. In *Proceedings of COLING 2004*.

Truckenbrodt, H. (1995). *Phonological Phrases: Their Relation to Syntax, Focus and Prominence*. PhD thesis, MIT.

Vallduví, E. (1990). *The Informational Component*. PhD thesis, University of Pennsylvania, Philadelphia,USA.

Vallduví, E. (1993). Information packaging: A survey. Technical Report HCRC/RP-44, Centre for Cognitive Science & Human Communication Research Centre, University of Edinburgh.

Vallduví, E. and Engdahl, E. (1996). The linguistic realisation of information packaging. *Linguistics*, 34:459–519.

van der Sandt, R. (1992). Presupposition projection as anaphora resolution. *Journal of Semantics*, 9:333–377.

von Stechow, A. (1981). Topic, focus and local relevance. In Klein, W. and Levelt, W., editors, *Crossing the Boundaries in Linguistics*, pages 95–130. Reidel, Dordrecht.

von Stechow, A. (1982). Structured propositions. Technical report, SFB, University of Konstanz.

von Stechow, A. (1989). Focusing and backgrounding operators. Technical Report 6, Fachgruppe Sprachwissenschaft, Universität Konstanz.

von Stechow, A. (1991). Current issues in the theory of focus. In von Stechow, A. and Wunderlich, D., editors, *Semantik – Ein internationales Handbuch zeitgenössischer Forschung*, pages 804–824. de Gruyter, Berlin/New York.

White, M. (2004a). Efficient realization of coordinate structures in Combinatory Categorial Grammar. To appear in Research on Language and Computation.

White, M. (2004b). Reining in CCG chart realization. In *Proceedings of the 3rd International Conference on Natural Language Generation*.

White, M. and Baldridge, J. (2003). Adapting chart realization to CCG. In *Proceedings of the 9th European Workshop on Natural Language Generation*, Budapest, Hungary.

Wood, M. M. (1993). *Categorial grammars*. Routledge, London.

Wood, M. M. (2000). Syntax in Categorial Grammar: An introduction for linguists. ESSLLI 2000, Birmingham, England. ESSLLI coursebook.

Zeevat, H. (1988). Combining Categorial Grammar and unification. In U.Reyle and C.Rohrer, editors, *Natural Language Parsing and Linguistic Theories*. D.Reidel Publishing Company.

Zeevat, H., Klein, E., and Calder, J. (1987). Unification Categorial Grammar. In Haddock, N., Klein, E., and Morrill, G., editors, *Categorial Grammar, Unification Grammar and Parsing*. Centre for Cognitive Science, University of Edinburgh.

Zubizarreta, M. L. (1998). *Prosody, Focus and Word Order*. MIT Press, Cambridge, MA.

www.ingramcontent.com/pod-product-compliance
Lightning Source LLC
LaVergne TN
LVHW042332060326
832902LV00006B/117